Beginning Creek

Beginning Creek

Mvskoke Emponvkv

Pamela Innes, Linda Alexander
and Bertha Tilkens

University of Oklahoma Press : Norman

Library of Congress Cataloging-in-Publication Data

Innes, Pamela Joan.
Beginning Creek: Mvskoke emponvkv / Pamela Innes, Linda Alexander, and Bertha Tilkens
p. cm.
Includes bibliographical references and index.
ISBN 0-8061-3583-2 (pbk.: alk. paper)
1. Creek language—Grammar. 2. Creek Language—Conversation and phrase books. 3. Creek language—Study and teaching. I. Title: Mvskoke emponvkv. II. Alexander, Linda, 1917– III. Tilkens, Bertha, 1936– IV. Title.

PM991.I56 2004
497'.385—dc22

2003061803

The paper in this book meets the guidelines for permanence and durability of the Committee on Production Guidelines for Book Longevity of the Council on Library Resources, Inc. ∞

1 2 3 4 5 6 7 8 9 10

Contents

Illustrations

Figures

Diagrams

Tables

Preface

This text is the outcome of several years of teaching Mvskoke in Oklahoma. Our classroom experience has shown us that there is a need for an introductory textbook that will guide students as they learn the language of the Muskogee and Seminole people. Many of the structures and units of the language are radically different from those encountered in English. Thus, a text to which students may refer for information and explanation will be helpful for those wanting to understand and use the language.

The order of topics throughout the chapters in this book will help students acquire a basic knowledge of the structure of Mvskoke, a working vocabulary, and information about Mvskoke culture. The exercises in each chapter require students to utilize the concepts and rules just presented. Many of the exercises reinforce spoken use of the language by demanding interaction with other students, the teacher, or a fluent speaker.

The chapters build upon one another. Chapter 1 presents the sound and writing systems of Mvskoke. Chapter 2 presents the language's tonal patterns, and chapter 3 introduces students to the basic word order of a Mvskoke sentence. In chapter 4, students are introduced to means of marking the definiteness and indefiniteness of nouns in Mvskoke, to adjective formation and placement in sentences, and to the formation of diminutive noun forms. Chapter 5 shows students how to construct sentences containing adverbs. Chapters 6 through 11 cover denotation of subject and object, the past tenses, and question formation.

Each chapter narrative is followed by a vocabulary list, a set of conversational sentences, a set of exercises, an essay, and suggestions for further reading. The vocabulary in each chapter focuses on a particular aspect of Muskogee-Seminole life and culture, and the essay follows through on that theme. Students are supplied with nouns and verbs that will allow them to participate in simple conversations about these topics. The conversational sentences center on the vocabulary and essay themes and provide students with yet another means of enhancing their speaking ability.

After completing the chapters and exercises, students will be able to formulate and understand sentences containing singular subjects and objects and past tense formations, and they will be able to distinguish questions from declarative sentences. We have reserved plural subjects and objects for a second textbook, because they require the use of very different forms for many common verbs, as well as additional forms of the suffixes and prefixes introduced in this volume. We believe it is best to introduce singular subject and object forms and provide a solid background in basic Mvskoke grammar before introducing the more advanced plural forms.

The majority of the essays in the chapters were written by Bertha Tilkens, who participates in traditional activities and has learned about Muskogee and Seminole culture from her elders. Pam Innes wrote the first two essays, which describe the relationships among different Southeastern languages in the family to which Mvskoke belongs and inform students about Muskogee and Seminole history. Linda Alexander, who is Bertha Tilkens's mother, wrote the essay for chapter 10, regarding preexisting Muskogee-Seminole knowledge and the effects of Anglo-European education on Muskogee and Seminole children. These essays are intended as introductions to each topic, and students are encouraged to seek out further sources about items that pique their interest.

The titles listed in the Suggested Readings sections and in the bibliography are meant as resources for students who wish to explore Mvskoke further; the bibliography covers all the references used in the writing of this text. Many of the articles and books listed there utilize linguistic notations and terminology and may be beyond the range of interest of most students. We offer them, however, because many of these are seminal works in the field of Mvskoke linguistics and may be of interest to some students.

Two read-only compact discs (CD ROMs) are included with this book to help learners hear the cadence and flow of Mvskoke. They contain examples of spoken Mvskoke, including sentences, stories, and a form of oratory heard at ceremonial grounds (stompgrounds), as well as Muskogee music.

CD A also contains sound files necessary to complete some of the exercises in the book. The voice most often heard speaking on the CDs is Linda Alexander's. The stompground speech was made by Andrew Alexander. Jimmy Gibson sings the stompdance song, and Linda Alexander sings the hymns. Further examples of stompdance songs and church hymns in Mvskoke are available at shops and gift stores in the Muskogee Creek and Seminole Nations.

We encourage you, the student, to use the language as often as you can in your daily life. Only through repeated practice and use will you be able to retain and master the language forms and structures covered in the text. Although learning Mvskoke may, at first, seem a daunting task, it is possible. If you run into periods of frustration or have difficulty with some of the concepts, we encourage you to keep trying and keep working at the problem. Learning a new language is time consuming and takes a good deal of effort. We support you in your endeavor to learn Mvskoke and hope that this book helps you to do so.

In this text, two spellings are used to refer to the people who speak the language—always identified as "Mvskoke"—analyzed here. Those who are not Mvskoke speakers most frequently use the spelling "Muskogee" to refer to the Mvskoke-speaking population. From the mid-1700s on, European powers dealt with representatives of the Muskogee population, and the United States government now recognizes the Muskogee (Creek) Nation, whose members make up a large portion of Mvskoke speakers in Oklahoma. "Mvskoke" is the spelling often preferred by members of the population itself because it utilizes the alphabet adopted by the population and is a distinctive marker of identity. As we are writing both from within and outside of the population and are speaking to those who are and are not members, we use both spellings in this text.

Acknowledgments

This book is the culmination of several years of work. It was begun at the urging of Dr. Loretta Fowler, then chair of the Department of Anthropology at the University of Oklahoma. She had envisioned that the book could become a basic text for use in the Mvskoke language courses taught at the university, and we certainly hope that it will be used in that venue. She took the time to read through very early drafts of some of the first chapters, for which we thank her.

Our colleagues teaching the other Native American language classes at the University of Oklahoma in the mid-1990s, Marcia Haag (Choctaw), Gus Palmer (Kiowa), and Laura Anderson and the late Bobby Blossom (Cherokee), were great morale boosters and applauded our efforts to finish this book. Our discussions about teaching strategies, material presentation, and which points to emphasize in each language were insightful and helpful. We sincerely thank each of them and those who are now teaching the language classes at the university. Dr. Morris Foster was one of the faculty members sponsoring the first Mvskoke language classes, and we acknowledge his help in founding the classes that led to this book.

We have each had a great number of teachers from among the Muskogee and Seminole Nation communities. Pam's thanks go first and foremost to her co-authors, Bertha Tilkens and Linda Alexander. Without their friendship, guidance, teaching, humor, knowledge, and patience, this book could not possibly have been completed, nor would Pam have made so many friends in the Muskogee and Seminole communities. Among the other people whose friendship, knowledge, and use of Mvskoke have helped Pam learn about the language are John Proctor, Thomas Yahola, Felix Gouge, George Bunny, Margaret Mauldin, Kelly Bell, Myrtle Monday, the late Toney Hill, the late Tema Tiger, and others too numerous to name.

Throughout the writing of this manuscript, Pam's parents, Robert and Joan Innes, were tremendously supportive. They also pushed and prodded at times, keeping the work moving. Without their love and support, the book would probably still be a work in progress.

Linda Alexander learned about Muskogee and Seminole culture and language from her father, Waddie Gibbs. Manie Cumseh, Linda's mother, died early in Linda's childhood, so her father became the primary caregiver in her life. He believed strongly in the traditional ways and did not speak English in the home. Linda also wishes to acknowledge the role her brother, George Gibbs, played in her acquisition of Muskogee and Seminole tradition. He encouraged her participation in traditional ceremonies and provided her with insights he gained from his own experiences in the Seminole community.

Bertha Tilkens was taught about Muskogee and Seminole culture and language by her grandparents Waddie Gibbs and Rosey Alexander. They provided her with guidance and encouragement, and the insights they shared with her influence her to this day.

We all wish to thank Andrew Alexander, Jimmy R. Gibson, and Marvin Alexander for their assistance in compiling the information on the accompanying CDs. Andrew kindly performed a speech in the style that one might hear at the ceremonial grounds, which has a cadence quite different from ordinary Mvskoke speech. Jimmy led a song that one would hear at the ceremonial grounds, which should give listeners a sense of the rhythm and sound experienced at the dances. Marvin did a wonderful job of recording and arranging the tracks on the CD. Without his work and skills, the recording would not have been possible.

Ultimately, the people we thank most are our students. You have made us realize how important the maintenance of the language is, how it can be taught through a variety of means, and how meaningful teaching others can be. We sincerely hope that you will find this book useful in learning how to use the language in real-life situations, with other Mvskoke speakers. If there are errors or omissions in the book, they are Pam's responsibility, as she was in charge of typing all the sentences and vocabulary items. Any mistakes in the linguistic discussions are also hers.

Beginning Creek

CHAPTER 1

The Mvskoke Alphabet and Phonemes

This chapter introduces the Mvskoke alphabet and the phonemes of the language. **Phonemes** are the sounds of a language that speakers recognize and expect to hear. When you use the alphabet and produce the phonemes of Mvskoke correctly, Mvskoke speakers will be able to read what you write and understand what you say.

Though there are some exceptions, many of the sounds of Mvskoke are similar to those found in English. For this reason, many of these sounds can be represented by letters of the English alphabet. The alphabet used to write Mvskoke is a revised version of the one adopted by the Muskogee Creek Tribe in the late 1800s. The Mvskoke alphabet represents most of the sounds of the language and provides an efficient spelling method for the writing system. As you will see in later chapters, however, the Mvskoke alphabet does not portray all of the nuances found in the language—some sound qualities are not visibly represented in written Mvskoke text.

The letters of the Mvskoke alphabet and their phonemic representations are given in table 1.1. Linguists use these phonemic symbols as a means of representing the sounds in Mvskoke. The phonemic symbols are used throughout this chapter and in the pronunciation guide for each entry in the glossaries at the end of this book. When the phonemic symbols appear, they indicate that a particular type of sound is being discussed—for linguists, this symbolism provides a great deal of information about the

TABLE 1.1. The Mvskoke Alphabet and Its Phonemes

Mvskoke Alphabet Symbol	Phonemic Symbol	Mvskoke Alphabet Symbol	Phonemic Symbol
a	/a:/	n	/n/
c	/č/	o	/o/
e	/ɪ/	p	/p/
ē	/i:/	r	/ɬ/
f	/f/	s	/s/
h	/h/	t	/t/
i	/e:/	u	/u/
k	/k/	v	/a/
l	/l/	w	/w/
m	/m/	y	/y/

way in which the sound is produced.[1] Although the phonemic system offers the reader, too, a great deal of information about the sounds in a word, few literate Mvskoke (Creek) people use it. The majority of written Mvskoke has been and is currently produced using the Mvskoke alphabet. For this reason, it is this alphabet that we use throughout the text.

In order to use the alphabet appropriately, a student needs to learn three general rules. First, Mvskoke *i*, *r*, and *v* do not represent the same sounds these letters symbolize in English. Second, each sound represented by a letter in a Mvskoke word is pronounced—there are no silent letters. And third, the consonants *w* and *y* are never written at the end of a syllable. However, you may *hear* /w/ and /y/ at the end of a syllable, as in *cokv* 'book', which is occasionally pronounced [čowga]. Most of the time, but not always, when you hear /w/ or /y/ at the end of a syllable, the vowel will be written as a diphthong. (Diphthongs are discussed later in this chapter.) You should try to quickly master the sounds of the Mvskoke language and become familiar with the Mvskoke alphabet, because this will save you a great deal of time and frustration.

1. For more information about linguistic representations of speech sounds, consult Ladefoged 2000a and 2000b or Fromkin and Rodman 1998, as listed in the bibliography. Ladefoged's works describe the ways linguists categorize various kinds of sounds, how sounds are produced, and how they are represented. Fromkin and Rodman 1998 is an introductory textbook that covers much of the same information in a less technical fashion.

Consonants

In Mvskoke orthography, *c, f, h, k, l, m, n, p, r, s, t, w,* and *y* are consonants. Most of the Mvskoke consonants in this group sound almost identical to the English consonants represented by the same letters. For instance, *f, h, l, m, n, s, w,* and *y* of the Mvskoke alphabet represent sounds similar to the sounds English speakers associate with these letters.

But not all of the letters represent the same sounds that the letters in the English alphabet do. In the Mvskoke alphabet, *c* /č/ represents the sound of *ch* in the word "such." This form of /č/ is described as **unaspirated**, which means that no puff of air is released with the sound. (You can see the difference between the aspirated and unaspirated forms of /č/ by holding a piece of paper in front of your mouth as you pronounce the words "cheese" and "such." The paper will vibrate after you have produced the /č/ of "cheese" and will remain still after the /č/ of "such." The paper vibrates because the /č/ of "cheese" is aspirated—it is followed by a puff of air.) In English, a /č/ at the beginning of a word is always aspirated. You will need to concentrate on making an unaspirated /č/ at the beginning of a Mvskoke word.

Another letter that represents a sound you would not expect is *r* /ł/. The *r* of Mvskoke orthography represents a sound that does not occur in English. To make this sound, place your tongue in position as though you are going to make the /l/ of "lean." Instead of making the /l/, force air over the top of your tongue and let the air exit off the sides of your tongue. You should hear a sound similar to saying *th* and /l/ all at once (like saying "thlee," which is the Mvskoke word *rē* 'arrow', instead of "three"). When you make *r* /ł/ correctly, you will hear only the sound of the air as it is pushed out between the edge of your tongue and the roof of your mouth. Watch and listen carefully to your instructor or other Mvskoke speakers as they make this sound—try to imitate what they are doing. You will find that some, primarily younger Mvskoke speakers pronounce this sound like the English *th* of "thing," but the older and more preferred pronunciation is the one we have described.

The Mvskoke consonants *c, k, p,* and *t* have a sound quality that varies from what English speakers tend to consider normal for these consonants. This is because the sounds represented by these letters change depending on the sounds that surround them. In order to know how to produce these consonants correctly, one needs to understand a quality of sounds called **voicing**. **Voiced sounds** are produced when your vocal cords vibrate as you say the sound. (You can check to see whether a sound is voiced or not by placing your fingers on your throat, around your Adam's apple. If you feel a vibration in your throat as you make a particular sound, then the sound is voiced.)

In Mvskoke, as in English, all vowels are voiced. So are the sounds represented by *l, m, n, w,* and *y* in the Mvskoke alphabet. Generally, the sounds represented by *c, k, p,* and *t* are voiced and unaspirated when they occur between two of these sounds (vowels or *l, m, n, w,* and *y*). Therefore, when *c, k, p,* and *t* occur between two voiced sounds, *c* will sound like the *j* /dž/ of "judge"; *k* will sound like *g* /g/ of "beg"; *p* will sound like *b* /b/ of "web"; and *t* will sound like *d* /d/ of "bed."

You also may hear that *c, k, p,* and *t* seem to be voiced when they begin a word. The consonants appear to be voiced because the voicing of the vowel begins before the consonant has been finished. Thus, the voicing of the vowel has influenced the sound of the preceding (voiceless) consonant. You should remember this, because the voiced versions of these consonants are not different phonemes in Mvskoke; when you hear /dž/, /g/, /b/, or /d/ at the beginning of a word, you will need to spell the word with an initial *c, k, p,* or *t,* respectively.

When *c, k, p,* and *t* are not bracketed by voiced sounds, they are voiceless and unaspirated. **Voiceless sounds** are produced when your vocal cords do not vibrate as you say the sound. (If you put your fingers to your throat as you produce the sound, you should not feel any vibration.) In these cases, the Mvskoke letter *c* will sound like *ch* of "such," Mvskoke *k* will sound like the English *k* of "take," Mvskoke *p* will sound like the English *p* of "cup," and Mvskoke *t* will sound like the English *t* of "bit." *C, k, p,* and *t* are also voiceless and unaspirated when they occur as the final consonant in a syllable, even if this causes them to be between two voiced sounds. For instance, the *k* in *vklopis* 'I am swimming', which is the final sound in the first syllable, is voiceless and unaspirated even though it occurs between two voiced sounds. The glossaries show syllable divisions within words, and you should check those sources if you are uncertain whether a *c, k, p,* or *t* is the final sound in a syllable.

Vowels

The vowels of Mvskoke are represented by *a,ē, e, i, o, u,* and *v*. The sounds represented by most of these letters differ from their English values. **Vowel length**, or the length of time a vowel sound is held, is important in Mvskoke. Some of the letters used to represent Mvskoke vowels show that the vowel is long, whereas others indicate that the vowel is short. The long vowels of Mvskoke each have a corresponding short version, and it is as long-short pairs that we introduce the vowels here.

Vowel length is tremendously important in Mvskoke. Speakers pay close attention to vowel length, for it is a meaningful distinction in the language. For instance, vowel length and tonal accent (introduced in chapter 2) are the only items that differentiate *pose* /posí/ 'grandmother' from *pose* /pó:si/ 'cat'. One of the key differences between these words is the length of the *o*—the *o* of 'cat' is held for a longer time than is the *o* of 'grandmother'. The pitch of the syllables within these words is different as well, but vowel length is still very important in enabling a speaker to understand which of the two words you are producing.

Another important quality of Mvskoke vowels, and one that differentiates them from English vowels, is the fact that the majority of Mvskoke vowels represented by single alphabetic symbols are **pure vowels**. This means that there is almost no movement of the tongue or jaw while the sound is being produced. The majority of English vowels represented by single alphabetic symbols are diphthongized—they are produced with some movement—and are not pure vowels.

To illustrate the difference between a pure vowel and a diphthongized vowel, pronounce the word "go" very slowly. You should feel your mouth move as you pronounce the *o* of this word: your jaw will move upward and your lips will move until they are pursed. If you listen carefully, it will sound as though the initial /o/ is followed by a /w/. Now, try pronouncing the word without moving your mouth once you have begun the *o* portion—you are now producing the Mvskoke vowel *o* /o/. Notice that there is no "w-quality" in the Mvskoke pronunciation of the vowel sound, in comparison with the usual English pronunciation. It will probably take you some time to get used to producing pure vowels, but it is necessary if you wish to speak like your instructor.

The Mvskoke vowel *i* /e:/ is usually pronounced like the *ay* of "say," but without movement of the jaw or tongue. The English pronunciation of "say" involves jaw and tongue movement as the vowel is produced. Mvskoke speakers keep their mouth in a relatively fixed position as they make this sound, which makes this a pure vowel in Mvskoke. You will need to pay attention to your pronunciation of this vowel, as the tendency will be to pronounce it as a diphthong. However, in order to produce this vowel correctly according to Mvskoke usage, you should not move your jaw or tongue much while making this vowel sound, thereby producing a pure vowel.

The first Mvskoke vowel of the alphabet, written as *a*, sounds like the /a/ of "father." This vowel is long—the sound is held for a long time. You should pay close attention to your CDs or to the speaker with whom you are working in order to get used to hearing long vowels. (In the pronunciation guides in the glossaries, which use the phonemic writing system, this vowel is represented by /a:/, an *a* followed by a colon. The colon indicates that this, or any other vowel it follows, is long.)

The short vowel that corresponds to *a* is *v* /a/. Mvskoke *v* sounds like the *u* in "but." Occasionally, *v* has the quality of the /a/ in "father," just as Mvskoke *a* does. However, even when we English speakers might think it has the same sound, it is short—Mvskoke *a* and *v* are very different to a Mvskoke speaker, on the basis of their length.

Mvskoke *ē* and *e* are the long and short members of another length-based vowel pair. Mvskoke *ē* /i:/ is the long vowel. This vowel always has the sound of *ee* in "beet," held for a long time. The short vowel, Mvskoke *e* /i/, can be pronounced in two ways: most often, it sounds like the *ee* of "beet," but there are times when it sounds like the *i* of "bit." In either case, the sound is held for a short length of time. You should concentrate on listening for the length of the vowel sound, so that you will know which of these vowels, *e* and *ē*, is being produced.

Mvskoke *i* /e:/ can be pronounced in two ways. Generally, as we mentioned earlier, it represents the sound of *ay* in "say," but it may also be pronounced as the sound of *e* in "bet." Mvskoke *i* /e:/ tends to have the quality of *e* in "bet" when it is added to verbs to show that "I" am the person performing the action. We will cover this use of Mvskoke *i* at a later point. This vowel does not have a short version and is generally held for a fairly long length of time.

Mvskoke *o* /o/ represents both a short vowel and a long vowel. In its short version, Mvskoke *o* /o/ sounds like the *o* in the English "so," but without any "w-quality," which is characteristic of the English pronunciation of this vowel. It has a long variant, which is represented by the same symbol in the Mvskoke alphabet, *o* /o:/. The long form also sounds like *o* in "so," again without a "w-quality," but is held longer than the short form. Because there is no mark that signifies whether the *o* is long or short, you will have to listen carefully to your instructor.

Mvskoke *u* is always short. This vowel sound is like the *oo* of "look." *U* is a relatively uncommon vowel and appears to be a variant of the short /o/ of Mvskoke.

Diphthongs

Diphthongs are combinations of vowel sounds in the same syllable. An example of a diphthong that we use in English is the /oy/ of "boy." If you pay attention to your mouth as you produce the /oy/ sound, you will notice that your lips, tongue, and jaw move. It is that movement which tells you that the sound you have just produced is a diphthong—the parts of your mouth are moving during the production of the sound. We tend to hear this sound as though it is a single vowel, but it is not.

There are three diphthongs in Mvskoke. The first of these is written as *oe* or *ue*. It has the sound of /oy/ in "boy," and is evident in forms of the word for water: *oewv* and *uewv*. A second diphthong is written as *eu*. This diphthong sounds like the /eu/ in "reuse," as evident in the Mvskoke word *cēmeu* 'you'. The third diphthong is written as *vo*. It begins with the sound of /u/ in "hut" followed by the sound of /o/ in "so." This diphthong occurs in the word *vhvoke* 'door'. Diphthongs are relatively uncommon in Mvskoke, and they have no long forms.

Each of the nouns and verbs presented in the vocabulary section of this chapter is pronounced for you in tracks 39–64 on CD A of the accompanying set. Listen carefully to these words, for they contain all of the sounds except /ł/ and the diphthongs. Practice repeating these words after Linda pronounces them, for they will help you to become used to the different sounds and the cadence and rhythm of Mvskoke.

Representative Two- and Three-Letter Syllables

A Sample of Two-Letter Syllables

ca	ce	cē	ci	co	cu	cv
fa	fe	fē	fi	fo	fu	fv
ha	he	hē	hi	ho	hu	hv
ka	ke	kē	ki	ko	ku	kv
la	le	lē	li	lo	lu	lv
ma	me	mē	mi	mo	mu	mv
na	ne	nē	ni	no	nu	nv
pa	pe	pē	pi	po	pu	pv
ra	re	rē	ri	ro	ru	rv
sa	se	sē	si	so	su	sv

ta	te	tē	ti	to	tu	tv
wa	we	wē	wi	wo	wu	wv
ya	ye	yē	yi	yo	yu	yv
af	ef	ēf	if	of	uf	vf
ak	ek	ēk	ik	ok	uk	vk
al	el	ēl	il	ol	ul	vl
am	em	ēm	im	om	um	vm
an	en	ēn	in	on	un	vn
ap	ep	ēp	ip	op	up	vp
as	es	ēs	is	os	us	vs
at	et	ēt	it	ot	ut	vt

A Sample of Three-Letter Syllables

hak	hek	hēk	hik	hok	huk	hvk
hal	hel	hēl	hil	hol	hul	hvl
has	hes	hēs	his	hos	hus	hvs
lak	lek	lēk	lik	lok	luk	lvk
mak	mek	mēk	mik	mok	muk	mvk
man	men	mēn	min	mon	mun	mvn
mas	mes	mēs	mis	mos	mus	mvs
mat	met	mēt	mit	mot	mut	mvt
nak	nek	nēk	nik	nok	nuk	nvk
sak	sek	sēk	sik	sok	suk	svk
tak	tek	tēk	tik	tok	tuk	tvk
hvr	hvt	kas	let	nvr	pen	pok
pon	rak	rof	tor	tos	yek	yvt

Vocabulary

Terms for People

Mvskoke	English
honvnwv	man
hoktē	woman
cepanē	boy

hoktuce	girl
estuce	child
pipuce	baby
este vculē	old man
hoktvlē	old woman
honvnwv ehicv	married man
hoktē ehessē	married woman

Verbs

(The symbols in brackets following the Mvskoke infinitives are covered in later chapters.)

Mvskoke	English
yvkvpetv {I}	to walk
letketv {I}	to run
hvlketv {I}	to crawl
omiyetv {I} *or* vklopetv {I}	to swim
svtohketv {I;3}	to drive
liketv {I}	to sit
ohliketv {I;3}	to ride
tvmketv {I}	to fly
wvkketv {I}	to lie down
hueretv {I}	to stand
selaksēketv {I}	to yell or scream
kerretv {I;II}	to know (someone or something)

An Introductory Conversation

Hoktet 1: Hensci!	Woman 1: Hello!
Hoktet 2: Hensci!	Woman 2: Hello!
Hoktet 1: Estvnko?	Woman 1: How are you?
Hoktet 2: Vnhēnrētos. Mvn centv?	Woman 2: I am fine. And you?
Hoktet 1: Estvnkewiseks.	Woman 1: I am fine.
Hoktet 2: Naket cehocefkvtē?	Woman 2: What is your name?
Hoktet 1: ________ cvhocefkvtos.	Woman 1: My name is ___________.

Fig. 1.1. Getting ready for the Buffalo Dance, to be led by singer Toney Hill. The dancers, who have lined up and are walking toward the dance ground, are led by Burt Tilkens and Jimmy R. Gibson (at far right). The other dancers pictured are, in pairs behind the dance leaders, Bertha Tilkens and Anna Cooper, Simon Harry and Marvin Squires, and Bonnie Gibson and Mary Cully. *Photograph by Linda Alexander.*

Exercises

Exercise 1

Turn back to Table 1.1, which lists the Mvskoke alphabet and its phonemes. Listen closely as the instructor makes the sound of every character. Imitate him or her as best you can. The alphabet is also pronounced on CD A, accompanying this book. Imitate the speaker on the CD as closely as possible. Repeat the entire alphabet three or four times.

Exercise 2

Turn to the list of two-letter syllables on page 9.

For the first part of the exercise, determine which syllables contain or may contain a long vowel. Repeat these syllables after the instructor, making certain that you produce a long vowel as you pronounce them.

For the second part of the exercise, determine which syllables contain or may contain a short vowel. Repeat these syllables after the instructor, making certain that you produce a short vowel as you pronounce them.

Exercise 3

Turn to the list of three-letter syllables on page 10. Repeat the syllables after the instructor. Write down the syllables that are pronounced with a long vowel.

Exercise 4

Listen to the "Exercise 1-4" file on CD A. Pronounce the words after the speaker. Then write down the one- and two-syllable words pronounced by the speaker. Look these words up in the Mvskoke-to-English glossary and provide the definitions for them.

Exercise 5

Working with a partner, pronounce the vocabulary words in this chapter and give their meanings. Listen to your partner's pronunciation of the vocabulary words. Critique your partner's pronunciation, remembering which words caused pronunciation problems or questions for you or your partner. Ask your instructor to repeat these words again in class.

Exercise 6

Working with a partner, pronounce the following phrases. Repeat those phrases containing letters that may represent either long or short versions of sounds, pronouncing them first with the short version, then with the long. Check the glossary if you are uncertain whether a *k*, *p*, or *t* ends a syllable. Listen to your partner's pronunciation of the phrases. Note which phrases cause you and your partner trouble. Ask your instructor to repeat these phrases in class.

1. cetto mekko
2. efv hvtkat
3. honvnwvt wakkes
4. eto rakkan
5. tolose palen

6. vhvoke lvstēn
7. uewv okofkē
8. tvklike svkmorkē
9. estenkehute
10. perro okvtafkes

The Muskogee Language Family

Mvskoke is one of several languages that were originally spoken in the southeastern United States. Technically, Mvskoke refers to the language spoken by members of the Muskogee (Creek) Nation, to distinguish it from a closely related language, Seminole. Mvskoke and Seminole, however, very closely resemble each other in their sound systems, their writing systems, and the majority of the vocabulary used to refer to items and actions in the world. Therefore, this text should be considered an introduction to the Seminole language as well as to Mvskoke.

Linguists are able to show relationships between languages by comparing word lists, sound systems, and grammars. From such analyses, linguists have found that Mvskoke is one of eight related languages spoken by American Indian peoples who originally lived in the southeastern United States. The related languages are considered to be part of a **language family**, which means that the languages all sprang from the same ancestral language (just as a family is related through its ancestors). The ancestral language is called a **proto-language**.

The family tree for the languages in the Muskogean language family is shown in diagram 1.1. This graphic shows that certain languages within the family are more closely related to each other than they are to the other members of the family. Choctaw and Chickasaw, Alabama and Koasati, Mikasuki and Hitchiti, and Mvskoke and Seminole are each more closely related to the other language in the pair than they are to the other languages in the family. Each pair belongs to a common branch descending from the parent language, Proto-Muskogean.

Because these languages are connected, you will find that many of the sounds, some of the grammatical rules, and some of the vocabulary of one of them sounds similar to the sounds, rules, and words of one or more of the other, related languages. Each is a distinct language, however, so it is not entirely possible to translate the statements of a speaker of another of the languages without some training or experience. It is often possible, however,

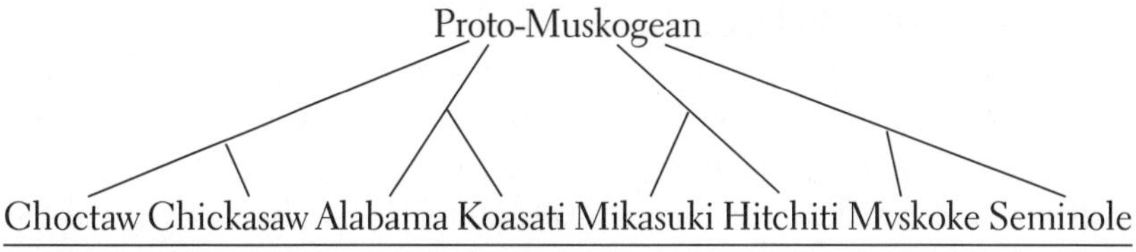

Diagram 1.1. The Muskogean Language Family

to understand some of what a speaker of another, closely related language is saying. If the languages are distantly related (that is, do not share the same line of descent from the parent language), then it will be more difficult to understand what a speaker is saying.

As you might expect, Proto-Muskogean is no longer spoken. It was the language that gave rise to each of the eight daughter languages, but in doing so, it fell out of use. As groups split off from the original speakers of Proto-Muskogean, their languages changed so much that they resemble Proto-Muskogean only slightly. Linguists are working to reconstruct Proto-Muskogean. They work from the sounds, words, and grammatical rules of each of the daughter languages to discover the sounds, rules, and words that must once have been used in Proto-Muskogean. This is a lengthy, involved process, but perhaps someday linguists will be able to re-create the original parent language of the Muskogean language family.

Suggested Readings

For more information about the sounds in Mvskoke and related languages, interested readers might wish to consult Mary Haas's "Nasals and Nasalization in Creek" (1977a) and her "Tonal Accent in Creek" (1977b), as well as Jack B. Martin and Margaret McKane Mauldin's *A Dictionary of Creek/Muskogee* (2000:xix–xxiii). All three works are listed in the bibliography. The Haas articles are somewhat technical but offer an insightful analysis of the rules governing the sounds and stress patterns in the language. Martin and Mauldin's work provides an easy-to-read pronunciation guide and discussion of nasalization in Mvskoke, which we have not discussed here.

Those interested in exploring the Muskogean language family and the relationships between its languages may want to consult Karen M. Booker's articles "The Loss of Preconsonantal *k in Creek/Seminole" (1988) and "More on the Development of Proto-Muskogean $*k^{w}$" (1993); Haas's "The

Classification of the Muskogean Languages" (1941), "The Position of Apalachee in the Muskogean Family" (1949), and "Southeastern Languages" (1979); and Pamela Munro's "Introduction: Muskogean Studies at UCLA" (1987) and "The Muskogean II Prefixes and their Significance for Classification" (1993). Because of their reliance on demonstrating similarities and correspondences among the languages in the family, readers may find these sources more technical than they would like.

Lyle Campbell's *American Indian Languages* (1997), Campbell and Marianne Mithun's *The Languages of Native America* (1979), and Michael K. Foster's "Language and the Culture History of North America" (1996) explore language family groupings throughout North, Central, and South America. These sources offer explanations of how languages are placed within particular families, and Foster and Campbell each discuss the inferences archaeologists and anthropologists draw about population movements and prehistory from language family groups.

CHAPTER 2

Tonal Accent

As in all other languages, there is a particular cadence or rhythm to spoken Mvskoke. The rhythm of Mvskoke is somewhat different from the rhythm of English, and you will need to become familiar with Mvskoke's cadence in order to pronounce words and sentences correctly.

The rhythm of Mvskoke is caused by arrangements of tonal accent in the words and sentences. **Tonal accent** refers to the way in which syllables in words are pronounced at different pitches—in some places the speaker's voice will go up or down in tone as he or she pronounces a syllable. For instance, most speakers pronounce the English interjection "uh-oh" with a higher tone on the first syllable ("uh") than on the following syllable ("oh").

In Mvskoke, the pitch contours of the syllables in a word are fairly regular and in some cases determine the meaning of the word. Tone is thus a very important feature to attend to when learning to pronounce Mvskoke words. This is very different from English, where stress—the amount of vocal force used when pronouncing a word or syllable—is more important than tone. You will need to listen consciously for the tonal qualities of the words your teacher is producing and remain intent on re-creating those tonal qualities when you say the words.

Light and Heavy Syllables

In order to understand how syllable pitches are organized in Mvskoke words, it is necessary to consider the different types of syllables that may occur. There are two forms of syllables in Mvskoke, light syllables and heavy syllables. **Light syllables** (abbreviated "L") are composed of a short vowel alone, a consonant followed by a short vowel, or a short vowel followed by a consonant. The words in examples 1, 2, and 3 all contain light syllables (the syllables are separated by raised dots when the word is presented in its phonemic form, following its Mvskoke spelling).

1.	efv	i·fa	'dog'
2.	coko	co·ko	'house'
3.	este	is·ti	'person, man'

In example 1, the first syllable is made up of a single short vowel; it is a light syllable for this reason. Light syllables made up of a consonant followed by a short vowel are evident in the second syllables of examples 1, 2, and 3 and the first syllable of example 2. A short vowel followed by a consonant is found in the first syllable of example 3.

Heavy syllables (abbreviated "H") are composed of a long vowel alone, a consonant followed by a long vowel, or a vowel (either long or short) between two consonants. Heavy syllables demonstrating these different forms of construction are found in examples 4, 5, and 6.

4.	ayo	a:·yo	'hawk'
5.	hēyvn	hi:·yan	'here'
6.	wakkes	wa:k·kis	'he/she/it is lying down'

Example 4 has an initial heavy syllable, the long vowel *a*, followed by a light syllable. The first syllable of example 5 is a heavy syllable constructed of a consonant followed by a long vowel. The heavy syllable form consonant-short vowel-consonant is found in the second syllables of examples 5 and 6, whereas the form consonant-long vowel-consonant is found in the first syllable of example 6.

When determining whether a syllable is heavy or light, remember that *a* and *ē* are long vowels and will cause their syllables to be heavy syllables. Because *i* is a diphthong ending in the consonantal sound /y/, it forms a heavy syllable when it follows a consonant but is considered a light syllable if it is the only sound constituting the syllable (that is, it acts as a short vowel-consonant combination). Further examples of the different forms of light and heavy syllables are presented in tables 2.1 and 2.2.

TABLE 2.1. Structures of Light Syllables

Short Vowel Alone	Consonant-Short Vowel	Short Vowel-Consonant
e	fe	ef
v	fv	vf
o	fo	of
u	fu	uf
		er

TABLE 2.2. Structures of Heavy Syllables

Long Vowel Alone	Consonant-Long Vowel	Consonant-Vowel-Consonant
ē	fē	fek
a	fa	fēk
o (long form)	fo	fok
i	fi	fik

KEY SYLLABLES AND TONAL PATTERNING

In general, Mvskoke tonal accent is governed by the number and structure of the syllables within a word. All Mvskoke words containing more than one syllable have one key syllable. A **key syllable** is a syllable that governs the tone levels of the syllables around it. A small number of syllables in Mvskoke are always key syllables, but the majority of Mvskoke syllables may or may not play the role of key syllable in a word. Syllables that always act as key syllables are covered later in this chapter and in subsequent chapters. Ultimately, the key syllable in a word determines where the highest tone is, and other syllables have tones lower than the key syllable's.

Words with Only Light Syllables

In words that end in a light syllable and that do not contain one of the small number of syllables that are always key, the location of the syllable that governs the tonal accent pattern in the word generally depends upon how many light syllables precede the end of the word. When the word is made up only of light syllables, the last even-numbered light syllable plays the role of the key syllable. If the key syllable is the next-to-last (penultimate) syllable in the word, then the syllable will have a higher tone than the syllables that come before it and follow it, as in examples 7 and 8.

7.	cvpvwv			
	ca·pá·wa	LLL	i-2-d	'my maternal uncle'
8.	pohetv			
	po·hí·ta	LLL	i-2-d	'to hear'

In these and subsequent examples, the syllables in the word, separated by raised periods, and the kinds of syllables they are (heavy or light) are presented in the second line. The key syllable is indicated by an accent (´), or tone mark—here, the mark over the */a/* in *ca·pá·wa* and over the */i/* in *po·hí·ta*. Also given in the second line are the tones of the individual syllables. Tones are indicated by numbers, with the higher tones represented by lower numbers. Thus, a syllable with a tone of 2 has a higher pitch than one with a tone of 3. Tones represented by 23 or 24 are falling tones—the tone begins high and drops before the next syllable is produced. Initial syllables are produced with a tone, indicated by *i*, that is slightly lower than the tone of the syllable they precede. The symbol *d* represents a very low tone.

When the last even-numbered light syllable is the last syllable in the word, all preceding syllables, except those having the "initial syllable tone," have the same relatively low tone, as is shown in examples 9 and 10.

9.	cofe			
	co·fí	LL	3-3	'rabbit'
10.	vmefuce			
	am·i·fu·cí	LLLL	i-3-3-3	'my puppy'

The tone of the initial syllable in example 10 is slightly lower than the tone of all the syllables following it, so it has an *i* tone designation. In example 9, however, the initial syllable is pronounced in the same tone as the syllable following it.

All four of the preceding examples show that the syllables preceding the key syllable are either lower in tone than the key syllable or are at the same tone. Any syllables following the key syllable are lower in tone and are produced with less force. In cases where the tonal accent is highest on the penultimate syllable, as in examples 7 and 8, the final syllable will have a very low tone.

Words with Light and Heavy Syllables

In words that contain some heavy syllables but end in a light syllable, the placement of the key syllable is determined by the number of light syllables following the heavy syllables. If one light syllable follows the last heavy syllable, then stress and higher tone will be placed on the penultimate heavy syllable. Examples 11 and 12 show how stress and higher tone are applied to the penultimate heavy syllable. Note that even though example 12 has more than one heavy syllable, only the penultimate heavy syllable receives the tone level appropriate for a key syllable.

11.	honvnwv			
	ho·nán·wa	LHL	i-2-d	'man'
12.	hoporrenkv			
	ho·poł·łín·ka	LHHL	i-3-2-d	'penny'

If multiple light syllables follow the last heavy syllable, then the final even-numbered light syllable, counting from the heavy syllable forward, will be the key syllable. Examples 13 and 14 involve words in which at least one heavy syllable is followed by multiple light syllables.

13.	tafvmpuce			
	ta:·fam·pu·cí	HHLL	i-3-3-3	'wild onion'
14.	mvhakv-cuko			
	ma·ha:·ka·cú·ko	LHLLL	i-3-3-2-d	'school'

Note that the key syllable in example 13 is the last (the even-numbered) light syllable and not either of the heavy syllables. Also note that the first syllable, even though it is a heavy syllable, has the tone *i*, which is slightly lower than the syllables that follow it.

These rules about locating the key syllable work for the majority of Mvskoke words, but there are exceptions. For instance,

15.	este			
	ís·ti	LL	2-d	'person or man'

has a tone pattern of 2-d, with the higher pitch on the first light syllable, rather than on the second. In some words with a combination of heavy and light syllables, there may be tonal features on more than one syllable. In example 16,

16.	sasvkwv			
	sâ:·sak·wa	HHL	24-3-d	'goose',

sasvkwv has a tonal pattern of 24-3-d. The highest tone, followed by a descent in pitch, is placed on the first heavy syllable (as indicated by the circumflex symbol [^] over the *a*). A moderately high tone is placed on the second heavy syllable, and the lowest tone on the final, light syllable. Because of exceptions like these, it is crucial to pay attention to the placement of the tonal mark in the pronunciation guide for each new word you will learn in this book. The general pattern for the position of the key syllable in words that do not contain an "always key" syllable is given in the following list:

If a word contains an even number of light syllables, then the final syllable is the key syllable.
If a word contains an odd number of light syllables, then the penultimate syllable is the key syllable.
If a word contains one light syllable following the last heavy syllable, then the last heavy syllable is the key syllable.
If a word contains multiple light syllables following the last heavy syllable, then the final even-numbered light syllable, counting from the last heavy syllable, is the key syllable.

"Always Key" Syllables

As mentioned earlier, some syllables always play the role of key syllable—for example, verb syllables modified for aspect (introduced in chapter 3), the second person suffix (introduced in chapter 6), and the negating suffix (introduced in chapter 10). The majority of these syllables are added to verbs, which are covered in chapters 3 through 11. If a word has more than one of these "always key" syllables, then the first of them will have the highest tone. All following key syllables will be lower in tone, but they will have a higher tone than their surrounding syllables. Thus, the first always key syllable in a word will have a higher tone than any other syllable. Any following syllables that are not always key syllables may take the same tone as the preceding key syllable or may drop in tone. Examples 17, 18, and 19 present words containing one or more of the always key syllables.

17.	hompeckvnks			
	hom·píc·kanks	HHH	i-2-3	'you were eating'
18.	hompeckvnks			
	hôm·píc·kanks	HHH	24-3-4	'you ate'
19.	hompeckekomvts			
	hom·píc·kí·ko·mats	HHLLH	i-2-3-4-4	'you weren't eating'

In example 18, the falling tonal quality of the first syllable (*hôm*) is meaningful. It is the falling tone that signals that the act has been completed. (You will learn more about this in chapter 9.) Thus, paying attention to tonal quality can be very important in Mvskoke.

Both examples 18 and 19 contain more than one always key syllable. In example 18, the first such syllable (*hôm*) has a falling tone, and the second such syllable (*píc*) has a high tone. In example 19, the second syllable (*píc*) has a high tone, as does the third syllable (*kí*). In both of these words, the first syllable with a tonal quality marked by an accent, an always key syllable, has the highest tone, while the next always key syllable has a tone one step lower than the preceding syllable. Thus, in example 18, the first syllable has a 24 tonal quality (note that it begins with a high tone, indicated by the 2), and the second syllable has a tonal quality of 3. In example 19, the second syllable has a tonal quality of 2, and the following syllable, a tonal quality of 3. The syllable or syllables following the last always key syllable have the tonal quality of 4 in both examples, showing that these non-key syllables are even lower in pitch than the second key syllable in the word. Thus, the tonal quality tends to descend for each consecutive key syllable in a word.

Vocabulary

Numbers

Mvskoke	English
hvmken	one
hokkolen	two
tutcēnen	three
osten	four

cvhkēpen	five
ēpaken	six
kolvpaken	seven
cenvpaken	eight
ostvpaken	nine
palen	ten
palen-hvmkentvlaken	eleven
palen-hokkolohkaken	twelve
palen-tutcenohkaken	thirteen
palen-ostohkaken	fourteen
palen-cvhkēpohkaken	fifteen
palen-ēpohkaken	sixteen
palen-kolvpohkaken	seventeen
palen-cenvpohkaken	eighteen
palen-ostvpohkaken	nineteen
pale-hokkolen	twenty

Verbs

Mvskoke	English
vhvmkvtetv {I;II} *or* vhvnkvtetv {I;II}	to count
kerretv {I;II}	to know
sē emmvhayetv {I}	to practice
mecetv {I;3}	to try, attempt something
em etetakuecetv {I;D}	to prepare
vtotketv {I}	to work (at a job)

Conversational Sentences

Hoktet 1: Hensci.	Woman 1: Hello.
Hoktet 2: Hensci. Stvnko?	Woman 2: Hello. How are you?
Hoktet 1: Vnhēnrētos. Enkv?	Woman 1: I am well. And you?
Hoktet 2: Vnhēnrekotos. Cvkv ennokkētos.	Woman 2: I am not well. My head hurts.
Hoktet 1: Heleswvn ceyacv?	Woman 1: Do you want some medicine?
Hoktet 2: Mvnks. Cvkv ennokkēt wikvrēs.	Woman 2: No. My headache will go away.

Figure 2.1. Getting ready for the Ribbon Dance, Greenleaf Ceremonial Ground, Okemah, Oklahoma, August 1985. Left to right: Muriel Wright, Linda Alexander, Bertha Tilkens, Susan Alexander. Muriel Wright and Susan Alexander are Linda's granddaughters, and Bertha Tilkens is her daughter. *Photograph courtesy of Bertha Tilkens and Linda Alexander.*

Exercises

Exercise 1

Determine the correct placement of the key syllable in the following words. Once you have determined which syllable is the key syllable, list the tones of the preceding and following syllables. (Note: None of these words contains a syllable that always plays the role of a key syllable.)

1. nokwv
2. cvlvkloketv
3. ele-ohsehoyetv
4. vpvllakv
5. tvklike
6. hvyetv

7. cvto
8. pvkpvkoce
9. fuswv
10. hoyv

Exercise 2

Choose ten syllables from the two-letter syllable list on page 9. Decide whether these syllables are light or heavy or may be either. For syllables that may be either light or heavy, pronounce them first as light syllables, then as heavy syllables.

Exercise 3

Working with a partner, randomly select five words from the Mvskoke-to-English glossary at the end of the book. Pronounce each word you have selected. Have your partner write the word as you pronounce it. As you are pronouncing the word, focus on producing truly long vowels, as necessary, and place the tonal accent on the syllables as you were taught in this chapter. You may be asked to pronounce the words you selected in class, so you should note which words you chose.

Exercise 4

Using the syllables from the two- and three-letter syllable lists in chapter 1, create five two-syllable "words." Then, using the same lists, create five three-syllable "words." Finally, create five four-syllable "words" using the two- and three-letter syllables. Now, for each "word" you have created, break the word into its syllables and show which is the key syllable, as was done in the examples in this chapter. Practice pronouncing your "words," placing the highest tonal accent on the syllable you have determined is the key syllable in each word. Be prepared to spell the "words" you have created and pronounce them in class.

Exercise 5

Listen to the file "Exercise 2-5" on CD A. Write each word the speaker pronounces and then determine where the tonal accent falls in each word. Mark where the tonal accent is by placing a tone mark (´) over the appropriate syllable in the word you have spelled. None of these words has an always key syllable.

Exercise 6

Practice the conversational sentences from chapters 1 and 2, as pronounced on CD A. Focus on re-creating the long vowels and the tonal contours of each word. When you feel you have mastered the pronunciation of the two conversations, practice them with another student. Your teacher may ask you to play one of the roles in one of the conversations in class.

A Brief History of the Muskogee

The people who have come to be known as the Muskogee (Creek) and Seminole Nations of Oklahoma are descended from people who originally inhabited the southeastern United States. Before their removal to Oklahoma in the mid-1800s, the Creek and Seminole people inhabited a region that has become the states of Alabama, Georgia, and Florida. The Poarche Band of Creek in Alabama and the Florida Seminoles managed to escape removal and still live in their aboriginal territory today.

Archaeological and historical evidence suggests that the Creeks, Seminoles, and speakers of the other Muskogean languages are descendants of the Mississippian peoples, who flourished from about 700 A.D. until European contact in 1528. People of the Mississippian cultures built towns with mounds—large earthen constructions that occasionally held ceremonial structures or houses of the elites—and they maintained tremendous trade networks stretching from the panhandle of Florida to the Great Lakes region and the middle Great Plains. Their artwork, especially engraved shells, pottery figurines, and carved stone, suggests that they had a social hierarchy and a highly developed religious system. Early Spanish explorers wrote about chiefdoms among the Southeastern people, but these apparently did not survive long into the postcontact era. It is interesting, however, that the words for the highest leaders of the religious institutions and towns among Mvskoke speakers are translated as 'king' or 'chief', which may be a holdover from the chiefdoms of old. It also has been suggested that the stompdance religion currently practiced by the Creek and Seminole people is a remnant of the Mississippian religion.

By the time Europeans were making sustained contact with the Creeks and Seminoles, tribal towns, rather than chiefdoms, were the political, religious, and social centers. Tribal towns were made up of clans consisting of several families, with each family working for the good of itself, its clan, and the town. Clan leaders played a role in the government of the tribal town, but decisions were made communally. The decisions made by one tribal town were not binding on others. Tribal towns were autonomous entities, but they often worked together when matters of great importance were to be undertaken.

Although there is still uncertainty about the date when the Creek Confederacy was formed, the Creeks had certainly devised this system of dealing with European powers by the late 1500s. This form of government, in which the tribal towns retained their autonomy but met as a group to consider decisions affecting all towns, allowed the Creeks and Seminoles to deal as a relatively united group with European governments and commercial entities.

Some of the issues the Creek Confederacy dealt with involved whether or not to go to war. Over the course of their history in the Southeast, the Creeks were involved in wars with the Choctaws, Yamassees, Chickasaws, and Cherokees. They also had their share of internal strife. The Creek War of 1813–14 was a struggle in which one faction, allied with the American army, fought against another, the Redsticks, who advocated warfare against all Euro-Americans. Those who were allied with the American army won, but with severe consequences for all Creeks. Even though those siding with American interests won the war, they were required to cede vast amounts of territory as restitution for damages to American settlers caused by the Redsticks.

The confederacy made many treaties with the British, Spanish, French, and American governments. Some of these treaties governed trade and the conduct of traders within Creek and Seminole territory. A number also dealt with land-use agreements. By the late 1700s and early 1800s, the states of Georgia and Alabama were pursuing treaties to obtain land from the Creeks. By 1811, the leaders of the confederacy had realized that giving away land was causing hardship for the Creek towns. At this time, the confederacy outlawed the selling of Creek land unless all leaders had ratified the sale.

Despite the law outlawing sales of Creek land, William McIntosh, a leader of half of the Creeks, signed a treaty with federal commissioners in 1825, selling all of the territory still held by the Creeks in Georgia and two-thirds of their land in Alabama in exchange for a large tract of land in Oklahoma (Indian Territory) (Debo 1941:89). McIntosh was killed for having made this sale, and it was overturned. Nevertheless, other Creek leaders were convinced to ratify a cession of most of their Georgia holdings in 1826. The states of Georgia and Alabama pressed for removal of the Creeks from their remaining land, in order to increase the numbers of white settlers within the states' boundaries. Pressure from government officials of these and the other Southern states led Creek leaders to sign a removal treaty in 1832 (Debo 1941:98).

As a result of passage of the removal treaty, approximately twenty-three thousand Creeks were forced to leave their homes in Alabama and Georgia for new land in Indian Territory (Debo 1941:103). Several thousand Creeks died during the long trek to Oklahoma. Those who survived found themselves in a new area with a different climate and ecology. However, they soon reestablished their towns, learned to farm and ranch in the new region, and began to grow in numbers.

The Seminoles had decided to move into the Everglades region of Florida, in the hope of escaping removal. They eluded capture and were victorious in many of the battles fought during the Seminole Wars of 1835–37. In the end, some Seminoles did relocate to Indian Territory when this option was offered in exchange for peace. They were given part of Creek territory in Oklahoma, a move that did not sit well with some Creeks at the time. Today, relations are generally good between the Creeks and Seminoles of Oklahoma. Those Seminoles who remained in Florida are recognized as a separate tribe, though they maintain ties with the Oklahoma Seminoles.

The progress that the Creeks and Seminoles were making in Oklahoma was disrupted by the American Civil War. Factions among the Creeks and Seminoles sided with the Confederate states and fought against their tribesmen who sided with the Union forces. When the war ended, both the Creeks and the Seminoles were forced to give up portions of their land in Oklahoma as reparation for damages caused by those who had sided with the Confederate army. Again, they set about rebuilding their towns and social institutions, for many of their settlements had been destroyed in the war.

In 1887, the United States government passed the Dawes Severalty Act. This act was designed to break up communally held Indian land by allotting approximately 160 acres to each person in a tribe. A census of the Creek and Seminole tribes was taken between 1896 and 1898. Tribes were supposed to be able to decide freely whether or not to undergo allotment, but government officials put great pressure on them. In the end, both the Creeks and the Seminoles appeared to accept allotment. All unclaimed land was then sold to white settlers and developers in the land grabs of the early 1900s.

The so-called allotment act divided the land holdings of town members and caused many towns to be dispersed. However, the Creeks and Seminoles continued to recognize town membership through participation in ceremonial grounds (commonly known as "stompgrounds") and churches previously associated with individual towns. The allotment act also made it difficult for the Creeks and Seminoles to continue their clan-based agricultural system of old. Although individuals and families still turned to clan relatives for assistance in times of need, clan relatives from a particular town were less able to help one another with daily activities, and the importance of the clan in providing social services diminished.

Nowadays, members of the Muskogee (Creek) and Seminole Nations are less reliant on agriculture and ranching for their economy than they were before World War II. Many Creeks and Seminoles work in industrial, service, and managerial positions throughout Oklahoma and other states. The Muskogee and Seminole Nations provide services to their members with the assistance of the United States government. Throughout their history, the Muskogee and Seminole people have worked diligently to better themselves, in spite of the setbacks they have faced in the past.

Suggested Readings

The patterning of tonal accent in Mvskoke has been well documented and discussed in work done by Mary Haas ("Tonal Accent in Creek," 1977b), Donald E. Hardy ("The Semantics of Creek Morphosyntax," 1988), and Jack B. Martin and Keith Johnson ("An Acoustic Study of 'Tonal Accent' in Creek," 2002). Haas's work, while using linguistic terminology, is accessible because of the large number of examples she provides. Tonal accent is just one of a number of features of Mvskoke word formation discussed in Hardy's text, but it is handled with a good deal of detail. Martin and Johnson's work involves the use of acoustic measurements to test Haas's (1977b) assertions about tonal accent in Mvskoke. The results of Martin and Johnson's study verify the majority of Haas's assertions, though they do suggest some modifications of her tonal patterning. Due to the clarity and general applicability of Haas's method of determining the location of tonal accent in Mvskoke words, we have continued to use her method without alteration in this chapter.

For those interested in Muskogee history, there are a number of very good references. The early contact period is discussed in a number of accessible works, including William R. Bartram's *Travels through North and South Carolina* . . . (1791), Benjamin Hawkins's "A Sketch of the Creek Country, in 1798 and '99" (1848), and John R. Swanton's "Early History of the Creek Indians and Their Neighbors" (1922). Bartram and Hawkins were travelers through Muskogee country in the late 1700s and early 1800s, and they provided some interesting descriptions of life in Muskogee towns at that time. Swanton offered a more academic look at early Muskogee history, relying on sources produced between the 1500s and the early 1800s.

The role of the Muskogee in the slave and fur trades is covered in Kathryn E. H. Braund's *Deerskins and Duffels* (1993) and Daniel H. Usner Jr.'s *Indians, Settlers, and Slaves in a Frontier Exchange Economy* (1992). Both books are well-researched accounts of the effects of trade on Muskogee life and society. Warfare, the rise of the Creek Confederacy, and other social changes caused by interaction in the trade economy and with Anglo-Europeans are discussed in works by Ross Hassig ("Internal Conflict in the Creek War of 1813–1814," 1974), Michael D. Green (*The Politics of Indian Removal: Creek Government and Society in Crisis,* 1982), David Corkran (*The Creek Frontier, 1540-1783,* 1967), and Angie Debo (*The Road to Disappearance,* 1941). Hassig focuses on the Creek War, Green discusses the political motivations behind some of the treaties made with and by the Creeks, and Corkran and Debo both chronicle Creek history in general, up to and following removal.

J. Leitch Wright Jr. (*Creeks and Seminoles,* 1986), Grant Foreman (*Indian Removal,* 1932), and Angie Debo (*And Still the Waters Run,* 1940; *The Road to Disappearance,* 1941) discuss the political and social changes that have occurred in Creek and Seminole society. Wright's book and Debo's 1941 work are general histories of the Creeks, covering both the pre- and post-removal periods. Debo's 1940 book and Foreman's cover the changes affecting all of the Southeastern tribes as a result of removal.

The rise of the Seminole people is discussed in William Sturtevant's "Creek into Seminole" (1971) and Wright's *Creeks and Seminoles.* Both authors cover the political and social factors that promoted the formation of the Seminoles as a group distinct from the Creeks. Both works chronicle the early history of the Seminoles, including the Seminole Wars.

CHAPTER 3

Simple Sentence Structure

The simplest sentence in Mvskoke is made up of one word, a verb. A **verb** is a word that tells you that some action is taking place or some state exists. In order to make a one-word Mvskoke sentence of this type, pieces of information in the form of affixes are added to the verb. **Affixes** are units of meaning that, in Mvskoke, may be added to words at three places: at the beginning of a word, where they are called **prefixes**; in the middle of a word, where they are called **infixes**; or at the end of a word, where they are called **suffixes**.

In a single-word sentence, several affixes may be attached (affixed) to the verb, which makes such sentences quite complex. We will begin with easier sentences and work our way up to more complex constructions. Each of the Mvskoke sentence examples presented in this book consists of three lines of information: (1) the sentence in Mvskoke; (2) a translation showing the location of the grammatical information contained in the sentence; and (3) a less technical translation of the sentence.

Word Order

If a Mvskoke sentence includes more than a single word, the order of the words may differ from their order in an English sentence. In a relatively simple Mvskoke sentence, the subject comes first, then (unlike in English) the object, if there is one, and, at the end, the verb. The **subject** and **object** of the sentence are noun phrases, which are made up of nouns (entities that we can think of as things, objects, and living beings) and their modifiers.

Some of the easiest sentences in Mvskoke involve only a subject and a verb, as in examples 1–3.

1. Efvt noces.
   dog-subject sleeping
   'A dog is sleeping'.

2. Honvnwvt yvkapes.
   man-subject walking
   'A man is walking'.

3. Foswvt tvmkes.
   bird-subject flying
   'A bird is flying'.

In example 1, *efvt* 'a dog' is the subject of the sentence and comes before the verb. *Noces* 'he/she/it is sleeping' is the verb and comes at the end of the sentence. Note that the /o/ of *noces* is long.

Mvskoke sentences may also contain an object, the thing being directly affected by the action that is taking place. The following are Mvskoke sentences of this type:

4. Estucet efvn celayes.
   child-subject dog-object touching
   'A child is touching a dog'.

5. Hoktet rakkon ohlikes.
   woman-subject horse-object riding
   'A woman is riding a horse'.

6. Ecot nokosen pohes.
   deer-subject bear-object hears
   'A deer hears a bear'.

In example 4, *estucet* 'a child' is the subject of the sentence—the child is the one performing the act of touching. As you can see, in examples 4, 5, and 6 the subject of the sentence is the first item in the sentence, preceding both the object and the verb. Again in sentence 4, *efvn* 'a dog' is the object of the sentence—it is the thing being touched. The object comes after the subject but before the verb in all three examples. In each example, the verb occupies the last place in the sentence.

The structure of a Mvskoke sentence is shown in diagram 3.1. All of the items within parentheses in the diagram are optional—they do not need to appear in a sentence. The only item that cannot be omitted from a Mvskoke sentence is the verb.

(Subject) (Subject Modifiers) (Object) (Object Modifiers) (Verb Modifiers) Verb

Diagram 3.1. Mvskoke Sentence Structure

Subject and Object Markers

In sentences 1 through 6, the subjects were marked by adding the suffix *-t* to the noun. For example, in sentence 3, the subject noun *foswv* 'bird' has the form *foswvt*. The objects in sentences 4, 5, and 6 were marked by adding the suffix *-n* to the noun. For example, in sentence 5, the object noun *rakko* 'horse' has the form *rakkon*. These markers do more than simply show the role a noun phrase is playing in a sentence, but for now you need to remember only that the suffix *-t* indicates the subject and the suffix *-n* indicates the object. Chapter 4 contains a more detailed discussion of these markers.

Verbs

The verbs presented in the preceding examples all have a similar structure. They are composed of (1) a verb stem, (2) a subject suffix, and (3) a declarative suffix. The **verb stem** is the part of the verb that contains the meaning. The **subject suffix** states who or what is performing the action. The **declarative suffix**, *-(e)s*, indicates that a statement is being made. These items will be represented in the second line of each Mvskoke example from now on. The verb stem is represented by an English translation of the activity being performed. The subject is marked by one of the following abbreviations: 1S for first person singular ("I"); 2S for second person singular ("you"—one person); and 3S for third person singular ("he/she/it"). The declarative suffix is indicated by the abbreviation "dec." Example 7 shows a sentence analyzed in this fashion.

7. Rakkot cepanen kērres.
   horse-subject boy-object know-3S-dec
   'The horse knows the boy'.

There are two different ways of indicating the subject in Mvskoke verbs—through the use of type I and II affixes. In chapters 1 through 5, we will work only with verbs that take type I affixes to indicate the subject. Type I affixes are placed after the verb stem—that is, they are suffixes. Type I suffixes are used on verbs that show that some activity is occurring, activity over which the subject has some control (type I verbs). Such verbs are covered in greater detail in chapter 6. Type I verbs are identified in this book by the roman numeral I in brackets, {I}, at the end of the verb entry. In both the text and the glossaries, the first symbol in the brackets indicates the way the subject is marked. Other symbols, separated by semicolons, may follow the first symbol. For example, the glossary entry for *vcelaketv* 'to touch, brush up against, tag' includes the designation {I;II}. This indicates that the subject performing the action of touching or brushing up against is marked by a type I suffix added to the Mvskoke verb and that the object is marked by another kind of affix. Object affixes are covered in chapter 7.

The Verb Stem

When you look up a Mvskoke verb in a dictionary or ask someone to give you the word for some action (smiling or laughing, for instance), you may receive the **infinitive form**—that is, the "to laugh, smile" form. In Mvskoke, the verb translated as 'to laugh, smile' is *vpeletv*; the suffix *-etv* tells you that this is the infinitive form. Changes must be made to the infinitive form in order to produce sentences that people will understand. For instance, if we did not change from the infinitive form in English, we would say, "the dog to run," rather than "the dog runs." In Mvskoke, to change from the infinitive form to the verb stem, which allows us to create meaningful sentences, we must first drop the *-etv* suffix. The following chart shows how the verb stem is derived from the infinitive in three examples:

English Translation	Mvskoke Infinitive Form	Stem (Infinitive Minus *-etv*)
to laugh, smile	vpeletv	vpel-
to stand	hueretv	huer-
to smell, sniff, or sense	vwenayetv	vwenay-

The verb stem must then be altered to form a meaningful sentence. To form a sentence involving an action that has not been completed (called the **incompletive aspect**), the first alteration that occurs is that the last vowel of the verb stem is lengthened (with some exceptions to be discussed later). When the last vowel of a verb stem is *o*, you must simply remember to hold the vowel sound longer, because there is no special alphabet symbol for a long *o* in the Mvskoke system, though short /o/ is distinguished from long /o:/ in the phonemic transcription. In verb stems in which *e* is the last vowel in the stem, the vowel is written as *ē* after lengthening has occurred. This is apparent in the following verbs:

Infinitive Form		Stem		Lengthened Vowel Form	
letketv	'to run'	letk-	'run'	lētk-	'running'
hecetv	'to see'	hec-	'see'	hēc-	'seeing'
esketv	'to drink'	esk-	'drink'	ēsk-	'drinking'

When the last vowel in a verb stem is *v*, it is written as *a* when it is lengthened:

Infinitive Form		Stem		Lengthened Vowel Form	
vyetv	'to go'	vy-	'go'	ay-	'going'
wvkketv	'to lie down'	wvkk-	'lie down'	wakk-	'lying down'
lvffetv	'to cut it up'	lvff-	'cut it up'	laff-	'cutting it up'

Verbs with the stem vowel constructions described in the next chart do not undergo vowel lengthening in the incompletive aspect. When you are presented with a verb that contains a long final stem vowel in the infinitive form, a diphthong as the final stem vowel, or a final stem vowel followed by *m*, *n*, or *l* in the same syllable, do not lengthen the vowel in order to show the incompletive aspect. Simply leave the vowel in the form in which it appears in the infinitive form of the verb.

Infinitive Form		Stem/Incompletive Aspect Form	
Verb with long final stem vowel:			
vcelaketv	'to touch'	vcelak-	'touching'
vwenayetv	'to sniff'	vwenay-	'sniffing'
Verb with diphthong as final stem vowel:			
liketv	'to sit'	lik-	'sitting'
hueretv	'to stand'	huer-	'standing'

Verb with *m, n,* or *l* following final stem vowel and in same syllable:			
tvmketv	'to fly'	tvmk-	'flying'
hvlketv	'to crawl'	hvlk-	'crawling'

If there is more than one vowel in a verb stem, only the final vowel is lengthened, provided it is not subject to any of the factors illustrated in the last chart. In the stem of *yvkvpetv* 'to walk', for example, there are two vowels: *yvkvp-*. Only the final vowel is affected in the lengthening process, making *yvkap-* the incompletive form. Notice that the first vowel is still *v*, a short vowel. The same process occurs in the following verbs, though length is not indicated for the *o* in *vklopetv:*

Infinitive Form		Stem		Lengthened Vowel Form	
yvkvpetv	'to walk'	yvkvp-	'walk'	yvkap-	'walking'
ahkopvnetv	'to play'	ahkopvn-	'play'	ahkopan-	'playing'
vklopetv	'to swim'	vklop-	'swim'	vklop-	'swimming'

As the following examples show, when verbs with more than one vowel are used in sentences, they undergo the same subject suffix and declarative suffix additions as the verbs discussed previously:

8. Cepanat ahkopanes.
   boy-subject playing-3S-dec
   'A boy is playing'.

9. Kaccvt yvkapes.
   tiger-subject walking-3S-dec
   'A tiger is walking'.

10. Echaswvt vklopes.
    beaver-subject swimming-3S-dec
    'A beaver is swimming'.

Type I Subject Suffix

Once the verb stem has been determined and the appropriate changes have been made to produce the incompletive form, a subject suffix (indicated by "3S," or third person singular, in the second lines of the following examples) is added to the verb stem. The **subject suffix** is a suffix added directly to the verb to provide information about who or what is performing the action. We do not use this kind of construction in English; instead, we rely on the subject being specified at some other point in the sentence (for example, "*we* are running" or "*you* are swimming"). In Mvskoke, the subject suffix is added to the verb between the verb stem and the declarative suffix.

Each of the subjects in the sentences we cover in this and the following two chapters is a third person singular subject—that is, one that can be represented by the pronoun "he," "she," or "it." The position of the subject suffix is represented in the second line of each Mvskoke example by the abbreviation 3S, which indicates that the subject is third person (the 3 in the abbreviation) and singular (the S in the abbreviation). As other subjects are introduced, their abbreviations will be explained.

In the following Mvskoke sentences, the third person singular subject suffix should come between the verb stems (in these cases, *homp-*, *wakk-*, and *mapohic-*) and the declarative suffix, *-es*. In Mvskoke, however, third person singular subjects are not marked by a suffix that has a pronounced form. Instead, theirs is a **null suffix**; it is as if no suffix has been attached.

11. Efvt hompes.
dog-subject eating-3S-dec
'A dog is eating'.

12. Honvnwvt wakkes.
man-subject lying_down-3S-dec
'A man is lying down'.

13. Cesset mapohices.
mouse-subject listening-3S-dec
'A mouse is listening'.

As you will see, in Mvskoke verbs taking type I suffixes, all other subjects are marked by adding a suffix that has a pronounced form immediately after the verb stem. In Mvskoke, then, the presence of a null type I suffix tells you that the subject is third person singular, because this is the only subject that is not marked by a pronounced suffix on the verb stem.

Declarative Suffix

The final piece of information about the verbs you will work with at this point has to do with the declarative suffix, *-(e)s*. The **declarative suffix** tells a listener or reader that the sentence is a statement and is not asking a question or giving an order. This does not necessarily mean that the statement is true, just that the speaker or writer is making a statement. In each of the following examples, the abbreviation "dec" marks the position of the declarative suffix.

14. Echaswvt omiyes.
    beaver-subject swimming-3S-dec
    'A beaver is swimming'.

15. Hokte ēhesset likes.
    woman married-subject sitting-3S-dec
    'A married woman is sitting'.

16. Toloset noces.
    chicken-subject sleeping-3S-dec
    'A chicken is sleeping'.

In these sentences, the declarative marker is the *-es* at the end of the verb. It is this *-es* that provides the information about the kind of sentence that has just been produced.

In some cases, the *e* of the declarative suffix *-es* is deleted. This causes the declarative suffix occasionally to be represented by an *-s*. For this reason, when the declarative suffix is discussed separately from a verb, it is represented as *-(e)s*. The parentheses around the *e* show that it may be omitted on some occasions. Situations in which the declarative suffix is indicated only by *-s* will be covered in later chapters. We will also cover other suffixes which show that a sentence is a question or a command.

Tracks 2–7 on CD B of the accompanying CD set provide examples of sentences containing a subject noun and a verb. Vowel lengthening and the placement of the declarative suffix also are evident in these sentences. As you listen to the sentences, pay attention to their rhythm and cadence, because these are slightly different from English.

Vocabulary

Terms for Animals

Mvskoke	English
wakv	cow
rakko	horse
efv	dog
pose	cat
sokhv	pig
tolose	chicken
sasvkwv	goose
cesse	mouse
rvro	fish
nokose	bear
eco	deer
hvlpvtv	alligator
fuswv *or* foswv	bird
kaccv	tiger
wotko	raccoon
echaswv	beaver

Verbs

Mvskoke	English
celayetv {I;II}	to feel, touch
vwenayetv {I;II}	to smell, sniff, sense
hecetv {I;II}	to see, look
pohetv {I;II}	to hear
pvpetv {I;3} *or* hompetv {I;3}	to taste
hompetv {I;3}	to eat
vcvlaketv {I;II} *or* vcelaketv {I;II}	to touch, brush up against
mapohicetv {I;D} *or* em mapohicetv {I;D}	to listen to
vyetv {I}	to go (singular subject)
esketv {I;3}	to drink
nocetv {I/II}	to sleep

Figure 3.1. Three generations of shell shakers at the Cherokee National Holiday, September 1990. Left to right: Linda Alexander, Bertha Tilkens, Anna Cooper. *Photograph courtesy of Bertha Tilkens and Linda Alexander.*

Rattles made from turtle shells or condensed milk cans are worn on the legs with padding. They are used during the dances held from April to September at different ceremonial grounds. Sometimes dancers perform outside the ground, as when invited to participate in other tribal celebrations such as the Cherokee National Holiday.

Conversational Sentences

Honvnwvt: Cehēciyvt vnhēnres. Likvs.	Man: It is good to see you. Have a seat.
Hoktet: Mvto.	Woman: Thank you.
Honvnwvt: Cewvnhkēte?	Man: Are you thirsty?
Hoktet: Ehi, cvwvnhkēs.	Woman: Yes, I'm thirsty.
Honvnwvt: Celvwēte?	Man: Are you hungry?
Hoktet: Mvnks, cvlvweks.	Woman: No, I'm not hungry.

Exercises

Exercise 1

Create ten original sentences with a subject and a verb, using the vocabularies from chapters 1–3. Read your sentences out loud to a partner. As your partner reads his or her sentences to you, translate each sentence.

Exercise 2

Create ten original sentences with a subject, an object, and a verb, using the vocabularies from chapters 1–3. Read your sentences out loud to a partner. As your partner reads his or her sentences to you, translate each sentence.

Exercise 3

With a partner, create an introductory conversation from the phrases in chapters 1–3. Practice the conversation until it sounds natural. Each of you should have at least nine sentences in your conversation.

Exercise 4

Determine what is wrong in each of the following sentences. Rewrite each sentence, correcting the error(s). Translate each of the sentences.

1. Rvron omiyes.
2. Sasvkwvt yvkapetv.
3. Efvn vwenayes hoktet.
4. Hoktvlet heces.
5. Pohes nokoset honvnwvn.
6. Pipucen hoktet celayes.
7. Honvnwv noces vculēt.
8. Sokhan letkes.
9. Rakkon ohlikes estucet.
10. Ehessē hoktet honvnwv ehicvn hēces.

EXERCISE 5

In the following drill, your teacher or a fellow student will begin with a simple sentence containing a subject noun and a verb. Repeat the sentence after the leader. The leader will then introduce a new noun from the vocabularies in chapters 1–3. You are to substitute that noun in the subject position of the simple sentence. An example is provided here:

Leader:	Efvt celayes.
Student:	Efvt celayes.
Leader:	Wakv
Student:	Wakvt celayes.
Leader:	Honvnwv
Student:	Honvnwvt celayes. [And so forth]

EXERCISE 6

In this drill, your teacher will begin with a simple sentence containing a subject noun and a verb. Repeat the sentence after your teacher. Your teacher will then introduce a new verb, in the infinitive form, from the vocabularies in chapters 1–3. You are to change the verb from its infinitive form and substitute the correct form in the verb position of the simple sentence. An example is provided as follows:

Teacher:	Hoktet lētkes.
Student:	Hoktet lētkes.
Teacher:	Yvkvpetv
Student:	Hoktet yvkapes.
Teacher:	Vyetv
Student:	Hoktet ayes. [And so forth]

EXERCISE 7

Find five pictures in magazines, books, or newspapers that show some of the kinds of people or animals from the vocabulary noun lists performing an activity listed in the vocabulary verb lists in chapters 1–3. Be certain that you can describe in Mvskoke what the person or animal is doing in each picture. Bring your pictures to class. Your teacher may ask you to describe the pictures.

The Number Four (Osten) *in Mvskoke Life*

The number four is important in the lives of many American Indian tribes. For the Mvskoke people, it not only represents the directions—east, west, north, and south—but also the seasons—winter, summer, fall, and spring.

In a ceremonial ground, also called a stompground, everything is done in a series of four. The dance ground is sometimes referred to as a square ground. How many sides in a square? Again, the number four.

Many dance grounds still have four brush arbors, just as they did a long time ago. One of the arbors faces east; this is usually the chief's (*mekko*'s) arbor. Why east? This is the direction in which the sun rises.

A committee is usually chosen to carry out certain ceremonial and administrative tasks for the ground. This committee is composed of four members.

Male members of the ceremonial ground take medicine four times.

The fire of the ceremonial ground will have four logs, one facing each of the four directions. Some people have the idea that traditional people worship the fire, but this is not true. The fire was given to Indian people by the Creator to provide light and warmth and to be used in preparing food. The fire thus represents a gift given by the Creator. When Mvskoke people dance, they are worshiping the Creator, not the fire.

You will also see four predominant colors at a ceremonial ground or on people's clothing: white, red, green, and black. These colors represent different things in life. White represents the beginning of life and purity. Red represents the sun, which gives light. Green represents the harvest, and black represents the end of life.

The songs that are sung will be in series of four different songs for some of the dances, such as the Friendship, Duck, and Double-Header Dances.

The traditional people and their culture are the backbone of the Mvskoke people. Baptist, Methodist, and Presbyterian churches have also been established in the Mvskoke community. In these churches, you see reminders of the traditional ceremonial grounds, such as churches facing east. A bell or hollowed-out bull's horn is sounded four times before services begin.

In the churches, the position of pastor is equal to that of chief (*mekko*). The deacon of the church is equivalent to a stick man, who is called this because he carries a three-foot-long stick as a badge of his position. The stick man's and deacon's jobs are to welcome visitors, to make sure groups are seated together, and to keep order during the ceremony. Both churches and ceremonial grounds recognize women's leaders as well.

Whether at a church or at a ceremonial ground, you will see that the number four appears many times.

Suggested Readings

Readers interested in other sources dealing with word order in Muskogean languages might find Michele Nathan's "Grammatical Description of the Florida Seminole Dialect of Creek" (1977:49–73, 135–45) to be of interest. The structures of Florida Seminole are generally consistent with the forms found in Mvskoke and Oklahoma Seminole. Nathan treats noun phrases separately from general sentence structure; hence the two sets of pages in the citation.

Those interested in the significance of the number four and other symbols in Muskogee life are directed to John R. Swanton's "Religious Beliefs and Medical Practices of the Creek Indians" (1928b:623–24) and Charles Hudson's *The Southeastern Indians* (1976:120–83). Of the two, Swanton's account is strictly about Muskogee use of symbols, especially the four directions and colors associated with them. Hudson covers symbolic practices shared by a number of Southeastern tribes.

Readers interested in exploring the prehistoric symbolism of the Muskogee and Seminole people are referred to the following works: "The Southern Cult and Muskhogean Ceremonial," by Antonio J. Waring (1968: 30–69), *The Southeastern Ceremonial Complex and Its Interpretation*, by James Howard (1968), and "The Ideology of Authority and the Power of the Pot" by Timothy R. Pauketat and Thomas E. Emerson (1991). Waring's and Howard's works focus on the range of symbols used by certain Mississippian groups and suggest some interpretations of these symbols. Pauketat and Emerson provide insights into the use of certain symbols during the Mississippian period and suggest that they tell us something about social factors in the Mississippian groups.

CHAPTER 4

Adjectives and Adjectival Phrases

Adjectives are words that describe a noun. In English, we place adjectives before the noun they are describing. For instance, in the sentence "The big dog is running," we place the adjective "big" before the noun "dog" in order to describe what the dog is like. In Mvskoke, adjectives follow the noun they describe. In examples 1, 2, and 3, the adjectives following the nouns are *rakkat* in sentence 1, *holwvkat* in sentence 2, and *hvlvlatket* in sentence 3.

1. Efv rakkat lētkes.
   dog big-subject running-3S-dec
   'The big dog is running'.

2. Cepane holwvkat wakkes.
   boy naughty-subject lying_down-3S-dec
   'The naughty boy is lying down'.

3. Echaswv hvlvlatket vklopes.
   beaver slow-subject swimming-3S-dec
   'A slow beaver is swimming'.

In a sentence with a subject and an object, the adjectives follow whichever of the two nouns they are modifying. For example, the sentence

4. Cepanat svtvn hompes.
boy-subject apple-object eating-3S-dec
'A boy is eating an apple'.

has both a subject (*cepanat*) and an object (*svtvn*). If we describe the boy as big, we end up with

5. Cepanē rakkat svtvn hompes.
boy big-subject apple-object eating-3S-dec
'The big boy is eating an apple'.

Notice that the adjective comes between the subject noun (*cepanē*) and the object noun (*svtvn*). If we describe the apple as being red, we get

6. Cepanat svtv catan hompes.
boy-subject apple red-object eating-3S-dec
'A boy is eating the red apple'.

Notice that the adjective comes after the object noun (*svtv*), which is the noun to which the adjective is referring (the apple is being described as red).

When the subject and object nouns in a sentence are being described, the order shown in diagram 4.1 is observed. This order is followed in examples 7, 8, and 9, in which both the subject and the object are modified.

(Subject Noun) (Subject Adjectives) (Object Noun) (Object Adjectives) Verb

Diagram 4.1. Sentence Structure with Modifed Subject and Object

7. Cepanē rakkat svtv catan hompes.
boy big-subject apple red-object eating-3S-dec
'The big boy is eating the red apple'.

8. Hvlpvtv hotososat rvro lowaken hompes.
alligator skinny-subject fish weak-object eating-3S-dec
'The skinny alligator is eating a weak fish'.

9. Hoktē hotososat hvccuce lvokan hēces.
woman thin-subject stream deep-object sees-3S-dec
'The thin woman sees the deep stream'.

Adjectival Endings

Just as with verbs, changes must be made to adjectives to produce a form that a Mvskoke speaker will understand. In the glossaries, most adjectives are presented in a form ending in *ē* (e.g., *lvstē* 'black'). To create an adjectival form from the glossary form so that the adjective may be used to modify a noun in a sentence, the long *ē* ending must be changed. There are two types of changes that can be made, one which shows that you are speaking about a definite noun (such as "*the* horse") and another which shows that you are speaking about an indefinite noun ("*a* horse").

Although we present definite and indefinite nouns as distinct categories in Mvskoke, these categories are not always so clear-cut when people are speaking to others. In English, we are obligated to specify whether a noun is definite or indefinite unless we use a pronoun ("I, you, he/she/it," etc.), a personal name, or a plural noun. In Mvskoke, however, the indefinite form of the noun is sometimes used in ways that we would consider to apply to a definite noun, and vice versa. Although we will consistently translate nouns as either definite or indefinite in the second line of each example, you may hear speakers using the indefinite form to refer to a definite object in the world. The definite-indefinite noun distinctions do not occur in all languages in the world or in the majority of Native American languages.

Definite Nouns

In English, a noun is definite when the article "the" is used to introduce it. In the English sentence "The dog is running," because the noun "dog" is preceded by "the," we know that a specific dog's action is being described. This becomes clear when you think of situations in which you might say this sentence. For example, someone asks you, "Which of the animals is running?" In your response, "The dog is running," you are making a definitive statement about which one of several kinds of animals is running. This sentence could also occur as a statement about something you see. In that case, you have a specific, definite dog in mind—you are watching a particular dog run.

It is possible to show that you have a particular, definite noun in mind when you create a sentence in Mvskoke. To do so, write and pronounce the noun as it appears in the glossaries. No ending is added to the noun. Because the lack of an ending means that the subject or object is a definite noun, this information is included in the second line of each example. Thus, when unmodified, or definite, nouns are used, as they are in examples 10 and 11, each noun's translation is followed by "definite_subject" or "definite_object" (abbreviated "def_subj" or "def_obj").

10. Wakv noces.
cow-def_subj sleeping-3S-dec
'The cow is sleeping'.

11. Hoktē vholocē hēces.
woman-def_subj cloud-def_obj sees-3S-dec
'The woman sees the cloud'.

When a definite noun is modified by an adjective, the *ē* of the adjective's glossary form is changed to *a*. Once the adjective's final vowel has been changed, either *-t* or *-n* is added to the end of the adjective. The *-t* suffix is added to adjectives describing the subject. The *-n* suffix is added to adjectives describing the object. Thus, in the Mvskoke sentence

12. Cepanē rakkat hompes.
boy big-def_subj eating-3S-dec
'The big boy is eating'.

the adjective *rakkē* has been changed to *rakkat*. In example 13,

13. Este vculat rakko pvfnan ohlikes.
man old-def_subj horse fast-def_obj riding-3S-dec
'The old man is riding the fast horse'.

the adjectives *vculē* and *pvfnē* have been changed to show they are referring to a definite subject and object, respectively. The *ē* found in the glossary form of each of these adjectives, both of which modify definite nouns, was changed to *a*, and the subject or object adjective suffix (*-t* or *-n*) was then added to the adjective.

These changes take place on the final adjective modifying the noun. Several adjectives can follow nouns in Mvskoke, just as they can precede nouns in English. In this case, only the ē of the last adjective in the series is changed. All of the other adjectives remain in their glossary-entry form. The following is an example of a sentence in which one noun is modified by more than one adjective:

14. Nokose rakkē lvstat hompes.
bear big black-def_subj eating-3S-dec
'The big black bear is eating'.

Notice that *rakkē* 'big', which is the first adjective, is in the form in which it appears in the glossary. *Lvstat* 'black' has been changed from its glossary-entry form, *lvstē*; its final vowel, *ē*, has changed to *a*, and the subject adjective suffix *-t* has been added. The same rules apply in sentence 15, even though the adjectives are modifying the object (and therefore the object adjective suffix *-n* has been used):

15. Honvnwv rakko rakkē yekcē pvfnan ohlikes.
man-def_subj horse big strong fast-def_obj riding-3S-dec
'The man is riding the big, strong, fast horse'.

Any time more than one adjective follows a noun, the vowel change and the addition of the subject or object adjective suffix affect only the last adjective.

Indefinite Nouns

It is also possible to speak about indefinite nouns in Mvskoke. In English, these nouns are preceded by the article "a" or "an" or by no article in the case of mass nouns—those denoting things that cannot be counted, such as water, sand, or oatmeal. These articles suggest that you are talking about a generic example of that kind of noun, and not to any specific item. For instance, in the English sentence "A bear is eating an apple," there are two indefinite nouns, "bear" and "apple." The speaker is not talking about a particular bear or a particular apple. "A bear" could be any bear, and "an apple" could be any apple.

In Mvskoke, when an unmodified indefinite noun is used, the noun is suffixed with either a *-t* or an *-n*. If the indefinite noun is the subject of the sentence, *-t* is used. If the indefinite noun is the object of the sentence, *-n* is used. Example 16 demonstrates the use of an unmodified indefinite noun in the subject position (in this and all following examples, indefinite nouns are signified by "ind_subj" or "ind_obj"):

16. Sasvkwvt tvmkes.
goose-ind_subj flying-3S-dec
'A goose is flying'.

Example 17 demonstrates the use of unmodified indefinite nouns in both the subject and object positions:

17. Nokoset sokhvn vwenayes.
bear-ind_subj pig-ind_obj smells-3S-dec
'A bear smells a pig'.

When a sentence contains an indefinite noun modified by an adjective, the ē of the adjective's glossary form is shortened to *e*. The subject or object adjective suffix is then added to the altered adjective. This is shown in example 18:

18. Nokose rakket svtv caten hompes.
bear big-ind_subj apple red-ind_obj eating-3S-dec
'A big bear is eating a red apple'.

Notice that *rakkē* 'big' has been changed: its ē was shortened and the subject adjective marker *-t* was added. A comparable change has occurred on *catē* 'red', except that the object adjective marker *-n* was added instead of the subject marker.

When more than one adjective is used to describe an indefinite noun, the changes are made to the final adjective in the series. For instance, in the Mvskoke sentence

19. Nokose vcvkē lvstet pvhe kvrpan hompes.
bear short black-ind_subj grass dry-def_obj eating-3S-dec
'A short black bear is eating the dry grass'.

nokose 'bear' is followed by two adjectives, *vcvkē* 'short' and *lvstē* 'black'. Of these two adjectives, only *lvstē* is changed—its ē is shortened and the subject adjective marker is added. *Vcvkē* is not altered because it is not the last adjective in the series.

DIMINUTIVES

In Mvskoke, it is not always necessary to use a separate adjective to describe something as "little." Often, a noun will be described as little by the addition of a **diminutive suffix**, which in Mvskoke is *-uce*. If the noun being described as little is not modified by any other adjectives, then the diminutive suffix is added directly to the noun. Occasionally, changes must be made to the noun in order to add the diminutive suffix. The final vowel of nouns ending in *a*, *ē*, *e*, *i*, and *v* is deleted. Once the final vowel is deleted, *-uce* is added. As with the other adjectives described earlier, if *-t* or *-n* is added to the end of the *-uce* suffix, then the noun is translated as an indefinite noun. If *-t* or *-n* is not added, then the noun is translated as a definite noun. Some examples of the steps nouns ending in *a*, *ē*, *e*, *i*, and *v* go through to become diminutized are given in the following chart:

Original Noun Form	Final Vowel Deleted	Diminutized Form
kolēppa 'firefly'	kolēpp	kolēppuce 'the little firefly' or kolēppucet/kolēppucen 'a little firefly'
cvstvlē 'watermelon'	cvstvl	cvstvluce 'the little watermelon' or cvstvlucet/cvstvlucen 'a little watermelon'
custake 'egg'	custak	custakuce 'the little egg' or custakucet/custakucen 'a little egg'
eslafkv 'knife'	eslafk	eslafkuce 'the little knife' or eslafkucet/eslafkucen 'a little knife'

Nouns ending in *o* do not have their final vowel deleted. Instead, the diminutive suffix is modified slightly, to *-ce*, and is added directly to the end of the noun. As with nouns ending in other vowels, indefinite nouns are indicated by the addition of *-t* or *-n*, and definite nouns are indicated by the addition only of the diminutive suffix. Some examples of this type of diminutization are as follows:

Original Noun Form	Indefinite Diminutive	Definite Diminutive
rvro 'fish'	rvroce 'the little fish'	rvrocet/rvrocen 'a little fish'
kono 'skunk'	konoce 'the little skunk'	konocet/konocen 'a little skunk'

When the diminutive suffix is to be added to nouns modified by other adjectives, the diminutive suffix is attached to the final adjective. There are two versions of the diminutive suffix that can be attached to adjectives. The first of these, *-us*, can be used on almost every adjective. The final vowel of the adjective is deleted, the suffix is added, and then the definite or indefinite form of the adjective ending is added (*-at/-an* or *-et/-en*). Here is an example of the way an adjective diminutized by *-us* is modified to refer to a definite noun:

Original adjective form:	afvckē 'happy'
Delete final vowel:	afvck
Add diminutive suffix:	afvckus
Add definite noun ending:	afvckusat

The final form, *afvckusat*, is now ready to be used in a sentence. Note that the diminutive is abbreviated "dim" in the second line of example 20:

20. Honvnwv afvckusat vpēles.
man happy-dim-def_subj smiling/laughing-3S-dec
'The happy little man is smiling/laughing'.

The process of diminutizing an adjective that modifies an indefinite noun is very similar to that undergone by an adjective modifying a definite noun:

Original adjective form:	yekcē 'strong'
Delete final vowel:	yekc
Add diminutive suffix:	yekcus
Add indefinite noun ending:	yekcuset/yekcusen

This form can now be used in a sentence such as the following:

21. Efv nokose yekcusen enlētkes.
dog-def_subj bear strong-dim-ind_obj running_away-3S-dec
'The dog is running away from a strong little bear'.

Though almost all adjectives can take the *-us* diminutive suffix, some can take a different form of the diminutive suffix, *-uce*. Adjectives taking this form of the diminutive suffix are those that may be considered nouns or parts of nouns in the diminutized form. For instance, *cvmpē* 'sweet' becomes either 'a little sweet (thing)' or 'cookie' when it takes the diminutized form *cvmpuce*. Adjectives of this sort are uncommon, and the majority of adjectives take the *-us* form of the diminutive suffix.

To form diminutized noun-adjective combinations with this suffix, drop the final vowel of the original adjective form and then add *-uce*. If an indefinite noun is being diminutized, add *-t* or *-n*, depending on its role in the sentence (subject or object). If a definite noun is being diminutized, add nothing to the end of the diminutive suffix. The following examples demonstrate the steps adjectives go through to take the *-uce* suffix:

Original adjective form:	fvmpē 'smelly'
Delete final vowel:	fvmp
Add diminutive suffix:	fvmpuce

This adjective can now be used in a sentence:

22. Kono fvmpuce hompes.
skunk smelly-dim-def_subj eating-3S-dec
'The smelly little skunk is eating'.

When an indefinite noun is being modified with *-uce*, the same steps are followed before the indefinite ending is added to the adjective:

Original adjective form:	cvmpē 'sweet'
Delete final vowel:	cvmp
Add diminutive suffix:	cvmpuce
Add indefinite ending:	cvmpucet/cvmpucen

At this point, the diminutized adjective can be used in a sentence such as this one:

23. Hoktet sem vtehkv cvmpucen norices.
woman-def_subj pie sweet-dim-ind_obj cooking-3S-dec
'The woman is cooking a sweet little pie'.

Vocabulary

ADJECTIVES

Mvskoke	English
rakkē	big
cutkosē	little
cekfē	thick
tvskocē	thin (not of a person)
hotososē	slim, thin (of a person)
mahē	tall
kocoknē	short
pohkē	loud
cvyayvkē	quiet
pvfnē	fast
hvlvlatkē	slow
tvphē	wide
lopicē	nice, kind
holwvyēcē	mean
honnē	heavy
tvhoknē *or* tohoknē	light (in weight)
hiyē, hayē	hot
kvsvppē	cold
lvokē	deep (of water)
cahkē	shallow (of water)
yekcē	strong, loud
lowakē	weak
nehē	fat
hotosē	tired
feknokkē	sad
afvckē	happy
hēnrē	good
holwvkē	bad, naughty

Natural Objects

Mvskoke	English
eto	tree
stvpokhe	bush
ekvnhvlwuce	hill
hvcce	river
hvccuce	stream
uewv, oewv, owv	water
oskē	rain
hvse	sun
vholocē	cloud
hotvle	wind
sotv	sky
pvhe	grass

The Four Directions

Mvskoke	English
honerv *or* kvsvppofv	north
hvsossv	east
wvhvlv *or* lekothofv	south
hvsaklatkv	west

Conversational Sentences

Honvnwvt: Fettv stvnko?	Man: How is it outside?
Hoktet: Hayowvnt hēnres.	Woman: It is nice.
Hayowvnt hiyes.	It is hot.
Oskētos.	It is raining.
Kvsvppētos.	It is cold.
Hoktet: Naken estomet cvnkv?	Woman: What have you been doing?
Honvnwvt: Vtotkiyvnks. Naken estomet cvnkv?	Man: I have been working. What have you been doing?
Hoktet: Cokvn vketēciyvnks.	Woman: I have been studying.
Vmvnickv ceyacv?	Do you need help?
Honvnwvt: Mvnks, stvnkitos.	Man: No, I'm fine.

Figure 4.1. Preparing for the men's stickball game (Little Brother of War), Greenleaf Ceremonial Ground, September 1989. *Photograph courtesy of Bertha Tilkens and Linda Alexander.*

Men from other ceremonial grounds are invited to play in this game, which takes place after the last dance of the season for the ceremonial ground. The field is set up like a football field with goals at the east and west ends. The players are divided into two teams, East and West. The first team to reach twenty-one points wins the game. Men use sticks made from hickory wood bent over at one end and laced with leather. Each stick looks like a small lacrosse stick, and two are used during the game. The ball, made from string and leather, is about the size of a golf ball.

Exercises

EXERCISE 1

Use the nouns, adjectives, and verbs listed below to create twenty sentences. Of the twenty sentences, ten must have an indefinite subject and ten must have a definite subject. If you create sentences with an object, you may choose whether the object is definite or indefinite.

Nouns	Adjectives	Verbs
honvnwv	rakkē	letketv
eto	lvokē	esketv
sasvkwv	lowakē	yvkvpetv

vholocē	hvlvlatkē	tvmketv
pipuce	kvsvppē	hvlketv
wakv	pvfnē	mapohicetv
nokose	cvyayvkē	wvkketv
rakko	mahē	hueretv
hvcce	kocoknē	hompetv
uewv/oewv	honnē	pohetv

Exercise 2

Create twenty sentences from the vocabulary in chapters 1–4. Each of these sentences must have both a subject and an object. Of the twenty sentences, half must have indefinite subjects with multiple adjectives and half must have definite subjects with multiple adjectives. The objects must be split between definite, multiple-adjective objects and indefinite, multiple-adjective objects.

Exercise 3

Identify each of the meaningful units in the following sentences. You should create ten lines similar in form and content to the second line in each example presented in the text.

1. Wotkocen pvhe tvskocan hompes.
2. Cepanē holwvkat selaksēkes.
3. Cesse tvskocuset pose nehē hvlvlatken pohes.
4. Efv hotvle vwenayes.
5. Estucet ekvnhvlwuce ayes.
6. Foswv yekcat eto mahan tvmkes.
7. Sasvkwv omiyes.
8. Eco stvpokhe kocoknen papes.
9. Hoktē ehessuce svtohkes.
10. Hoktuce yvkapes.

Exercise 4

Translate the following sentences into Mvskoke. Pay attention to the indefinite or definite nature of the nouns. After translating the sentences, recite them to a partner.

1. The man is walking.
2. The tall man is riding a slow horse.
3. A little woman is eating chicken.
4. The big mean bear smells the small weak skunk.
5. The baby hears the wind.
6. A loud strong goose is brushing up against the tall tree.
7. A quiet man is listening.
8. A heavy woman is sitting on the big fast horse.
9. The girl sees the deep river.
10. The fat happy pig is drinking some cold water.

Exercise 5

In this exercise, your teacher or a fellow student will begin with a simple sentence containing at least one definite noun. Repeat the sentence after the leader. The leader will then present you with an adjective. You are to form the adjective to modify the definite noun, which may be either the subject or the object. The leader will then present you with another adjective. You will then substitute that adjective for the one you used in the previous sentence. An example of exercise 5 is as follows:

Leader:	Nokose hompes.
Student:	Nokose hompes.
Leader:	lvstē
Student:	Nokose lvstat hompes.
Leader:	rakkē
Student:	Nokose rakkat hompes. [And so forth]

Exercise 6

In this exercise, your teacher or a fellow student will begin with a simple sentence containing at least one indefinite noun. Repeat the sentence after the leader. The leader will then present you with an adjective. You are to form the adjective to modify the indefinite noun, which may be either the subject or the object. The leader will then present you with another adjective. You will then substitute that adjective for the one that you used in the previous sentence. An example of exercise 6 is given here:

Leader:	Wotko pvhen hēces.
Student:	Wotko pvhen hēces.

Leader: mahē
Student: Wotko pvhe mahen hēces.
Leader: lanē
Student: Wotko pvhe lanen hēces. [And so forth]

Exercise 7

Translate the following sentences, containing diminutives, into Mvskoke. Pay attention to the specific or generic nature of the diminutized noun.

1. The bear smells a little mean beaver.
2. A tall boy is riding the little black horse.
3. The quiet big tiger sees the little mouse.
4. A little old man is walking.
5. The little dog is drinking cold water.
6. The cow brushes up against the little bush.
7. A naughty little girl is swimming.
8. A fat little goose is flying.
9. An old woman is going to the little shallow river.
10. The heavy little pig is eating grass.

Exercise 8

Add a new adjective to each adjectival phrase in the following sentences. Your adjective must be the rightmost adjective in at least five of the sentences. In these five sentences, you will need to adjust the endings on the adjectives in the phrase. Translate your sentences into English after you have added an adjective.

1. Honvnwvt echaswv hvlvlatkan hēces.
2. Estuce afvcket wakkes.
3. Nokose rakkat hvcce cahkan pohes.
4. Eco tvskocet hotvle kvsvppan vwenayes.
5. Wakv rakkē lopicat pvhe mahan hompes.
6. Pipuce nehat hvlkes.
7. Este vculet rakko kocoknē pvfnan ohlikes.
8. Sasvkwv pohket tvmkes.
9. Hoktē yekcat honvnwv hotososē holwvyēcan mapohices.
10. Toloset stvpokhe cutkosen vcvlakes.

Colors

Four colors predominate in traditional Mvskoke thought: red, black, blue, and white. Each color symbolizes a number of items. Red symbolizes the direction east, the sun, the sacred fire, blood, and success. Black symbolizes the direction west, the moon, and death. Blue symbolizes the direction north, cold, trouble, and defeat. White symbolizes the direction south, warmth, peace, and happiness.

Red represents the sun, which provides light and warmth. The direction in which lives Hesaketv Messē, the "Giver of Life," or God, is east. This is also the color of the sacred fire, which is the lifeline in Mvskoke traditional belief. This fire not only provides warmth and light but used to be the way to cook meals—which are also essential in maintaining life.

Red is also important because it is the color of blood, which was shed for the survival of others. Warriors and others involved in saving people would shed their blood or give their lives to protect their women and children. In traditional belief, losing blood by scratching one's arms and calves cleanses the body of impurities.

For these reasons, red is the dominant color. Red represents everything that is accomplished through Hesaketv Messē and shows that you can live a successful life.

Black represents darkness. For this reason, it is used to represent the moon, which gives off no warmth or light. It is also used to represent death, which occurs when warmth leaves the body.

Blue represents the north, which is cold. It also represents trouble, which casts a shadow over the area.

White represents the south, a place of warmth. Peace and happiness were always the goals of the Mvskoke people, who originally came from the south. When one is peaceful and tries to maintain happiness, one is said to be "walking the white path of peace."

Suggested Readings

Those interested in other sources concerning the construction of noun phrases in Mvskoke should consult Michele Nathan's "Grammatical Description of the Florida Seminole Dialect of Creek" (1977:49–73). Nathan's discussion is applicable here because the noun phrase structures she describes are similar to those found in Mvskoke.

Further information about the formation of diminutive nouns in Mvskoke is presented in Donald E. Hardy's "The Semantics of Creek Morphosyntax" (1988:75–81). The relationship between the diminutive and undiminutized versions of the nouns is covered nicely in Hardy's analysis. He also discusses the adjective suffixes as they show whether the noun being modified is definite or indefinite (1988:281–88).

Readers interested in the variance in use of the definite and indefinite noun forms in Mvskoke are referred to Stephan Schuetze-Coburn's "Exceptional *-t/-n* Marking in Oklahoma Seminole Creek" (1987). This article offers some insights into when and why speakers may use the definite and indefinite forms but also shows that the use of these forms is variable. Again, strict categorization of the different noun forms as proving a definite or an indefinite reference is not supported by Schuetze-Coburn's work, just as we stated earlier that it is not a hard-and-fast rule.

Readers interested in color symbolism among the Mvskoke are referred to the books and articles listed in the Suggested Readings section of chapter 3.

CHAPTER 5

Adverbs

Adverbs are words that describe how an action is being performed. In the English sentence "The boy is singing slowly," the word "slowly" is playing the role of an adverb because it is describing how the boy is singing. In English, most adverbs are indicated as such by the suffix *-ly*, which distinguishes adverbs from adjectives. For instance, the concept of "slowness" occurs in both an adjectival and an adverbial form—that is, it can be used to describe a noun, as in "a slow boy," or it can be used to describe the way an action is being carried out, as in "the snail is moving slowly." The use of the *-ly* suffix in English helps listeners understand whether "slow" is being applied to a noun or to a verb.

A similar situation exists in Mvskoke. Many of the words you learned to use as adjectives in chapter 3 can also be used as adverbs. As in English, the distinction between adjectives and adverbs in Mvskoke is shown by the use of different suffixes.

Adverb Formation

In order to use a descriptive word as an adverb, some changes must be made to the form of the word as it is presented in the glossaries at the end of this book. The majority of descriptive words are presented in the glossaries with a final ē, as in *hvlvlatkē* 'slow'. For these words, little has to be done to produce a form that Mvskoke speakers will recognize as an adverb. The only change that has to be made is to add an *-n* to the end of the word. Thus, *hvlvlatkē* (the initial form) becomes *hvlvlatkēn* (the adverbial form).

It also is possible to derive adverbs from some words that are presented in the glossaries in an infinitive, or verb, form ending in *-etv*. To change these words into adverbs, simply drop the *-etv* suffix and add *-ēn*. In this way, *ēyvcayēcetv* 'to be careful' becomes *ēyvcayēcēn* 'carefully'.

Once the adverbial form is created, the word can be used in a sentence. In order to describe how the boy is running in the following Mvskoke sentence,

1. Cepanat lētkes.
   boy-def_subj running-3S-dec
   'The boy is running'.

we simply place the adverb before the verb it is describing. Thus, to state that the boy is running slowly, sentence 1 becomes

2. Cepanat hvlvlatkēn lētkes.
   boy-def_subj slowly running-3S-dec
   'The boy is running slowly'.

Notice that *hvlvlatkēn* 'slowly' is in the adverbial form (it has a final *-ēn*) and that it occurs before the verb. The position of the adverb in a Mvskoke sentence is thus different from its position in an English sentence.

It is possible to create sentences that contain both adjectives and adverbs. When this occurs, the endings on the adjectives and the adverbs serve to designate which is which. For example, the following sentence contains *cvyayvkē* 'quiet' as both an adjective and an adverb:

3. Cepanē cvyayvkat cvyayvkēn ahkopanes.
   boy quiet-def_subj quietly playing-3S-dec
   'The quiet boy is playing quietly'.

The adjective form of *cvyayvkē* (the *quiet* boy) takes the *-at* suffix. This ending shows that it is describing a definite noun, which is the subject of the sentence. The adverbial form of *cvyayvkē* (is playing *quietly*) ends in *-ēn*, which shows that it is an adverb.

The differences between the adjectival and adverbial endings are important in helping to distinguish a descriptive word's role in a Mvskoke sentence.

The final adjective in a noun phrase (noun plus modifiers) is always marked to show whether the adjectives in the noun phrase are describing the subject or the object of the sentence (the *-t* and *-n* suffixes). When the noun described by the adjective(s) is definite, the vowel before the *-t* or *-n* suffix of the final adjective in the phrase is changed to *a*. When the noun described by the adjective(s) is indefinite, the vowel before the *-t* or *-n* suffix of the final adjective in the phrase is *e* (not *ē*). These suffixes and vowels distinguish adjectives from adverbs because adverbs always end in *-ēn* (note this has a long *e*). Thus, in the following sentence, which contains an adjective describing an indefinite object noun, it is the difference in vowel length that shows which word is the adjective and which is the adverb.

4. Hoktē atvmo lvsten hvlvlatkēn svtohkes.
woman-ind_subj car black-ind_obj slowly driving-3S-dec
'A woman is driving a black car slowly'.

Here, *lvsten,* the adjective describing a property of the car (the indefinite object noun), ends in *-en*. The adverb, *hvlvlatkēn,* however, ends in *-ēn*, which shows that it is describing how the car is being driven. Because of the vowel length differences, we can be certain that *hvlvlatkēn* is describing how the car is being driven and is not referring to a property of the car itself (that is, describing a slow black car).

Vocabulary

Colors

Mvskoke	English
lanē	green or yellow
catē	red
holattē	blue
hvtkē	white
lvstē	black
sopakhvtkē	gray
oklanē	brown
yvlahomv	orange

pvrkomv *or* okcatē	purple
catosē	pink

Days of the Week

Mvskoke	English
Mvnte	Monday
Mvnte enhvyvtke	Tuesday
Ennvrkvpv	Wednesday
Nvrkvpv enhvyvtke	Thursday
Flati	Friday
Nettvcako ecuse	Saturday
Nettvcako *or* Tvcakuce	Sunday
mucv-nettv	today

Verbs

Mvskoke	English
takketv {I;II}	to kick
nvfketv {I;II}	to hit
vhopvketv {I;II} *or* vhepvketv {I;II}	to push
ahvlvtetv {I;II}	to pull
lvtketv {II/I}	to fall
vwiketv {I;II}	to drop (one object)
atvkkesetv {I;II}	to pick up (one object or person)
esetv {I;II}	to take (one object)
emetv {I;3;D}	to give something to someone
akketv {I;II}	to bite
korretv {I;3}	to dig
yvhiketv {I}	to sing
opvnetv {I}	to dance

Note that a special type of verb is included in this vocabulary list: *lvtketv* 'to fall', a type {II/I} verb. When verbs have both type I and type II conjugations, as denoted by a forward slash in their entries, they may be modified using either of two different kinds of subject markers. Type II subject markers are introduced in the next chapter.

The {II/I} verb introduced in this chapter, *lvtketv* 'to fall', is generally modified with the addition of type II subject markers. For that reason, the symbol for type II affixes is listed first in the entry. However, because *lvtketv* can also be conjugated with the addition of type I subject-marking suffixes, this type is listed in the verb entry, too. Because *lvtketv* is conjugated less frequently with the type I suffixes, type I subject markers are listed as the second choice, following the slash.

In later chapters, you will be introduced to other verbs that may take either type I or type II affixes to show the subject of the sentence. Speakers tend to deal with verbs as though they are primarily type I or type II verbs, even when they may be modified either way. Therefore, you should pay attention to which symbol comes first in the brackets. The first symbol shows which set of subject markers is most often used to modify the verb.

Conversational Sentences

Honvnwvt: Stvmen ayeckv?	Man: Where are you going?
Hoktet: Neskv-cokon ayetowis.	Woman: I'm going to the store.
Tvlofvn ayetowis.	I'm going to town.
Honvnwvt: Naken estowvhanskv?	Man: What are you going to do?
Hoktet: Naken apowvhan ayetowis.	Woman: I'm going shopping.
Mvhakv-cokon ayetowis.	I'm going to school.
Vtotkvhanat ayetowis.	I'm going to work.
Centv ayetv ceyacv?	Would you like to go?
Honvnwvt: Enka, cecakites cvyacewitēs.	Man: Yes, I would like to go with you.
Mvnks, ayetv cvyaceks.	No, I don't want to go.

Exercises

Exercise 1

Identify each of the meaningful units in the following sentences. You should create ten lines similar in form and content to the second line in each of the examples presented in the text.

Figure 5.1. Feather Dance performed by male members of the Greenleaf Ceremonial Ground, September 1989. This dance is usually done during the Green Corn Ceremony. Notice the layout of the ground and the brush arbors. *Photograph courtesy of Linda Alexander and Bertha Tilkens.*

1. Kaccv hotosē holwvyēcat pvfnēn lētkes.
2. Pipuce efv kocoknē oklanen yekcēn nafkes.
3. Mucv-nettv hoktvlē hvlvlatkēn opanes.
4. Rakkot eto lanē mahan takkes.
5. Tolose hvtket wakv lvsten lowakēn vcvlakes.
6. Honvnwv ehicv sokhv catosan ēses.
7. Hoktuce nehat cepanē pohken holwvkēn vhopakes.
8. Foswv sopakhvtket tvmkes.
9. Estuce hēnrēn yvhikes.
10. Hvlpvtv lanat eco rakkan ahvlates.

Exercise 2

Add an adverb to each of the following sentences. Try to incorporate an adverb that makes sense in the sentence.

1. Pipucet efucen atvkkēses.
2. Honvnwv vculat opanes.
3. Stvpokhe pvrkomat latkes.
4. Rakko lvstet eto cutkosan ahvlates.
5. Cepanē holwvket hoktucen nafkes.
6. Wotko rakkē sopakhvtkat uewv kvsvppan ēskes.
7. Sasvkwv hoktē vhopakes.
8. Sokhv catosat eto oklanen vcvlakes.
9. Hoktvlē mahat yvhikes.
10. Echaswv hvtket vklopes.

Exercise 3

Translate the following English sentences into Mvskoke.

1. The tall man is drinking the cold water slowly.
2. A short cow is eating the green grass quickly/fast.
3. The married man is singing loudly.
4. The loud married man is singing loudly.
5. The big pink pig is biting a short chicken meanly.
6. A gray horse is running happily.
7. The skinny brown dog is looking sadly at the boy.
8. The old man is kicking the tree weakly.
9. A black bear is falling down heavily.
10. The baby touched the dog nicely.

Exercise 4

Working with a partner, pronounce the Mvskoke sentences you made in exercise 2. Each of you should critique your partner's pronunciation and grammar. If you disagree on any of the sentences, write down how and why your sentences differ. Discuss these differences in class.

Exercise 5

Translate the following Mvskoke sentences into English. When a word has more than one possible meaning, include all forms by separating them with slashes (/). Then, working with a partner, compare your translations. If you disagree on any of the translations, write down how and why your translations differ and ask about these sentences in class.

1. Hvlpvtv rakkē lanat rvrocen hompes.
2. Eco oklanet cvyayvkēn hueres.
3. Hoktvlat oewv kvsvppan hvlvlatkēn ēskes.
4. Efv kocoknē hvtket korres.
5. Estucet pipucen holwvyēcēn atvkkēses.
6. Wotko nehet eto oklanan vcvlakes.
7. Eto tvhoknat tvhoknēn latkes.
8. Hvcce tvphē lvokat pvfnēn lētkes.
9. Honvnwvt foswv pvrkomen hēces.
10. Honvnwv ehicat lowakēn yvhikes.

Exercise 6

Find the problem(s) in each of the following sentences. Change the problem(s) to form grammatically correct, sensible Mvskoke sentences. Translate your sentences into English, including all meanings of words that have multiple translations.

1. Mahē honvnwvt sopakhvtkē nokosen hēces.
2. Pose rakkēt nehat cessen pohes.
3. Cepanē hotosēt yvhikes.
4. Foswv pvhe cekfan lowaken vhvlates.
5. Hoktē rakkat hvlvlatkēn opvnkes.
6. Honvnwet stvpokhen lanan feknokkēn vcelakes.
7. Cepanēt sasvkwv hvtkan afvckēn vwiketv.
8. Kaccv yvlahomat ayes.
9. Honvnwvt holwvyēcat efocen lvstan nafkes.
10. Hoktuce kocoknat rvro catan vhericetv atvkkēses.

Exercise 7

Translate the following short story from Mvskoke to English and answer the questions with Mvskoke sentences. You may need to check the glossary and conversational sentences in earlier chapters for the meanings of some of the words in the story and questions. After translating the story, tell the story, in Mvskoke, to a partner. Compare your translation and your answers to the questions with your partner's.

Nvrkvpv enhvyvtke, efv oklanē rakkat pvfnēn lētkes. Efv "Max" hocefketos. Cepanē efv hēces. Cepanē kocoknat "George" hocefketos. Max tolose lanen vwenayes. Tolosuce hvlvlatkēn yvkapes. Tolose hvlvlatkat efv pohes. Efv tolose akkes. Tolose lanan efv yekcēn takkes. George selaksēkes. Max tolosuce vwikes. Tolosuce pvfnēn tvmkes.

1. Efv hocefkēte?
2. Stimvt efv akkv?
3. Tolose enheckv estomētomv?
4. Naken efv hēcetomv?
5. Efv hvlvlatkēn lētkv?
6. Estimvt selaksēkv?
7. Cepanē hocefketē?
8. Tolose efv lowakēn takketomv?

Exercise 8

Working with a partner, create a short conversation using the conversational sentences provided in the chapters up to this point. Together, the two of you should have at least twelve lines in your conversation. Practice this conversation until you are both comfortable with it. Your teacher may ask you to perform your conversation in class.

Clans in Mvskoke Life

According to a Mvskoke (Creek) legend, a great fog once covered the Mvskoke. Unable to see, they were dependent on their sense of touch. In looking for food, the people became separated. They knew about each other's existence, so they stayed within calling distance. Then one day a great wind came from the east and began to clear away the fog. The first group of people who were able to see the land and the various things around them clearly were called the Wind Clan (Hotvlkvlke).

The rest of the groups each adopted the first animal they saw. Today, the Mvskoke and Seminole Nations have nine clans: Wind (Hotvlkvlke), Alligator (Hvlpvtvlke), Bear (Nokosvlke), Tiger (Kaccvlke), Deer (Ecovlke), Sweet Potato (Vhvlvkvlke), Raccoon (Wotkvlke), Beaver (Echaswvlke), and Bird (Foswvlke).

Clan relationship is as important to Mvskoke people as other blood relationships. Clan relationship is determined through the maternal (mother's) side of the family. If your mother belongs to the Alligator Clan, then you and your siblings belong to this clan. If you are a female, your children will belong to your clan. If you are a male, your children will belong to their mother's clan, not yours. Exceptions are made if you are adopted by the tribe or if your mother is non-Indian and your father is Mvskoke. In the latter case, you may use your father's ancestry.

In keeping with the maternal side's importance in determining clan relationship, the role of the father in children's lives was usually played by the mother's brother. He would teach the male children how to hunt and fish and would be responsible for disciplining the children. The father would also help, but his primary responsibility was to his sisters' children.

Clan identity governed whom one could marry. People from the same clan were absolutely forbidden to marry, because it would have been like marrying a close relative. When two people were interested in each other and thought about getting married, elders from each sweetheart's family would gather to discuss their lineages. If the two families shared a clan connection in the recent past (maybe both the girl's and the boy's mother's fathers were from the Bear Clan), then the couple was considered to be too closely related. Only if shared clan relations were long ago in the couple's ancestry were the two allowed to marry.

Clan loyalty was very important for tribal members. Clan members used to believe in revenge for any offense against any other member of their clan. For example, if a clan member was murdered, clan relatives had the duty to avenge the murder. The revenge was exacted by a blood relative from the victim's mother's line. If for some reason the murderer could not be executed, then another member of his or her clan took the murderer's place, usually voluntarily.

Before removal, the clans had particular areas in which they stayed at ceremonies. Today, you will see different clan members sitting at various places in the ceremonial grounds. They work together, however, to ensure that traditional ways are preserved and observed.

Suggested Readings

Unfortunately, there are few sources available for readers interested in further information about adverbial phrases in Mvskoke. Michele Nathan, in her "Grammatical Description of the Florida Seminole Dialect of Creek" (1977: 131–34) writes about adverbial forms in Florida Seminole, but she does not discuss to any great extent the manner of creating adverbial forms in that language.

The importance of the clan in Creek society cannot be overstated. Readers interested in the roles played by the various clans should consult John R. Swanton's "Social Organization and Social Usages of the Indians of the Creek Confederacy" (1928a:107–241) or George Stiggins's *Creek Indian History* (1989: 64–68). Although both sources discuss the activities in which clan relationships were of vital importance historically, readers should be aware that clan relations have decreased in importance in many of the activities described in the sources. The importance of other social groups for establishing and maintaining a Creek or Seminole identity (that is, membership in the Muskogee Creek Nation or the Seminole Nation) is explored by Pamela Innes ("Demonstrating that One Can Work within Two Communities," 1997a), Jason Baird Jackson ("Everybody Has a Part, Even the Little Bitty Ones," 1996), and John H. Moore ("The Mvskoke National Question in Oklahoma," 1988). Many of the social groups described in these works have become important for maintaining Creek and Seminole identity as the importance of the clan has waned.

CHAPTER 6

Singular Subject Affixes and Stative Verbs

Up to this point, you have been asked to create sentences with only one type of subject, the third person singular ("he," "she," or "it"). In this chapter, you will learn how to use two other singular subjects, "I" and "you." In type I verbs, these two subjects are shown by adding suffixes to the verb, just as a third person singular subject is. Verbs that use suffixes to indicate the subject of the sentence have {I} or {I;some other symbol(s)} following the pronunciation guide in their glossary entries.

First Person Singular Subject with Type I Verbs

The first person singular subject, abbreviated "1S" in the second line of the examples, is translated as 'I'. To use the 1S subject on a type I verb to make a declarative sentence in Mvskoke, the verb stem is modified for the incompletive aspect (the last vowel in the stem is lengthened), then the 1S type I subject suffix *-i-* is added to the verb stem, and finally the declarative suffix *-(e)s* is added. Thus, as shown in the following example, to make a sentence from the verb *vpeletv* 'to laugh, smile', the final vowel in *vpel-* is lengthened, *-i-* is added, and the declarative suffix *-s* is added:

Infinitive form of verb 'to laugh'	vpeletv
Derive verb stem	vpel-
Create incompletive aspect form	vpēl-

Add 1S suffix (*-i-*)	vpēli-
Add declarative ending	vpēlis

After all of these changes have been applied, a complete sentence is formed:

1. Vpēlis.
laughing/smiling-1S-dec
'I am laughing/smiling'.

The same steps are followed when an object is present in the sentence. The difference between the sentences you have made up to this point and the sentences made with the 1S subject is that a subject noun is generally not specified in a sentence containing a 1S subject. The subject, "I," is found in the verb and does not have to be present at another point in the sentence. For instance, in the sentence

2. Kafe hiyen ēskis.
coffee hot-def_obj drinking-1S-dec
'I am drinking the hot coffee'.

the subject, "I," occurs only in the verb. Occasionally, *vne* 'I, me' can be used before the verb to stress that *I* am the person doing the action. This is generally used for special emphasis, as in the following sentence:

3. Vnet taklike noricis.
I-def_subj bread-ind_obj cooking-1S-dec
'*I* am cooking bread'.

This sentence might have been produced when, in a previous statement, someone else had been credited with cooking the bread. The identity of the person performing the action, in this case "I," is being strongly marked by the use of *vne*. Notice that even when *vne* is used in the sentence, the 1S suffix is still added to the verb.

Second Person Singular Subject with Type I Verbs

The second person singular subject, abbreviated "2S" in the second line of the examples, is translated as 'you (sg.) [one person]' in the final line of each example. To use the 2S subject with a type I verb to make a declarative sentence in Mvskoke, the verb stem is first modified for the incompletive aspect (the last vowel in the stem is lengthened). Next, the 2S type I suffix, *-eck-*, is added. To the ears of English speakers, this suffix sounds as if it should be spelled **-etsk-*.[1] This is because the sound represented by *c* is altered when it precedes a *k*, so we hear it as a [ts] combination followed immediately by [k]. Remember to write this sound as *ck*, however. Finally, the declarative suffix is added. As with the third person singular type I suffix, when the second person singular type I suffix is added to a verb, the declarative suffix has the *-es* form.

The second person singular suffix is an "always key" syllable. Thus, when the 2S type I suffix is added to a verb, it will take the highest tone in the verb, unless the falling tone grade (discussed in chapter 9) is operating on the verb. If a number of syllables follow the 2S type I suffix, their tones will descend from the tone level of the 2S suffix.

The steps in the formation of a type I verb, *pvsetv* 'to sweep', with the 2S subject, is as follows:

Infinitive form 'to sweep'	pvsetv
Obtain verb stem	pvs
Create incompletive aspect form	pas
Add 2S subject suffix	paseck
Add declarative suffix	paseckes

Once all of these steps have been completed, a grammatically complete construction like the following has been formed:

4. Paseckes.
   sweeping-2S-dec
   'You (sg.) are sweeping'.

Like the 1S subject, the 2S subject can be used in sentences in which an object is used. Because the 2S subject is found in the verb construction, no other mention of the subject need be found in the rest of the sentence. Thus, a sentence with a 2S type I subject and an object will look like this:

1. Linguists mark ungrammatical or incorrect constructions by placing an asterisk before the ungrammatical form.

5. Coko rakken hayeckes.
house big-ind_obj building-2S-dec
'You (sg.) are building a big house'.

Notice that 'you' occurs nowhere else in the sentence than as a suffix on the verb. Also note that 'big house' is marked as the object (it has the indefinite object marker *-en*), so you know that a big house is being built by someone specified as the subject of the sentence.

As with the 1S type I subject, it is possible to insert a pronoun to emphasize that a second person singular subject is performing the action. The second person singular pronoun, *cēme*, stresses that *you* are the person doing the action, as in the following example:

6. Cēmet coko rakken hayeckes.
you (sg.)-def_subj house big-ind_obj building-2S-dec
'*You* (sg.) are building a big house'.

Again, this usage emphasizes who is performing the action. It adds extra weight to the information about who the subject is.

Stative Verbs

So far, we have looked at type I verbs, which are active verbs denoting that some activity is occurring. Another set of verbs also exists in Mvskoke and many other Native American languages. These are **stative verbs,** or verbs that describe states of being. In essence, they are like adjectives that have the characteristics of verbs. Stative verbs describe how someone or something looks or feels.

Stative verbs in Mvskoke are somewhat different from the type I verbs that we have discussed up to this point. Some verbs in Mvskoke, including the stative verbs, use type II affixes—that is, prefixes—to show who or what is playing the role of the subject. Stative verbs, in other words, are type II verbs. In the glossaries, verbs using type II subject prefixes are indicated by {II} or {II; some other symbol(s)} after the pronunciation guide in their entry.

There are three sets of subject prefixes that may be used with stative verbs, depending on which sound occurs at the beginning of the verb. These sets of prefixes are listed in table 6.1. In all three sets, the prefix is placed at the beginning of the verb stem. As you can see from the table, no audible type II prefix is used to mark the 3S subject, just as no audible type I suffix is used to mark the 3S subject.

TABLE 6.1. Type II Prefixes Used with Three Categories of Stative Verbs

Subject	Verbs Beginning with Consonant or *e*	Verbs Beginning with *ē*	Verbs Beginning with Any Vowel Other than *e* or *ē*
1S 'I'	cv-	vca-	vc-
2S 'you (sg.)'	ce-	ecē-	ec-
3S 'he/she/it'	–	–	–

When the subject prefix is added to a verb beginning with *e* or *ē*, the first vowel is deleted from the stem. This is shown in examples 7 and 8, which contain the verbs *enhonrē* 'to be hopeful' and *ētvsē* 'to be a little different'.

7. Cvnhonrēs.
   1S-to_be_hopeful-dec
   'I am hopeful'.

8. Vcatvsēs.
   1S-to_be_a_little_different-dec
   'I am a little different'.

Stative Verbs with 1S Subjects

Many stative verbs are listed in the glossaries in an adjectival form (that is, they end in *-ē* rather than *-etv*). To form a stative verb such as *cvpakkē* 'to be angry' for a 1S subject, we begin by adding the 1S type II prefix to the verb. Because this verb begins with a consonant, we will use the prefix *cv-*, which gives us *cvcvpakkē*.

In order to complete the verb, we need to add the declarative suffix *-s*. Adding this suffix gives us an entire sentence:

9. Cvcvpakkēs.
   1S-to_be_angry-dec
   'I am angry'.

If the verb begins with a vowel, you must note which vowel is in the initial position. The following are examples of how verbs beginning with vowels are constructed in the first person singular. The first example involves *enokkē* 'to be sick', a verb beginning with *e*. The form of the 1S prefix is *cv-*, because *e-* is the first sound of the verb.

Drop initial *e* from *enokkē* 'to be sick'	-nokkē
Add appropriate form of 1S prefix	cvnokkē
Add declarative suffix	cvnokkēs

This results in the sentence

10. Cvnokkēs.
 1S-to_be_sick-dec
 'I am sick'.

Verbs beginning with ē go through similar steps, as shown in the following example, where *ēhotkē* 'to be dangerous' is formed with a 1S subject. The 1S prefix form is *vca-*, because the verb begins with *ē*.

Drop initial ē from *ēhotkē* 'to be dangerous'	-hotkē
Add appropriate form of 1S prefix	vcahotkē
Add declarative suffix	vcahotkēs

This leads to the final sentence form:

11. Vcahotkēs.
 1S-to_be_dangerous-dec
 'I am dangerous'.

The next list gives the final example of a type II verb beginning with a vowel sound to be constructed with a 1S subject. This verb, *vculē* 'to be old', begins with neither *e* nor *ē*, which leads us to select the 1S subject prefix form *vc-* from those presented in table 6.1.

Obtain verb stem 'to be old'	vculē
Add appropriate form of 1S prefix	vcvculē
Add declarative suffix	vcvculēs

Once the declarative suffix is added, the verb is in its final form and is a complete sentence:

12. Vcvculēs.
    1S-to_be_old-dec
    'I am old'.

If a verb begins with a consonant, use the same prefixes that apply when a verb begins with *e-* (see table 6.1). When these prefixes are applied to a verb beginning with a consonant, the verb stem remains unchanged—nothing is removed. For instance, the verb *wvnkē* 'to be thirsty' is formed in the first person singular like this:

Obtain verb stem 'to be thirsty'	wvnkē
Add appropriate form of 1S prefix	cvwvnkē
Add declarative suffix	cvwvnkēs

The form after the addition of the declarative suffix is a complete sentence:

13. Cvwvnkēs.
    1S-to_be_thirsty-dec
    'I am thirsty'.

Use of Auxiliary Verbs

Many Mvskoke sentences contain a type I or type II verb followed by a form of a second verb, *ometv* 'to be', as part of the construction. We employ this construction in English, too. The sentence "The dog is running" contains two verbs, "is" and "running." In English constructions, "is" plays a role similar to that of *ometv* in the Mvskoke sentences. In Mvskoke sentences containing *ometv* and another verb, *ometv* is called an **auxiliary verb**, which means that it is not the main verb of the sentence; some other verb is actually the primary action.

When *ometv* is used, a suffix, *-t,* is added to the primary verb, which shows that the subject is the same for both the main verb and the auxiliary verb.[2] The same-subject suffix is denoted by "ss" in the second line under the Mvskoke sentence in the following example. A modified form of *ometv*

2. In designating the *-t* suffix added to the primary verb as a same-subject marker, we are taking only one of several possible meanings associated with suffixed *ts* in Mvskoke. For more information about the alternative meanings of the *-t* suffix, readers are directed to Hardy 1988:336–404.

then follows as a suffix added after the same-subject suffix (*-t*). In present tense declarative sentences containing verbs with singular subjects, the form of *ometv* that is used is always *os*.[3] Thus, sentence 13, an example using a type II verb, may also take the following form:

14. Cvwvnkētos.
1S-thirsty-ss-aux_vb-dec
'I am thirsty'.

Note that the presence of the auxiliary verb is marked by the abbreviation "aux_vb" in the second line of example 14. Auxiliary verbs will be noted in this way in subsequent examples.

Auxiliary verbs can also be used in sentences containing type I verbs. Again, the inclusion of an auxiliary verb in these sentences does not change their meaning, but it does necessitate the use of the same-subject suffix, *-t*, on the main verb of the sentence. Example 15 is a sentence containing both a type I primary verb and an auxiliary verb:

15. Echaswvt hompetos.
beaver-ind_subj eat-3S-ss-aux_vb-dec
'A beaver is eating'.

Stative Verbs with 2S Subjects

The steps followed to produce sentences with correctly formed verbs using the 2S type II subject prefixes are the same as those listed earlier for the 1S type II subject. The only difference involves the form of the prefix added to the verb stem. Verbs beginning with *e* use the prefix *ce-* to denote a 2S subject (see table 6.1). The verb stem is changed in that the initial vowel (*e*) is dropped before this prefix is added. Once the vowel has been dropped, the 2S subject prefix is added to the verb stem. The final step in the process involves adding the declarative suffix. The following example using the verb *etkolē* 'to feel cold' shows how this is done:

3. The meaning of the *os* auxiliary in Mvskoke is fairly complex. Although in this text we translate the auxiliary as some form of 'to be', Donald E. Hardy (1992) suggests that this verb may have several other translations. He provides greater information about items in the sentence than is provided here.

1. Delete initial *e* from *etkolē* 'to feel cold'	-tkolē		
2. Add appropriate 2S prefix	cetkolē		
3. Add declarative suffix	16a.	Cetkolēs. 2S-to_feel_cold-dec 'You (sg.) are feeling cold'.	

or

4. Add same-subject suffix	cetkolēt	
5. Add modified form of *ometv*	16b.	Cetkolētos. 2S-to_feel_cold-ss-aux_vb-dec 'You (sg.) are feeling cold'.

Verbs beginning with a consonant use the same form of the 2S prefix as verbs beginning with *e*. When this prefix is added to verbs beginning with a consonant, however, there is no need to delete anything from the verb stem before adding the prefix. Thus, a type II verb with an initial consonant will be formed in the following manner. In this example, the verb to be modified is *lvwē* 'to be hungry':

1. Obtain verb stem 'to be hungry'	lvwē	
2. Add appropriate 2S prefix	celvwē	
3. Add declarative suffix	17a.	Celvwēs. 2S-to_be_hungry-dec 'You (sg.) are hungry'.

or

3. Add same-subject suffix	celvwēt	
4. Add modified form of *ometv*	17b.	Celvwētos. 2S-to_be_hungry-ss-aux_vb-dec 'You (sg.) are hungry'.

In the preceding examples, forms 16a and 16b and forms 17a and 17b each mean the same thing. The difference is simply the use of the auxiliary verb in sentences 16b and 17b.

If the verb begins with a vowel other than *e* or *ē*, then nothing is removed from the verb stem before the 2S type II prefix *ec-* is added. For instance, the verb *vcvkē* 'to be stunted, dwarfish', takes the *ec-* prefix because it begins with the vowel *v*. The steps taken to modify *vcvkē* to create a sentence with a 2S subject are as follows:

1. Obtain verb stem 'to be stunted, dwarfish'	vcvkē	
2. Add appropriate 2S prefix	ecvcvkē	
3. Add declarative verb suffix	18a.	Ecvcvkēs. 2S-to_be_stunted-dec 'You (sg.) are stunted'.
or		
3. Add same-subject suffix	ecvcvkēt	
4. Add modified form of *ometv*	18b.	Ecvcvkētos. 2S-to_be_stunted-ss-aux_vb-dec 'You (sg.) are stunted'.

Similar steps are taken to modify a type II verb beginning with *ē* for a 2S subject. Note that *ētvsē* 'to be a little different' undergoes exactly the same steps as those just listed for *vcvkē*:

1. Obtain verb stem 'to be a little different'	ētvsē	
2. Add appropriate 2S prefix	ecētvsē	
3. Add declarative verb suffix	19a.	Ecētvsēs. 2S-to_be_little_different-dec 'You (sg.) are a little different'.
or		
3. Add same-subject suffix	ecētvsēt	
4. Add modified form of *ometv*	19b.	Ecētvsētos. 2S-to_be_little_different-ss-aux_vb-dec 'You (sg.) are a little different'.

Stative Verbs with 3S Subjects

Despite the fact that third person singular subjects are not shown by adding an audible type II prefix to the verb stem (see table 6.1), a 3S prefix is still considered to be present. Because the type II 3S prefix is a null prefix, the only changes that have to be made to the verb in order to form a complete sentence are either (1) simply to add the declarative suffix to the end of the adjectival form of the verb (the form ending in ē) or (2) to add the same-subject suffix *-t* to the verb stem and then add the modified form of *ometv*. Because the 3S subject is not marked by any audible type II prefix, verbs beginning with vowels and consonants are constructed in the same manner. Unless the identity of the subject of the sentence is already known to both speaker and listener, a pronoun is often included in sentences containing type II 3S subjects, in order to make clear what or who is being described. In examples 20 and 21, stative verbs have been formed for a 3S subject:

20. Honvnwv hvlvlatkētos.
man-def_subj 3S-to_be_slow-ss-aux_vb-dec
'The man is slow'.

21. Wakv fvmpētos.
cow-def_subj 3S-to_be_smelly-ss-aux_vb-dec
'The cow is smelly'.

Notice that in both examples, the subject of the sentence has been specified ('the man' and 'the cow', respectively). Thus, the listener has been given specific information about who or what the subject is.

TYPE II POSSESSION MARKERS

Type II affixes—that is, prefixes—can be used to mark possession of certain nouns. Ownership of many **inalienable nouns**, items that cannot really be "disowned," such as relatives and body parts, is often shown by using a prefix on the noun itself. When this is the case, the glossary entry for the noun will have {II} after the noun. This means that a type II prefix must be used to show that a certain person (I, you, he/she/it) owns or is closely related to that item.

Several of the kinship terms presented in the vocabulary for this chapter show relationship through type II prefixes. When the nouns are presented in the glossary, they are presented with a 3S possessive prefix, *e-*, that is a discernible prefix separable from the noun itself. It is the initial *e-* of *ervhv* 'his/her older same-sex sibling' which shows that this term is referring to "his" or "her" sibling, not "mine" or "yours." When an inalienable noun is to be possessed by any other subject, the initial *e* of the 3S form is dropped and the appropriate type II prefix is chosen for the initial sound of the remaining noun stem. Thus, because the unpossessed form of *-rvhv* 'older same-sex sibling' begins with *r* after the 3S possessive prefix has been dropped, the correct 1S type II prefix added to the noun to show possession is *cv-*, because the noun stem begins with a consonant (see table 6.1). The 1S possessed form of 'my older same-sex sibling' is thus *cvrvhv*.

Nouns that are noted as being type II possessed nouns cannot, generally, exist in an unpossessed form. It is not grammatically correct to use *-rvhv* without a possessive prefix, even if the possessor is mentioned in the sentence. Thus, for a man to say 'I see my older brother', he must use both the possessive prefix *cv-* on the possessed noun and the subject suffix on the verb. This leads to a construction like the following:

22. Cvrvhv hēcis. (man speaking)
    1S-older_brother see-1S-dec
    'I see my older brother'.

Even though you may know that the speaker is referring to his brother because of previous clues in the conversation, the term for his older brother must still contain the possessive prefix.

A man's term for his sister, *ēwvnwv*, differs from most other kinship terms in that the vowel of the 3S possessive prefix is long. When the 1S or 2S prefix is added to this noun, their vowels also are long. The possessive forms used with this word, then, are distinct from the type II possessive forms used with most other nouns, as shown in the following list, which compares the various possessed forms of *ēwvnwv* with the possessed forms of *epose* 'grandmother'.

'My sister' (said by a man)	cawvnwv
'Your sister' (said to a man)	cēwvnwv
'His sister'	ēwvnwv
'My grandmother'	cvpose
'Your grandmother'	cepose
'His/her grandmother'	epose

Notice that the long vowel length of the 3S possessive prefix in *ēwvnwv* is maintained in the 1S (*ca-* rather than *cv-*) and 2S (*cē-* rather than *ce-*) possessed forms as well. The short vowel quality of the 3S possessed form of *epose* is maintained in the 1S and 2S forms.

Vocabulary

Kinship Terms

Mvskoke	English
epoca {II}	grandfather
epose {II}	grandmother
erke {II}	father
ecke {II}	mother
ervhv {II} *or* ervhv vculicat {II}	a man's older brother
ecuse {II} *or* ecerwv mvnetosat {II}	a man's younger brother
ecerwv {II}	a woman's brother
ervhv {II} *or* ervhv hoktvlēcat {II}	a woman's older sister
ecuse {II} *or* ecuse mvnetat {II}	a woman's younger sister
ēwvnwv {II}	a man's sister
eppuce {II}	a man's son
eccus honvnwv {II}	a woman's son
eccuste {II}	a man's daughter
eccus hoktē {II}	a woman's daughter
epvwv {II}	maternal uncle
erkuce {II}	paternal uncle
eckuce {II}	maternal aunt
epose {II}	paternal aunt
enahvmke {II} *or* enahvnke {II}	cousin (male or female)

Verbs

Mvskoke	English
vpeletv {I}	to laugh or smile
hvkihketv {I}	to cry (of one)
cokopericetv {I;D}	to visit

vyepetv {I;II} *or* enkvpvketv {I;D}	to leave or go away from
hvsvtecetv {I;3}	to clean (one thing)
etepoyetv {I;II}	to fight
etenherketv {I;II}	to make peace with each other
oponvyetv {I}	to talk
em oponvyetv {I;D}	to talk with someone
enkvpicetv {I;D}	to share with someone
vnokecetv {I;II}	to love someone
vsēketv {I;II}	to shake hands with, greet
penkvlē {II;D}	to be afraid, scared
fekhvmkē {II}	to be brave
nockelē {II} *or* nuckelē {II}	to be sleepy
vhonecē {II}	to be awake

Conversational Sentences

Honvnwvt: Stofvn vncokopericeckvrēte?	Man: When will you visit me?
Hoktet: Pvksen cencokopericares.	Woman: I will visit you tomorrow.
Honvnwvt: Pvksen cvcuset vncokopericvhanes.	Man: Tomorrow my younger brother will visit me.
Hoktet: Cvcerwvt vncokopericekotos.	Woman: My brother doesn't visit me.
Honvnwvt: Cencvmēroses.	Man: I'm sorry for you.
Hoktet: Etepoyēs.	Woman: We fight.
Honvnwvt: Cvcose etepoyekotos.	Man: I don't fight with my younger brother.
Hoktet: En hēnres.	Woman: That's good.
Honvnwvt: Etemēyackvkekvs.	Man: You should make up.
Hoktet: Enka, momarēs.	Woman: Yes, we will.

Exercises

Exercise 1

Translate the following sentences into Mvskoke. Then, working with a partner, read your Mvskoke sentences out loud. If you disagree with your partner's

Figure 6.1. Ribbon Dance leaders at Greenleaf Ceremonial Ground, August 1995. Right to left: Toni Wise, Bonnie Gibson, Anna Cooper, Bertha Tilkens. *Photograph by Linda Alexander.*

A committee of ceremonial ground members selects the women to lead the dance. The women serve as dance leaders for four years. The Ribbon Dance honors women on this day during the Green Corn Ceremony. The date of this dance is set by men who are selected to be leaders at the ground and who make the majority of decisions for the ceremonial ground.

translation, write down why you disagree and how your sentences differ. Discuss the differences in class.

1. I am drinking the cold water slowly.
2. You are singing loudly.
3. I see the big white cloud.
4. He is mean.
5. I am sleepy.
6. The wide river is deep.
7. A skinny man is singing.
8. You are strong.
9. The water is hot.
10. The tall fat man is talking to you.

Exercise 2

Identify each of the meaningful units in each of the following sentences, then provide an English translation of each. You should produce ten pairs of lines similar in form and content to the final two lines provided in each example in the text. When possible, note the gender of the subject and/or speaker in your translation.

1. Hvse hayēs.
2. Cvnockelēs.
3. Cvrvhv vculicat vpēles.
4. Cepanē feknokket penkvlētos.
5. Eppuce vhonecēs.
6. Cēwvnwv hotosat hvkihketos.
7. Cerke vnokēceckes.
8. Honvnwvt cvnahvmken vsēkis.
9. Hvcce lvokētos.
10. Ceccus hoktē vyēpeckes.

Exercise 3

Working with a partner, use the conversational sentences from the chapters you have covered to create a sensible conversation of at least forty sentences (you and your partner should be responsible for about twenty sentences each). Practice your conversation until it sounds natural. Repeat your conversation in front of the class.

Exercise 4

Create twenty original sentences using the vocabulary you have covered so far. You should create sentences with subject and object adjectives, adverbs, and 1S, 2S, and 3S subjects.

Exercise 5

Construct each of the verbs below with the specified subject, then translate the resulting sentence in English. Some of these verbs take type I subject suffixes; others take type II subject prefixes.

1. oponvyetv (1S)
2. wvkketv (2S)
3. tvhoknē (3S)
4. atvkkesetv (2S)
5. fekhvmkē (1S)
6. lvtketv (3S)
7. vhonecē (2S)
8. nocetv (1S)
9. afvckē (1S)
10. enokkē (2S)
11. etkolē (1S)
12. lopicē (2S)
13. vculē (3S)
14. korretv (3S)
15. opvnetv (2S)
16. hueretv (1S)
17. ēyvcayē (2S)
18. enhonrē (3S)
19. yvkvpetv (2S)
20. maketv (1S)

Exercise 6

Create twenty original sentences using stative verbs. Pronounce your sentences to a partner and ask him or her to translate your sentences. If your partner cannot translate your sentences, discuss why this is the case. If you have questions about your sentences or if there are misunderstandings that cause your partner to be unable to translate your sentences, ask your teacher about these in class.

Exercise 7

Translate the following story from Mvskoke to English and answer the questions with Mvskoke sentences. You may need to check the glossary and conversational sentences in earlier chapters for the meanings of some of the words in the story and questions. After translating the story, tell the story, in Mvskoke, to a partner. Compare your translation and your answers to the questions with your partner's.

"Cvcke, cvnockelēs," Sam maketos. Wakkes. "Cetkolēte?" cecke maketos. "Mvnks. Cvwvnkēs." "Uewvn ēskeckes," ecke makes. "Oponvkv ohhonayeckes." 'Locv Elvwēs' ecke Sam ohhonayes. "Hēnrētos," Sam makes. "Hvte noceckes" ecke maketos. Sam nocetos.

1. Estimvt nockelēte?
2. Naken oponvkv ecke Sam ohhonayetomv?
3. Sam etkolēte?
4. Ecke Sam vsēketomv?
5. Sam hvkihkv?
6. Naken Sam ēsketomv?

Mvskoke Kinship

Mvskoke people are related by blood and clan ties through their mother's line of ancestry. Therefore, it is sometimes difficult for people to determine their relationship to another Mvskoke person—are they clan relatives, blood relatives, or both? It is very important for a Mvskoke person to know his or her clan and family relations.

Because of the blood and clan relationships, Mvskoke people tend to have more grandmothers and grandfathers than most Euro-American people. From childhood, Mvskoke people are taught never to call an older person by his or her given name. Instead, children are taught to precede the elder's name with "aunt," "uncle," "grandma," or "grandpa." Because these terms apply to a number of people, confusion can occur unless knowledgeable traditional people are asked about one person's relationship to others. Those who are knowledgeable can explain how people are related by being maternal and paternal relatives or clan relatives.

All members of a person's mother's clan become relatives. The mother's brothers, sisters, aunts, and uncles become the child's uncles, aunts, grandmothers, and grandfathers, respectively. Younger members of the mother's clan will be called brothers and sisters. Members of a child's father's clan also become relatives. They, too, become the child's brothers, sisters, uncles, aunts, grandmothers, and grandfathers.

Because all people who are members of the same clan can claim some relationship to each other, marriage within the clan is discouraged. Every

Mvskoke person should know what his or her father's clan is as well, for marriage into that clan is also discouraged. For this reason, prospective boyfriends and girlfriends often have to answer questions about their parents' clan membership.

This practice of keeping track of clan membership and making certain that people marry outside their clan is becoming less common in the twenty-first century. Mvskoke people who are interested in tracing their clan membership should try asking an elder for help in determining what their mother's and father's clans are. People attempting to find out about their parents' clans will need to know their parents' names and perhaps the names of their grandparents and great-grandparents in order to help the elder place the clan membership. This kind of knowledge is an important part of knowing about a person's Mvskoke family history.

Suggested Readings

The meaning denoted by the use of one Muskogean subject set versus another (that is type I vs. type II) on a given verb is richer than has been presented in this chapter. This richness of meaning has led several linguists to investigate why various verbs take one set over another to denote the subject. Of the works that have emerged from this analysis, Pamela Munro and Lynn Gordon's "Syntactic Relations in Western Muskogean" (1982) provides a clear explanation of the uses of type I and type II affixes to denote agency and passivity in the subject role. Their findings are not derived solely from Mvskoke, however, and some readers may find the comparative approach difficult to follow.

Abigail Cohn ("Causative Formation in the Oklahoma Seminole Dialect of Creek," 1987:51–57) and Donald E. Hardy ("The Semantics of Creek Morphosyntax," 1988:197–203, 209–30) each investigate the various pronominal marker sets in Mvskoke. In both sources, the distinction between a subject's agency or passivity in the midst of the action denoted by the verb is viewed as playing a role in determining whether the type I or type II subject marker is used. This is very similar to the findings reached by Munro and Gordon. But because Cohn and Hardy discuss the use of the type I and type II subject markers only in Mvskoke, their works may be more helpful for readers of this textbook.

Mary Haas ("From Auxiliary Verb Phrase to Inflectional Suffix," 1977c) shows how the type I subject markers have been derived from auxiliary verb stems. Haas is primarily interested in showing that one of the subject marking sets used by most languages in the Muskogean family was formed by combining auxiliary verbs and an earlier, already existing subject marking set. The ways in which the auxiliary verbs and early subject markers combined have caused different forms of subject markers to develop in the Muskogean languages.

Further information about stative and active verbs in Mvskoke may be found in Hardy's 1988 article (pp. 277–99). There, Hardy discusses the difference between stative and active verbs, as well as how to modify both for a range of subjects, tenses, and aspects. The majority of these topics are covered in later chapters in this textbook.

Family relationships and their importance for members of the Muskogee and Seminole communities are discussed in John R. Swanton's "Social Organization and Social Usages of the Indians of the Creek Confederacy" (1928a:79–107) and Alexander Spoehr's *Kinship System of the Seminole* (1942) and *Changing Kinship Systems* (1947). Swanton described historical family relations and terminology among the Muskogee. Spoehr, in his 1942 book, described the kinship system in use among the Oklahoma Seminoles in the 1930s. He compared the Oklahoma Seminole system to that of the Florida Seminoles and attempted to discover what the prehistoric system might have been like. In his 1947 book, Spoehr investigated changes in the kinship system among the Muskogee (Creeks), comparing their kinship system in the early 1940s with earlier kinship system structures and with the kinship systems of two other Southeastern groups, the Choctaws and the Cherokees. Each of these works identifies family as an important structure in the Muskogee and Seminole communities at the time when the book was written, and the family remains important today.

CHAPTER 7

Verb Prefixes Denoting Singular Objects

In English, we have to use separate words to specify who or what is the subject of a sentence and who or what is the object of the sentence. In Mvskoke, it is possible to indicate both the subject and the object of a sentence by adding what are called **pronominal markers** to the verb. Depending on the verb, either a type I or a type II affix serves as the pronominal marker, denoting who or what is performing the action. That is, they work just the way the pronouns "I," "you," "he," "she," and "it" do in English. As you know from the previous chapter, the subject of a sentence (the person or thing performing the action) is indicated by adding a type I subject suffix or a type II subject prefix to the verb stem. When the object of a sentence (the person or thing affected by the action) is singular, it is indicated on the verb in the form of a prefix added to the front of the verb stem.

There are two types of objects, direct and indirect. **Direct objects** are those things that are directly affected by the action described in the sentence. **Indirect objects** are those things that are indirectly affected by the action described in the sentence. In English, singular direct and indirect objects may be noted by the pronouns "me," "you," and "him/her/it." Examples 1, 2 and 3 present sentences in which these pronouns designate the direct object:

1. John hit me!
   "John" is the subject, "me" is the direct object.

2. The bear sees you.
   "The bear" is the subject, "you" is the direct object.

3. Desmond heard him.
   "Desmond" is the subject, "him" is the direct object.

In each of these sentences, the subject is the person or thing causing the action to happen, and the direct object is the person or thing to which the action is being done.

Indirect objects are persons or things that are not immediately involved in the performance of the action. In English, singular indirect objects often occur after prepositions, as in examples 4, 5, and 6 (the indirect objects are shown in italics):

4. The man brought the kitten to *me*.

5. Her mother took the knife away from *her*.

6. The singer sang the song for *you*.

It also is possible for an indirect object to occur without a preposition, as in example 7:

7. That boy threw *you* the ball.

In each of the preceding examples, the indirect object is not immediately affected by the action because it is not the primary object upon which the action is being performed. Instead, the indirect object is the recipient of the action, which is being directly applied to something else that is somehow connected with the indirect object.

Both direct and indirect object pronouns are represented by prefixes in Mvskoke. The form of the prefix for a particular object depends upon the type of object (direct or indirect), the type of verb (type I or II), and the structure of the verb stem (whether it begins with a vowel or a consonant). We will begin with singular direct object pronouns prefixed to type I verbs.

Singular Direct Object Pronouns Prefixed to Type I Verbs

Verbs that use type I suffixes to indicate the subject of the sentence show the singular direct object of the sentence by adding the same prefixes that you

Table 7.1. Direct Object Prefixes for Type I Verbs

Subject	Abbreviation	Verb Stems Beginning with Consonant or *e*	Verb Stems Beginning with Any Vowel Other than *e*
1S 'me'	1Sdo	cv-	vc-
2S 'you'	2Sdo	ce-	ec-
3S 'him/her/it'	3Sdo	–	–

learned to use with type II verbs in chapter 5. Thus, with type I verbs, type II prefixes are used to indicate direct objects. Verbs of this type will have {I;II} following the pronunciation guide in their glossary entries. The I in the {I;II} symbol refers to the subject suffix; the II refers to the direct object prefix.

Remember that the form of the direct object prefix depends upon the form of the verb stem. Type I verbs whose stems begin with consonants or the vowel *e* take the prefixes presented in the third column of table 7.1. A second set of prefixes, also presented in table 7.1, is used to denote direct objects on type I verbs beginning with any vowel other than *e*. For all type {I;II} verbs, the order of meaningful units in the verb is as shown in diagram 7.1.

Type II Direct Object Prefix	Verb Stem	Type I Subject Suffix	Declarative Suffix

Diagram 7.1. Order of Constituents in a Type {I;II} Verb with a Direct Object

Type I Verbs Beginning with a Consonant or *e*

If a {I;II} verb begins with a consonant or *e*, then the singular direct object of the sentence (abbreviated Sdo) is indicated by adding to the verb stem one of the prefixes shown in table 7.1. The null prefix symbol (—) for the third person singular direct object prefix indicates that there is no audible form; it appears as if no prefix is added. But despite the absence of an audible prefix, one is considered to be in the direct object position in a null prefix form. When 1Sdo and 2Sdo prefixes are added to verb stems beginning with *e*, the initial *e* of the verb stem is dropped. Adding the 3Sdo prefix to a verb stem beginning with *e* causes no change, and the initial *e* is retained.

Examples 8a and 8b, 9a and 9b, and 10a and 10b show the construction of verbs beginning with consonants and utilizing singular direct object pronoun prefixes. In each case, the direct object (shown by the pronominal prefix) is the first item, the verb stem is second (in the incompletive aspect form), the type I subject suffix is third, and the declarative suffix ends the sentence. Examples 8a and 8b each have a first person singular direct object (1Sdo):

8a. Cvnafkeckes.
1Sdo-hitting-2S-dec
'You are hitting me'.

8b. Cepanē cvhopakes.
boy-def_subj 1Sdo-pushing-3S-dec
'The boy is pushing me'.

Examples 9a and 9b each have a second person singular direct object (2Sdo):

9a. Cehēcis.
2Sdo-see-1S-dec
'I see you'.

9b. Sokhvt cepohes.
pig-ind_subj 2Sdo-hear-3S-dec
'A pig hears you'.

The third person singular object prefix is considered to apply even when a noun has been specified as the direct object in the sentence, preceding the verb. When a noun has already been mentioned as an object in the sentence, the 3Sdo prefix ('it') refers to that noun. This structure would be redundant in English but is not so in Mvskoke. Thus, in example 10b, 'the bread' is specified as the object (the thing being eaten) and also is referred to on the verb stem (a 3Sdo is considered to have been applied to the verb). In example 10a, however, the 3Sdo prefix is referring to an item that has not been specified in the sentence.

10a. Honvnwv hvsvtēces.
man-def_subj 3Sdo-cleaning-3S-dec
'The man is cleaning him/her/it'.

10b. Tvklike hompis.
bread-def_obj 3Sdo-eat-1S-dec
'I am eating the bread'.

As you can see, in each case the order of the constituents added to the verb is exactly as specified in diagram 7.1: the direct object pronoun (*cv-*, *ce-*, or —) is first, the verb stem is second, the type I subject suffix is third, and the declarative suffix *-(e)s* is last. Note that in examples 8a and 8b, "me," which is denoted by a type II direct object prefix, is the one being hit and pushed. The object prefix is thus indicating the direct object of the verb. The same pattern exists in 9a and 9b, where the person referred to as "you" is the direct recipient of the action.

In examples 10a and 10b, however, there is some ambiguity. It is possible to translate 10a as 'The man is cleaning', without specifying that there is an object. This translation is possible because there is no audible prefix for 3S direct objects, so there is no certainty that a 3S direct object is being discussed. If a 3S object is considered to be part of the sentence in 10a, then that sentence may be translated as 'The man is cleaning him', 'The man is cleaning her', or 'The man is cleaning it'. This ambiguity occurs because, unlike English, Mvskoke does not designate the gender of third-person singular subjects or objects. For these reasons, when you are confronted by a type I verb that can take a direct object, but no object is specified in the sentence, you should provide translations with and without an object. For instance, 10a would be translated as:

10a. Honvnwv hvsvtēces.
man-def_subj cleaning-3S-dec
'The man is cleaning'.
or
man-def_subj 3Sdo-cleaning-3S-dec
'The man is cleaning him/her/it'.

The same prefixes that are applied to verbs beginning with consonants are also applied to verbs beginning with *e*. The forms that result from their application are shown in examples 11–13. In sentences 11 and 12, it is clear that when 1Sdo and 2Sdo prefixes are added to the verb, the initial *e* of the stem is deleted. In example 13, we see that when the 3Sdo prefix is added, the first vowel of the verb stem is not deleted. In this example, the first vowel of the verb *esketv* 'to drink' is also the stem vowel, which becomes *ē* after it has been lengthened in order to indicate the incompletive aspect.

11. Cepanē cvtepoyes.
boy-def_subj 1Sdo-fighting-3S-dec
'The boy is fighting me'.

12. Cepanē cetenhērketos.
boy-def_subj 2Sdo-making_up_with-3S-ss-aux_vb-dec
'The boy is making up with you'.

13. Hoktucet ēsketos.
girl-ind_subj 3Sdo-drinking-3S-ss-aux_vb-dec
or girl-ind_subj drinking-3S-ss-aux_vb-dec
'A girl is drinking it' *or* 'A girl is drinking'.

Just as was noted earlier for example 10a, example 13 is ambiguous with respect to the inclusion of a direct object. Hence, two different translations for 13 are possible, and both have been listed.

Type I Verbs Beginning with a Vowel Other than *e*

When a {I;II} verb begins in a vowel other than *e*, a different set of singular direct object pronoun prefixes is used. These prefixes are shown in table 7.1. When these prefixes are used, as in examples 14a and 14b, 15a and 15b, and 16a and 16b, the direct object prefix comes first, the verb stem is next, the type I subject suffix is third, and the declarative suffix -*(e)s* comes last. Verbs formed with a first person singular direct object are shown in examples 14a and 14b:

14a. Honvnwv vcvsēkes.
man-def_subj 1Sdo-greeting-3S-dec
'The man is greeting me'.

14b. Vcakkes.
1Sdo-biting-3S-dec
'He/she/it is biting me'.

Examples 15a and 15b use verbs containing a second person singular direct object:

15a. Ecvnokēces.
2Sdo-love-3S-dec
'He/she/it loves you'.

15b. Wakv ecvwenayes.
cow-def_subj 2Sdo-smelling-3S-dec
'The cow is smelling you'.

In sentences 14a and 15b, the subject has been specified by a noun in the sentence as well as by a suffix on the verb. In sentences 14b and 15a, information about the subject and object is located solely on the verb. When no subject noun is specified in a sentence involving a third person singular subject, your translation should reflect the ambiguity of the subject, just as the translations of 14b and 15a do.

In the next two examples, 16a and 16b, the subjects and direct objects are both third person singular. Also, in both cases, subject and object nouns, separate from the verb, are present.

16a. Hoktē pipuce atvkkēses.
woman-def_subj baby-def_obj 3Sdo-pick_up-3S-dec
'The woman is picking up the baby'.

16b. Rakko lvstat eton ahvlatetos.
horse black-def_subj tree-ind_obj 3Sdo-pulling-3S-ss-aux_vb-dec
'The black horse is pulling a tree (toward the speaker)'.

It would be possible to omit both the subject and object nouns, because the verbs in both sentences contain information about the subject and object. For instance, 16a could be rewritten as

16c. Atvkkēses.
3Sdo-pick_up-3S-dec
'He/she/it picks up him/her/it'.

As you can see, when the subject and object nouns are deleted from 16a, the resulting sentence, 16c, while grammatical, is very ambiguous. Sentences like 16c are used most frequently when the subject and object of the sentence are understood from previous statements.

Singular Dative Pronominal Prefixes on Type I Verbs

Singular dative pronominal prefixes generally refer to what we think of as indirect objects. The term **dative** means that the pronoun is marked as the

TABLE 7.2. Dative Object Prefixes for Use on Type I Verbs Beginning with *em*

Indirect Object	Abbreviation	Mvskoke Prefix
1S 'me, to me, for me', etc.	1SD	vm-
2S 'you, to you, for you', etc.	2SD	cem-
3S 'him/her/it, to him/her/it', etc.	3SD	em-

indirect object of a verb or as the direct object of some verbs and prepositions. Because the set of indirect object pronouns differs from the set used to denote direct objects on most verbs, it is called the dative pronominal set. It will often be necessary to use a preposition in the English translation of a Mvskoke verb containing a dative pronoun prefix (for example, "to me," "for you").

Type I and II verbs that take the dative pronominal set to denote their indirect or direct objects have {I;D} and {II;D}, respectively, following the definitions in their glossary entries. There are two sets of dative (D) prefixes: one set used with {I;D} verbs beginning with *em* (the set shown in table 7.2) and a second set used with {I;D} verbs beginning with all other vowel-consonant or consonant-vowel combinations and all {II;D} verbs (shown in table 7.3).

Dative Object Prefixes For {I;D} Verbs Beginning with *em*

Dative object prefixes used with type I verbs beginning with *em* are presented in table 7.2. When these are added to {I;D} verbs, the D object prefix comes first, the verb stem is second, the subject suffix is third, and the declarative suffix is last, as shown in diagram 7.2.

Dative Object Prefix	Verb Stem	Type I Subject Suffix	Declarative Suffix

Diagram 7.2. Order of Constituents in a Type {I;D} Verb Containing an Object

When the glossary entry for a {I;D} verb begins with *em* followed by a vowel, the initial *em* is dropped before the appropriate dative object prefix is added to the verb. In essence, the *em* in the glossary entry is the 3SD prefix, which indicates that the verb takes a dative object. Thus, to properly modify the verb for any other dative object, the 3SD prefix must be dropped and the proper prefix added.

In example 17, the verb *em vsehetv* 'to give a warning to' is used to create the sentence 'I am giving you a warning'. The order of the modifications to the verb necessary to form the sentence 'I am giving you a warning' is presented in the following list. First the *em* and the infinitive suffix of *em vsehetv* are dropped. Then the final vowel of the verb stem is lengthened (if appropriate), the 2SD object prefix is added to the verb stem (which now begins with *v*), the 1S suffix is added, and finally the declarative suffix is attached.

1. Infinitive form 'to give a warning to'	em vsehetv
2. Delete initial *em* and infinitive suffix *-etv*	vseh-
3. Lengthen final stem vowel	vsēh-
4. Add correct form of 2SD prefix	cemvsēh-
5. Add 1S suffix	cemvsēhi-
6. Add declarative suffix	cemvsēhis

The order of these components is presented in the second line of example 17:

17. Cemvsēhis.
cem-vsēh-i-s
2SD-give_a_warning_to-1S-dec
'I am giving you a warning'.

This pattern is repeated in examples 18 and 19, each of which uses a {I;D} verb beginning with *em* followed by a verb stem that begins with a vowel. In example 18, the verb stem appears very similar to its form in the glossary (*em etetaketv* 'to be ready for something'), but note that the 3SD prefix has been attached directly to the beginning of the verb.

18. Emetetakeckes.
em-etetak-eck-es
3SD-get_ready_for-2S-dec
'You are getting ready for it'.

In example 19, the 1SD prefix is attached directly to the stem of the verb *em vnvtaksetv* 'to look up at someone'. To form this construction, the initial *em* of the glossary entry is dropped before the 1SD prefix is added.

19. Honvnwv vmvnvtakses.
man-def_subj 1SD-looking_up_at (a person)-3S-dec
'The man is looking up at me'.

When a {I;D} verb begins with *em* followed by a consonant, the initial *em* is deleted from the verb stem before the dative prefix is added. The steps followed to form a verb beginning with *em* followed by a consonant are shown in the following list:

1. Obtain infinitive form 'to pray for'	em mēkusvpetv
2. Delete *em* and infinitive suffix *-etv*	mēkusvp-
3. Lengthen last stem vowel, if appropriate	mēkusap-
4. Add appropriate dative object prefix	cemmēkusap-
5. Add subject suffix	cemmēkusapi-
6. Add declarative suffix	cemmēkusapis

Performing each of these steps results in the form found in example 20.

20. Cemmēkusapis.
2SD-praying_for-1S-dec
'I am praying for you'.

The same steps were followed in creating examples 21 and 22, which use the verbs *em mvyattēcetv* 'to wave at' and *em ponvyetv* 'to talk to'.

21. Hoktet vmmvyattēces.
woman-ind_subj 1SD-waving_at-3S-dec
'A woman is waving at me'.

22. Vnet honvnwv emponayis.
I-def_subj man-def_obj 3SD-talking_to-1S-dec
'I am talking to the man/to him'.

When the glossary entry for a {I;D} verb begins only with *m*, the initial *m* is removed from the beginning of the verb stem before the D object prefix is added. This occurs because many of these verbs used to begin with an *e*, which appears already to have been deleted. An already deleted *e* is indicated in the pronunciation entry of the glossary by an *i* in parentheses (i) before the initial *m* of the verb. Replacing the deleted *e* causes the initial *m* to become the last sound of a syllable, so it will be separated by a raised period (·) from the next syllable in the verb. If a {I;D} verb may be pronounced with an initial *e*, such as *mvcvnēyetv* 'to peek at', which may also be pronounced *em vcvnēyetv*, then you should treat it as if its glossary entry begins with *em*.

Thus, in examples 23 and 24, the initial *m* of the verb stems *mvkerr-* 'to fool' and *mehak-* 'to wait for' are deleted before the correct prefixes and suffixes are added and the stem vowel is lengthened. Thus, there is only one *m* at the beginning of each of the verbs in examples 23 and 24, rather than two *ms*, as in **cemmvkērris* and **vmmehakeckes*, respectively.

23. Cemvkērris.
    2SD-fool-1S-dec
    'I am fooling you'.

24. Cvyayvkēn vmehakeckes.
    quiet-adv 1SD-wait_for-2S-dec
    'You are waiting for me quietly'.

Dative Object Prefixes for {I;D} Verbs That Do Not Begin with *em*

When a {I;D} verb begins with anything other than *em*, the dative prefix takes one of the forms shown in table 7.3. When these prefixes are added to {I;D} verbs, the dative object prefix comes first, the verb stem second, the subject suffix third, and the declarative suffix last. This follows the same constituent order as that shown in diagram 7.2.

When the {I;D} verb begins with *en* followed by a consonant, the *en* is dropped entirely from the stem before the dative prefix is added. Thus, in examples 25 and 26, which use the verbs *enlvksetv* 'to lie to' and *enfotketv* 'to whistle at', the verb stems are changed to *-lvks-* and *-fotk-*, respectively, before changes are made to the stem to indicate the incompletive aspect, the object and subject of the sentence, and the declarative mood.

25. Vnlaksecketos.
    1SD-lie_to-2S-ss-aux_vb-dec
    'You are lying to me'.

26. Honvnwvt cenfotkes.
    man-ind_subj 2SD-whistle_at-3S-dec
    'A man is whistling at you'.

When a {I;D} verb begins with any consonant or with a vowel-consonant combination other than *en*, no changes are made to the verb stem before the appropriate dative prefix is added. Examples 27 and 28 illustrate how dative

TABLE 7.3. Dative Object Prefixes for Use on Type {I;D} Verbs Not Beginning with *em*

Indirect Object	Abbreviation	Mvskoke Prefix
1S 'me, to me, for me', etc.	1SD	vn-
2S 'you, to you, for you', etc.	2SD	cen-
3S 'him/her/it, to him/her/it', etc.	3SD	en-

prefixes are added to verbs beginning with the vowels *i-* and *v-*, respectively. In neither case is a deletion made from the verb stem before the dative prefix is added. Example 27 uses the verb *imapohicetv* 'to eavesdrop on', and example 28 is constructed with the verb *vhēhketv* 'to growl at'.

27. Enimapohicis.
 3SD-eavesdrop_on-1S-dec
 'I am eavesdropping on him/her'.

28. Efv cenvhēhketos.
 dog-def_subj 2SD-growl_at-3S-ss-aux_vb-dec
 'The dog is growling at you'.

In example 29, the dative prefix is added directly to the verb stem, *pvlecetv* 'to return something', which begins with a consonant. Again, no changes are made to the stem before the dative prefix is added.

29. Rakko cenpvlēcis.
 horse-def_obj 2SD-return_to-1S-dec
 'I am returning the horse to you'.

DATIVE OBJECT PREFIXES AND TYPE II VERBS

In {II;D} verbs, the order of the verbal elements is dative prefix, type II prefix, verb stem, and declarative ending, as shown in diagram 7.3.

Dative Object Prefix	Type II Subject Prefix	Verb Stem	Declarative Suffix

Diagram 7.3. Order of Constituents in a Type {II;D} Verb Containing an Object

The prefix sets presented in tables 7.1, 7.2, and 7.3 are used on {II;D} verbs, depending upon the type II subject prefix attached to the verb. If the type II subject prefix is 1S or 2S, then the prefixes from table 7.2 or 7.3 are used. If the type II subject prefix is 3S (which is a null suffix; nothing appears to be added to the verb stem), then the dative prefix will be from table 7.1 if the verb begins with *em* followed by a vowel. If the type II 3S prefix is to be added to a verb beginning with anything other than *em* followed by a vowel, then the dative prefix will be from table 7.2 or 7.3. Whenever the type II 3S prefix is added to a {II;D} verb beginning with *em* or *en*, the verb stem undergoes the types of changes described previously for {I;D} verbs beginning with *em* or *en*. A guide to the appropriate table in which to find a particular type II prefix form is given in table 7.4.

When a type II prefix is added to a verb stem beginning with *em* followed by a consonant, the *em* is dropped, as in examples 31a and 31b, where the verb is *em penkvletv* 'to be afraid of'. Notice that the type II prefix is attached directly to the verb stem after the *em* is dropped in these examples.

31a. Cencvpenkvlētos.
2SD-1S-afraid_of-ss-aux_vb-dec
'I am afraid of you'.

31b. Efv cempenkvlētos.
dog-def_subj 2SD-3S-afraid_of-ss-aux_vb-dec
'The dog is afraid of you'.

The initial *em* of the verb is also dropped when a type II prefix is added to a verb stem beginning with *em* followed by a vowel, as in examples 32a and 32b, where the verb is *em enhotetv* 'to be uneasy about'.

32a. Hotvlen encvmenhotēs.
wind-ind_obj 3SD-1S-uneasy_about-dec
'I am uneasy about the wind'.

32b. Sasvkwv nokose emenhotētos.
goose-def_subj bear-def_obj 3SD-3S-uneasy_about-ss-aux_vb-dec
'The goose is uneasy about the bear'.

In sets 31a–31b and 32a–32b, dropping the *em* results in a verb stem that begins with either a consonant or the vowel *e*. Thus, the type II prefix chosen

TABLE 7.4. Guide to D Prefix Forms according to Verb Stem Structure

Type II Prefix Form	First Sound of Verb Stem	Table Giving D Prefix
1S, 2S	Any sound	7.2, 7.3
3S	Anything besides *em* followed by a vowel	7.2, 7.3
3S	*Em* followed by a vowel	7.1

to add to the stem comes from the set presented in table 6.1 for use with verbs that begin with a consonant or an *e* (for a review of the type II prefix sets, see chapter 6).

Notice that the form of the dative prefix differs between the examples in each pair. In both 31a and 32a, the dative prefix is taken from table 7.3. In 31b and 32b, the dative prefix is taken from table 7.2, yet the verbs are the same as those used in 31a and 32a. The dative prefixes differ in each case because the type II 3S prefix is null (it does not have an audible form on the verb stem), so the dative prefix attaches directly to the stem and not to the type II prefix. Thus, the dative prefixes used in sentences containing a type II 3S subject follow the same rules as those listed on pages 101–105 for their prefixation on {I;D} verbs.

A similar pattern is followed for {II;D} verbs beginning with *en* followed by either a consonant or a vowel. Such verbs have the *en* dropped from the verb stem before the type II prefix is added. An example of the changes made to a verb beginning with *en* followed by a consonant is provided in examples 33a and 33b, where the verb *enhomecē* 'to be mad at/hate' is used. As you look at example 33b, remember that the 3S subject is represented by a null prefix on type II verbs (there appears to be no 3S prefix).

33a. Cencvhomecēs.
2SD-1S-be_mad_at-dec
'I am mad at you'.

33b. Cvcerwv vnhomecēs.
my_brother-def_subj 1SD-3S-be_mad_at-dec
'My brother is mad at me'. (Woman speaking)

When a {II;D} verb begins with a vowel-consonant or consonant-vowel combination other than *em* or *en*, no changes are made to the verb stem before the type II prefix is added. Thus, the type II prefix to be added to the verb depends on whether the verb begins with any consonant or with the vowel *e* (not followed by *m* or *n*) or with any vowel other than *e* or *ē* (refer to chapter 6 for more detail).

Examples using {II;D} verbs beginning with consonants are given in sentences 34–36. In all cases, the verb stem is not changed before the type II prefix is added. In example 34, the verb is *heromosē* 'to be kind, generous to'.

34. Encvheromosētos.
3SD-1S-be_generous/kind_to-ss-aux_vb-dec
'I am generous/kind to him/her/it'.

The verb in example 35 is *lopicetv* 'to be nice, kind to'.

35. Cenlopicētos.
2SD-3S-be_kind_to-ss-aux_vb-dec
'He/she/it is kind to you'.

In example 36, the verb is *mvnhēretv* 'to enjoy'.

36. Cencvmvnhērētos.
2SD-1S-enjoy-ss-aux_vb-dec
'I enjoy you (what you are doing)'.

In these examples, the D prefix is added to a type II prefix (examples 34 and 36) or a verb stem (example 35) beginning with a consonant. The reason the dative prefix is added directly to the verb stem in example 35 is because the 3S subject prefix is null.

In example 37, the verb stem begins with a vowel other than *e* and with a vowel-consonant combination other than *em* or *en*. As in examples 34–36, no changes are made to the verb stem before the dative and type II prefixes are added. The verb in example 37 is *ohsolotketv* 'to slide toward'.

37. Cvnecohsolotkēs.
1SD-2S-slide_toward-dec
'You are sliding toward me'.

Type I and Type II Verbs Taking Third Person Direct Objects

Certain type I and II verbs take only third person singular direct objects. Many of these verbs refer to actions such as eating, drinking, and cooking that are generally performed only on nonhuman objects. Occasionally, however, the direct object of a verb taking only third person direct objects can be human—for example, the verb *aswiyetv* 'to pass (something) to someone' can be used to refer to passing a baby from person to person. Verbs taking only third person direct objects are identified by the symbol 3 in the position for the direct object in brackets: {I;3} or {II;3}. Example 38 contains a verb that can take only a third person singular direct object:

38. Tosēnv vcvnahēs.
salt_meat-def_obj 3SD-1S-run_out_of-dec
'I am running out of salt meat'.

The definition of *vnahetv* is 'to run out of something (such as food)'. The definition of the verb specifically states that the thing being run out of is not human. Thus, the only choice for a direct object for this verb is a nonhuman, third person noun.

Occasionally, a verb will allow only for a third person singular direct object of a sort that could be physically given to the indirect object. In other words, verbs of this sort allow for the movement of one item to another, as in example 39:

39. Vpeswv ascenwiyis.
meat-def_obj 3Sdo-to-2SD-pass_something-1S-dec
'I am passing the meat to you'.

In this sentence, 'the meat', which is a third person direct object not noted by an audible prefix on the verb, is being passed to 'you', which is indicated by a D object prefix. Note that the prefix *as-*, meaning 'to', precedes the 2SD prefix. In this verb, the prefix *as-* always comes before the dative object prefix.

Verbs such as *aswiyetv* that take third person direct objects and some type of indirect object are indicated by three symbols within the brackets in their entries in the glossaries. The entry for *aswiyetv*, for example, gives {I;3;D}. The bracket entry indicates that *aswiyetv* takes a type I subject, a third person

Figure 7.1. Buffalo Dance leaders, Greenleaf Ceremonial Ground, August 1988. Left to right: Jimmy R. Gibson, Farron Cully, Jack Wolf (the singer). The Buffalo Dance is held on the Saturday evening during the Green Corn Ceremony. Dancers are lined up two by two, pairs of men alternating with pairs of women. Children may also participate. *Photograph courtesy of Bertha Tilkens and Linda Alexander.*

direct object, and a type D indirect object. Some verbs may have {II;3;D} in their entries, which indicates that the verb takes a type II subject, a third person direct object, and a type D indirect object.

Vocabulary

Food

Mvskoke	English
hompetv	food
hompetv hakv	meal

vpeswv	meat
wakvpeswv	beef
sokhvpeswv	pork
tosēnv	salt meat/pork
tvklike	bread
vce tvklik kvmoksē	sour cornbread
cvtvhakv	blue bread
tvklik svkmorkē	fry bread ('fried bread')
wakvpesē	milk
wakvpesē neha	butter
kafe	coffee
vsse	tea
vce	corn
hockvte	flour
vsokolv	sugar
okcvnwv	salt
homuce	black pepper

Verbs

Mvskoke	English
noricetv {I;3}	to cook
svkmorecetv {I;3}	to fry
vsemetv {I;3;D}	to serve (something) to someone
hompetv {I;3}	to eat
esketv {I;3}	to drink
tvcetv {I;3}	to cut once
lvffetv {I;3}	to cut many times
nesetv {I;3}	to buy
wiyetv {I;3}	to sell
eteyametv {I;3}	to mix, stir
awotsvnetv {I;3}	to pour out a liquid
aswiyetv {I;3;D}	to pass (something) to someone
eyvcetv {II;3}	to like, want, need
em merretv {II;D}	to feel sorry for
vpohetv {I;D}	to ask someone
ahvlvtetv {I;II}	to pull in the direction of the speaker
vnahetv {II;3}	to run out of something

Conversational Sentences

Hoktē: Hensci.	Woman: Hello.
Honvnwv: Hensci.	Man: Hello.
Hoktē: Likepvsci. Celvwēte?	Woman: Sit down. Are you hungry?
Honvnwv: Ehi, cvlvwēs.	Man: Yes, I'm hungry.
Hoktē: Epohompvs. Hvtē hompetvn norihcis.	Woman: Eat with us. I just cooked some food.
Honvnwv: Vwenayayat hēnrēs. Cvtvhakatowv?	Man: It smells good. Is that blue bread?
Hoktē: Mvnks, tvklik kvmokse. Ceyacv?	Woman: No, it's sour corn bread. Do you want some?
Honvnwv: Ehi, mvto. Kafe oceckv?	Man: Yes, thank you. Do you have coffee?
Hoktē: Hēyvn kafe ocet. Vketēcet hayētos.	Woman: Here is some coffee. Be careful, it's hot.
Honvnwv: Vsokolvn wakvpesē asvnwiyvs.	Man: Pass me the milk and sugar.
Hoktē: Wakvpesē ecvmohcvnares.	Woman: I will pour the milk for you.
Honvnwv: Mvto. Hēnres rēskayat.	Man: Thank you. This tastes very good.
Hoktē: Hēyvt pvrko cencvtvhake. Ascempvlares.	Woman: Here are some grape dumplings. I will pass them to you.
Honvnwv: Pvrko cencvtvhakat hopvkat hofones. Cvposet hayyētowemvts.	Man: I haven't eaten grape dumplings in a long time. My grandmother used to make them.
Hoktē: Mowis pvrkoce hecetv yekcētos. Mvt oposwv hēnretontomat.	Woman: It is hard to find wild grapes. They make the best juice.
Honvnwv: Tayyes. Hecetv yekcētos.	Man: You are right. They are hard to find.

Exercises

Exercise 1

Find all of the meaningful units in each of the following sentences and then translate the sentences. When you have completed this task, you will have created lines similar to the second and third lines in many of the examples in the text.

1. Efvt ecakketos.
2. Cvrke kafe vsēmis.
3. Hoktē ehessē cecuse mvnetan encokoperices.
4. Tosēnv laffeckes.
5. Honvnwv mahet vcen wiyetos.
6. Wakv hotosē elvwan encvmerres.
7. Pipuce cvtvhakv ascenwikes.
8. Cepanet vcvhepakes.
9. Cvtakkecketos.
10. Ceppucet mapohicis.

Exercise 2

In each of the following entries, you will find a verb followed by a specific noun or an abbreviation for a subject and a direct object. Your task is to create a grammatically correct sentence by constructing the verb with the subject and direct object specified and placing the noun (if any is specified) and the verb in the correct order. Each of the verbs is listed in the Mvskoke-English glossary, which will help you determine the initial form of the verb stem and whether the direct object is indicated by a type II or a D prefix.

Verb	Subject	Object
1. etepoyetv	2S	1S
2. eyvcetv	3S	'bread'
3. atvkkesetv	1S	'child'
4. vwenayetv	'dog'	2S
5. pohetv	2S	'mouse'

6. esetv	'boy'	'cow'
7. vnahetv	2S	'tea'
8. vnokecetv	1S	2S
9. em vsehetv	'married man'	1S
10. em mēkusvpetv	2S	1S

EXERCISE 3

Each of the verbs below is formed with a subject and an object marked on the verb. From the forms of both prefixes, determine whether the verb is {I;II}, {I;D}, or {II;D}. After you have determined the types of subject and object markers necessary for use on the verb, modify it with a subject and object pair different from the one that is on the form provided in the exercise. Some of these verbs are not taken from the vocabulary lists, but they are presented in the glossaries.

1. Asvnwiyeckes.
2. Encemenhotēs.
3. Cemehakis.
4. Cvkērreckes.
5. Enlaksis.
6. Cvhēces.
7. Cvncelopicētos.
8. Envcohsolotkēs.
9. Cepvlēcis.
10. Cvtakkecketos.

EXERCISE 4

The following is a recipe for one of the foods eaten by Mvskoke people. Translate the recipe. You may want to try cooking this recipe at home. Enjoy!

Tvklik svkmorkē

2 C. hockvte
1 1/2 tsp. tvklik-espakkueckv
3/4 tsp. sote
1 C. wakvpesē tvlokfe
nēha

Hockvte, tvklik-espakkueckv, sote eteyameckes. Wakvpesē tvlokfe awotsaneckes. Eteyameckes. Vlke ēpaken poloksvn hayeckes. Poloksvn svkmorkeckes. Hompvs!

Fo-encvmpet munkat vsokolvt esyomen tvklik svkmorken hompeckes.

EXERCISE 5

Translate the following story. You may need to review the vocabulary and conversational sentences from earlier chapters or look up words in the glossary in order to translate some sentences.

Cofe holwvkat yvkapes. Cofe wakv lowakē hotososen hēces. Wakv pvhe oklanen pvfnēn hompes. "Hensci. Estvnko?" Cofe vpohetos. "Estvnkewiseks," wakv maketos. "Celvwēs," Cofe maketos. "Ehi, cvlvwēs," wakv makes. "Pvhe lanē mahen vcvnahēs. Pvhe oklanen hompis." "Pvhe lanen ocis," Cofe makes. "Stvmen ayeckv?" wakv vpoketos. "Tvlofvn ayetowis," Cofe maketos. "Pvhe lanen wiyis." "Pvhe lanen cvyacetos!" wakv maketos. "Tvlofvn ayis!" "Pvhe lanen wiyeckes," Cofe makes. "Pvhe hompeckes. Pvhe lanen tvlofvn nēseckes." "Ehi, tvlofvn ayis," wakv makes. Wakv Cofe vyēpes. Cofe vpēles. Cofe pvhe oklanen hompes.

EXERCISE 6

Translate the following story into Mvskoke.

I am visiting my cousin. He is big. He is strong. I am eating grape dumplings. "Are you hungry? Do you want some grape dumplings?" I ask my cousin. "Yes, I am hungry. I want some grape dumplings," he says. I share with my cousin. He is smiling. I am smiling. I am happy.

Food in Mvskoke Life

The Mvskoke people were agricultural people. They raised the food they ate. To preserve food, they used the methods of drying and canning. Their meat was usually dried so that it would not spoil and so that they could use it at a later time.

Corn continues to be a big part of the diet. It is used to make traditional foods such as hominy, dried corn, and *apvske*. The corn is gathered and dried. After it is dried, corn can be ground fine or coarse, parched, or left whole. Various traditional dishes require the dried corn to be treated in these different ways.

Two popular drinks are made from corn. One is *sofke* and the other is *apvske*.

Sofke is made by cooking finely ground dried corn in water and lye, often called ash drippings. The corn used to be ground by using a hollowed-out log, called a *keco*, and a pounder made from a log with a long handle, called a *kecvpe*. The pounder's top was heavier than the bottom, which fit into the hollow in the *keco*, in order to give it the weight to pound the corn into coarse or fine meal. Today, some people grind the corn in blenders or food processors, though this results in a coarser meal.

The ash drippings are made from the ashes of wood fires built for heating or cooking. Ash from blackjack oak is the best type to use to make the lye. Ashes are collected from the fire bed and checked to make sure that there are no foreign objects that might give a different taste to the lye. Water is poured over the ashes, which are held in a clean cloth. The resulting liquid is collected in a clean container. If done properly, the liquid will be clear, with a dark brownish color. This is used to flavor the *sofke*.

To make *apvske*, corn is put in a big kettle over an open fire. The corn is stirred constantly so that it does not burn but is instead parched to a brown color. The parched corn is then pounded into a very fine meal, resembling cornmeal. The pounded corn is put into an airtight container for storage. To make a drink, the *apvske* meal is combined with water and a little sugar.

Cornmeal, made by pounding dried corn into powder, is used to make sour cornbread. Cornmeal is mixed with water and left to sit for several days until the mixture becomes sour. This mixture is then used to make cornbread, which tastes tangy and rather sour. This bread is delicious when served with soup or meat.

The most popular types of meat are pork and dried beef. Most meat is either boiled or fried. Beef is dried by cutting it into thin strips, which are then salted and dried in the sun. The dried meat can be easily stored to be used at a later time. It is cooked in several changes of water (to remove most of the salt) until it is tender. The meat is then ground fine and cooked again with onions and grease.

The most popular bread served today is fry bread. It is popular among most Indian tribes.

Figure 7.2. Two Seminole women making *sofke*, a drink made from ground corn. *Photograph courtesy of the Western History Collections, University of Oklahoma Libraries, Seminole Nation Museum Collection.*

Other traditional foods are wild onions, possum grapes, pumpkins, and sweet potatoes. Each of these foods is popular with Mvskoke people.

Suggested Reading

The use and meaning of Mvskoke type II and D prefixes are discussed in Donald E. Hardy's "The Semantics of Creek Morphosyntax" (1988:204–9, 236–59). Hardy uses the designations established by Pamela Munro and Lynn Gordon ("Syntactic Relations in Western Muskogean," 1982) for all of the languages in the Muskogean family. He confines his discussion to the use of type II and D prefixes in Mvskoke, which makes his article more informative than Munro and Gordon's for students working only in Mvskoke. Each of the means of marking subject, object, and possessor on Mvskoke verbs and nouns is also presented in Jack Martin and Margaret McKane

Mauldin's *A Dictionary of Creek/Muskogee* (2000:xxvi–xxviii), though in less detail than in this text.

Unfortunately, few books have been published concerning traditional foods eaten by the Muskogee and Seminole people. Infrequently, recipes are printed in the *Muskogee Nation News*. The best way to learn about traditional Muskogee and Seminole foods is to ask a *hompetv hayv* 'cook' to teach you how to use the ingredients and create the wonderful dishes that have been part of Muskogee and Seminole culture for centuries.

CHAPTER 8

Recent Past Tense

In Mvskoke, aspectual information about an action—that is, whether it is done continually, is ongoing, or has been completed—may be indicated by **verb grades**. Verb grades are changes made to the verb stem. You are already acquainted with one grade, the lengthened grade, commonly abbreviated "l-grade," which causes the final vowel in a verb stem to be lengthened. The l-grade is associated with constructions that show that the action being spoken about in the sentence has not been finished (incompletive aspect). When the l-grade is used, a listener or reader understands that the speaker is talking about an action that is still occurring at the time to which the sentence refers.

The recent past tense, commonly referred to as the h-grade, is a verb grade in Mvskoke that both indicates that the action has been completed and denotes the time at which the action occurred. When the h-grade is used, it indicates that the action took place shortly before the statement was made. The h-grade signifies that only a short time has passed between when the action took place and when the statement is made.

The Mvskoke h-grade is known by this name because one of its forms is indicated by inserting the infix *-h-* between the stem vowel and the last consonant in the verb stem. **Infix** is the linguistic term for an item that is inserted into a word or a stem. As shown in table 8.1, the h-grade has three different infix forms, each used in verb stems with different constructions.

TABLE 8.1. H-Grade Infix Forms and Verb Stem Factors Determining Their Use

Infix form	Verb Stem Construction Determining Which Infix Form Is Used
-h-	Vowel-consonant
-i-	Geminate *k*s or two different consonants
-iy-	Geminate consonants other than *k*

H-INFIX

The h-infix form of the h-grade is used when the verb stem ends in a vowel-consonant pair. Many Mvskoke verb stems are of this type. When the verb stem ends in this way, an *h* is inserted between the final vowel and the final consonant. The tonal quality, but not the length, of the final vowel is affected by the insertion of the h-grade infix. The vowel's tone becomes high with the application of the h-grade. Suffixes and prefixes added to the verb are not affected by the h-grade. Thus, type I subject suffixes, the declarative suffix, and type II subject and object prefixes are added as usual.

The verb stem of *hecetv* 'to see', *hec-*, ends in a vowel-consonant pair: the final sounds in the stem are *e* and *c*, in that order. To create the sentence in example 1, 'I just saw you', an *h* is placed between the unlengthened vowel (*e*, not ē) and the consonant *c*, which leads to the form *hehc-*. The tone of the vowel *e* becomes high when the *h* is inserted. Because there is an object, 'you', the object prefix is added to the beginning of the h-graded verb stem (*cehehc-*). The type I 1S subject suffix and the declarative suffix are then added to produce the following sentence:

1. Cehehcis.
   2Sdo-see-h_grd-1S-dec
   'I just saw you'.

The same pattern occurs in examples 2 and 3, which are formed from type I verbs ending in a vowel-consonant pair, *yvkvpetv* and *noricetv*, respectively:

2. Pipuce yvkvhpes.
   baby-def_subj walk-h_grd-3S-dec
   'The baby just walked'.

3. Hoktet tvkliken norihces.
woman-ind_subj bread-ind_obj cook-h_grd-3S-dec
'A woman just cooked some bread'.

In these examples and all the others that follow, the fact that the h-grade is operating is indicated in the line immediately below the Mvskoke example by the abbreviation "h_grd" at the end of the verb stem translation. When you are asked to dissect Mvskoke sentences in which the h-grade is operating, you should use this strategy to show that the h-grade has affected the verb.

The h-infix works in a similar manner when it is added to type II verbs whose stems end in a vowel-consonant pair. For instance, the {II;D} verb in example 4, *enhomecetv* 'to be mad at', takes the h-infix when the immediate past and completive aspect are indicated. The h-grade does not affect the forms of either the type II or the D prefixes, nor does it affect the form of the declarative suffix. Only the verb stem itself is directly affected by the inclusion of the h-grade, in that the tone of the vowel before the *-h-* is high, and the *e* before the declarative suffix is short (the vowel is not ē). Notice that this pattern occurs in examples 5 and 6 as well, even though the verbs are *lopicetv* 'to be nice to' and *nockelē* 'to be sleepy'.

4. Cencvhomehces.
2SD-1S-be_mad_at-h_grd-dec
'I was mad at you (just now)'.

5. Honvnwv vnlopihces.
man-def_subj 1SD-3S-nice-h_grd-dec
'The man was just nice to me'.

6. Hoktuce nockehles.
girl-def_subj 3S-sleepy-h_grd-dec
'The girl was sleepy (just now)'.

In each of these examples, the vowel preceding the h-infix has a high tone.

I-Infix

The i-infix form of the h-grade is used when the verb stem ends in two different consonants (for example, *hompetv* 'to eat', which has the stem *homp-*) or in geminate *k*s (for example, *akketv* 'to bite', which has the stem *akk*-).[1] When the verb stem ends in either of these ways, the high-toned infix *-i-* is inserted between the two consonants. As with the h-infix, the final vowel is not lengthened when the i-infix form of the h-grade is used. Also, the forms of all prefixes and suffixes and the manner in which they are added to the verb stem remain the same as they have been to this point. Inserting the i-infix into *akketv* leads to a construction like that found in example 7:

7. Efv vcakikes.
dog-def_subj 1Sdo-bite-h_grd-3S-dec
'The dog just bit me'.

The verb stem of *hompetv* 'to eat' (*homp*-) ends in two different consonants (*m* and *p*), so it, too, takes the i-infix form of the h-grade. To create the sentence in example 8, 'You just ate', the i-infix, with high tone, is inserted between the last two consonants of the verb stem, leading to the form *homip*-. The subject suffix (*-eck*-) and the declarative suffix (*-es*) are then added. This results in the following sentence:

8. Homipeckes.
eat-h_grd-2S-dec
'You just ate'.

The same pattern is followed in examples 9 and 10. In both of these examples, the type I verb stems, *letk*- from *letketv* 'to run' and *esk*- from *esketv* 'to drink', also end in two different consonants (/tk/ and /sk/, respectively). In each case, the high tone i-infix is placed between the two final consonants, and the subject suffix and declarative suffix are then added as usual. The use of the i-infix form of the h-grade results in the following constructions:

9. Rakkot letikes.
horse-ind_subj run-h_grd-3S-dec
'A horse just ran'.

10. Pipuce wakvpesē kvsvppan esikes.
baby-def_subj milk cold-def_obj drink-h_grd-3S-dec
'The baby just drank the cold milk'.

1. **Geminate consonants** are pairs of the same consonant, such as the two *l*s in the verb *melletv* 'to point'.

The i-infix form of the h-grade may also be used in type II verbs whose stems end in two different consonants. Type II verb constructions using the i-infix are shown in examples 11–13.

11. Hoktē yekices.
woman-def_subj 3S-strong-h_grd-dec
'The woman was strong (very recently)'.

Notice that the i-infix is added between the two final consonants just as it was in examples 7–10, and it has a high tone. No changes are made to the type II subject prefix added to the verb stem, nor are changes made to D prefixes when they are used, as in example 12.

12. Mekko encvmenhonires.
chief-def_obj 3SD-1S-trust_in-h_grd-dec
'I trusted the chief (recently)'.

13. Cvlvtikes.
1S-fall-h_grd-dec
'I just fell'.

The i-infix affects only the verb stem. The final *e* of the verb is shortened, so that it is *e* in examples 11–13, rather than ē, before the declarative suffix is added.

Type II verb stems ending in geminate *k*s also take the i-infix form of the h-grade. In these verbs, the i-infix is inserted between the two *k*s, as is the case with type I verbs of this sort. All type II and D prefixes remain unaffected by the addition of the i-infix. In example 14, the {II;D} verb *encvpvkketv* 'to be mad at' is used with the i-infix form of the h-grade:

14. Cencvcvpvkikes.
2SD-1S-be_mad_at-h_grd-dec
'I was mad at you very recently'.

Because the final vowel of the verb stem is short in the infinitive form, the vowel of the verb stem remains short with the insertion of the i-infix between the two *k*s at the end of the verb stem. All prefixes and suffixes are added in their usual manner and take their usual forms.

Iy-Infix

The final form of the h-grade is used in verbs that end in geminate consonants other than *k*. For these verbs, insert an *i* between the two consonants and then replace the second consonant with *y*. Thus, the infix form appears to be *-iy-*, but this form is actually realized because of separate changes made to the verb stem. For all intents and purposes, however, you may consider the third form of the h-grade to be *-iy-*, with the /y/ taking the place of the second consonant in the geminate pair.

For example, when the type I verb *vmelletv* 'to point at' is formed in the h-grade, the verb stem (*vmell-*) is changed to *vmeliy-* with the addition of the *-iy-* infix. The vowel of this infix always carries a high tone. The subject and declarative suffixes are then added to the infixed verb stem. Thus, to create the sentence in example 15, 'You were pointing at me (very recently)', the verb undergoes the following changes:

1. Derive verb stem 'to point at'	vmell-
2. Drop final consonant of the pair	vmel-
3. Add h-grade geminate infix	vmeliy-
4. Add direct object (II) prefix	vcvmeliy-
5. Add subject suffix	vcvmeliyeck-
6. Add declarative suffix	vcvmeliyeckes

The resulting verb form may then be used as a sentence, as shown in example 15:

15. Vcvmeliyeckes.
    1Sdo-point_at-h_grd-2S-dec
    'You were pointing at me (very recently)'.

This pattern is repeated in example 16 to derive the recent past tense form of *korretv* 'to dig'. The only difference is that because there is no direct object, no type II or D object prefix is added to the verb stem. In all other respects, the verb in example 16 is treated just like the verb in example 15.

16. Efv koriyes.
    dog-def_subj dig-h_grd-3S-dec
    'The dog was just digging'.

A similar pattern is followed when the recent past tense infixes are applied to type II verbs ending in non-*k* geminate consonants. Any II or D prefixes added to the verb stem retain their usual form and are added in their usual order. The verb stem is modified in the same way described for type I verbs ending in geminate consonants other than *k*—the second consonant is dropped and the h-grade geminate infix *-iy-* is added. Finally, the declarative suffix is placed at the end of the verb. This is the sequence followed to create examples 17 and 18. In each of these examples, the infinitive form of the verb is presented in the first line so that you can ascertain that the verb stem ends in geminate consonants.

17. vnvttetv 'to get wounded' {II}
Vcvnvtiyes.
1S-get_wounded-h_grd-dec
'I was just wounded'.

18. em merretv 'to feel sorry for' {II;D}
Opanvn encemmeriyes.
dancer-ind_obj 3SD-2S-feel_sorry_for-h_grd-dec
'You felt sorry for a dancer recently'.

With the addition of the h-grade, you are now able to form sentences showing that an action has been completed and that it happened in the very recent past. Each form of the h-grade (the h-infix, the i-infix, and the iy-infix) denotes that this time frame and the completive aspect must be taken into account when the verb is translated. You should remember to mark the use of the h-grade in your sentence translations by placing "h_grd" at the end the verb stem translation.

Vocabulary

Ceremonial Ground Objects and People

Mvskoke	English
yvhikv	singer
opanv	dancer
locv	turtle, turtle shell
vpēttē	arbor

totkv	fire
heles hayv	medicine man
heleswv	medicine
hvpohakv *or* hvpo	camp
(o)pvnkv ēkvnv	'dance ground' (ceremonial ground)
(e)tokonhe	ball stick
Vce lanē posketv	Green Corn Ceremony
Yvnvsv opvnkv	Buffalo Dance
Nettv opvnkv	Ribbon Dance
mekko	chief
heneha	second chief
oponayv	speaker

Verbs

Mvskoke	English
ēlvwēcetv {I}	to fast
posketv {I}	to fast for the Green Corn Ceremony
opvnetv {I}	to dance
yvhiketv {I}	to sing
heleswv sēyocetv {I}	to take Indian medicine (medicine taken this way is both applied to the body and consumed)
vkvsvmetv {I;II}	to believe
mēkusvpetv {I}	to pray
pokkeccetv {I}	to play ball
vhonecetv {II}	to stay awake
nokricetv {I;3}	to burn
es enhomahtetv {I;D}	to lead a dance
hvpo hayetv {I;3}	to make camp
em enhonretv {I;D/II;D}	to believe in, trust, depend on (something or someone)

Conversational Sentences

Hoktet: Nērēyise stvnkisv?	Woman: What did you do last night?
Honvnwvt: Sayvtketvn ahyis.	Man: I went to a stompdance.

Figure 8.1. Buffalo Dance, Greenleaf Ceremonial Ground, August 1989. Toney Hill is the lead singer of the song to which the Buffalo Dance is performed. Burt Tilkens and Jimmy R. Gibson are leading the dancers. *Photograph courtesy of Bertha Tilkens and Linda Alexander.*

Stompdances are ceremonies made up of many dances, such as the Buffalo Dance, all performed in one evening. In these dances, men and women alternate in line, moving counterclockwise around a central fire. Children are allowed to follow the adults, often creating a long "tail" at the end of the line of dancers.

Hoktet: Stvmen cokorakkon ayeckv?	Woman: What ground did you go to?
Honvnwvt: Oce upofat cokorakkot vhyis. Poskaket Vce lanē emposkaketomen.	Man: I went to Hickory Ground. It was their Green Corn.
Hoktet: Nettv opvnka ayeckv?	Woman: Did you go to their Ribbon Dance?
Honvnwvt: Ehi, Flati hvnke.	Man: Yes, that was Friday.
Hoktet: Este sulket vnkv?	Woman: Were there many people there?
Honvnwvt: Ehi, este sulket follvnks. Cokorakkot este vnvcowe omepekv.	Man: Yes, many people were there. The ground has many members.

Hoktet: Senhomahteckisv?	Woman: Did you lead (a dance)?
Honvnwvt: Ehi, hvmken senhomahitis. Cawvnwv hoktvlēcat locv svmopanis.	Man: Yes, I led one time. My older sister shook shells.
Hoktet: Ceckvlketv vhohyv?	Woman: Did your parents go, too?
Honvnwvt: Ehi. Cvcke mowis opvneks. Cvrket ennokkēt vnken mvn enlikes.	Man: Yes. My mother didn't dance. She sat with my ill father.
Hoktet: Kerrisekatēs. En hēnrē hvnkv?	Woman: I didn't know (he was ill). Is he getting better?
Honvnwvt: Ehi. Vce lanē emposketv ayat hēcat enhēnrētomis.	Man: Yes. Going to the Green Corn made him feel better.

Exercises

Exercise 1

Translate the following sentences from Mvskoke into English. When translating the sentences, show the meaningful units as is done in the second line of each example in the chapter. Once you have identified the form of the h-grade present in the verb, determine the infinitive form of the verb. An example is provided for you.

Hokte mēkusvhpes.
woman-def_subj pray-h_grd-3S-dec
'The woman was praying'.
inifinitive form = mēkusvpetv

1. Cepanet pokkeciyes.
2. Heles hayv heleswvn vnehmes.
3. Ecafvcikes.
4. Heneha cvnhonires.
5. Kafe kvsvppan awotsvhneckes.
6. Vcvhonehces.
7. Oponayv cvyayvkēn lihkes.
8. Sasvkwv sopakhvtkē rakkat pvfnēn tvmikes.
9. Nettv opvnkv opvhnis.
10. Cecuset hvpo hahyes.

Exercise 2

Change the following sentences from l-grade to h-grade. Translate the sentences after you have changed them to the h-grade form.

1. Pipucet wakvpesē kvsvppen ēsketos.
2. Hvlpvtv rakkē vculet hvlvlatkēn omiyes.
3. Cvcket sokhvpeswvn nokrices.
4. Mekko posketos.
5. Ecahvlvtis.
6. Cenahvmke fekhvmkētos.
7. Pipuce atvkkesis.
8. Rakkot cetakkes.
9. Ceccuste hotosētos.
10. Honvnwv cvkērres.

Exercise 3

Choose ten type I verbs from the vocabulary introduced in chapters 1–8. Create ten sentences with these verbs, modifying each for the h-grade.

Exercise 4

Choose ten type II verbs from the vocabulary you have learned to this point. Use each verb in a sentence, modifying each for the h-grade.

Exercise 5

Create ten sentences containing type {I;II}, {I;D}, or {II;D} verbs modified for the h-grade. Try to include some adjectives and adverbs in your sentences.

Exercise 6

Working with a partner, create ten sentences in the l-grade, using verbs and nouns presented in chapters 1–8. Pronounce your sentences to your partner. Your partner is to change the verbs in your sentences into the h-grade form. Your partner should also translate your sentences after changing them to the h-grade. Record any sentences for which you and your partner disagree over the form of the sentence, the h-grade form of the verb, or the translation. Ask your instructor about these sentences in class.

EXERCISE 7

Translate the following simple story into Mvskoke. Each of the past tense sentences in the English version should be translated using the h-grade in the Mvskoke version.

> I know an old man. His name is Raccoon. He went to a stompground today. He listened to the speaker. He talked with the chief. He danced the Buffalo Dance. The medicine man gave him Indian medicine. Raccoon took the medicine. He stayed awake. His son played ball. Raccoon watched his son. His son played well. Raccoon was happy. He came home. He went to sleep.

Traditional Ceremonial Grounds

Ceremonial grounds are the backbone of the Mvskoke Nation. At the time of removal, there were forty-four tribal towns, each with its associated ceremonial ground—the place were town members performed their religious ceremonies. Today, all but three tribal towns have been dissolved, because of allotment and other forces that have caused people to live apart from one another. Ceremonial grounds, however, have continued to exist, because people still come together there to perform their traditional ceremonies.

A central feature at each ground is its fire. Originally, all the people of a tribal town shared the same fire, which was lit anew each year during the Green Corn Ceremony. During removal, the medicine men of most towns, using great care, brought their fires with them from the Southeast. Remember, the Creator gave the Mvskoke fire to give them light, warmth, and a means of preparing food.

Today, there are still seventeen active ceremonial grounds. All Mvskoke people, through their ancestors, belong to a ceremonial ground or tribal town. Membership in a ground or tribal town comes through the mother's line, just as clan membership does. If the mother's ground or tribal town is no longer active, a person may join his or her father's ground, where people will welcome the descendant of a member.

Each ground has its own rules, which each member must follow. The grounds begin their ceremonial seasons in April, and certain tasks must be done before the grounds are opened for the ceremonial season.

Each ground has a committee that oversees its operation and discusses matters relevant to the ground. These committees are responsible for selecting persons to fill positions within the ground. Each ground committee also decides the dates on which its ground's dances will take place, including the most important event of the season, the Green Corn Ceremony.

To get ready for the Green Corn, an Arbor Dance will be held one week beforehand. During this time the ceremonial ground is cleaned, and repairs are made if needed. New brush arbors are built in the ceremonial square in preparation for the Arbor Dance. The singers and women's leaders for the Ribbon Dance, as well as the men who will gather medicine to be used during the Arbor and Ribbon Dances, are selected at this time. These preparations are completed before the Arbor Dance is performed.

One week after the Arbor Dance, usually on the following Friday, the Ribbon Dance is performed. Ribbon Dance day is set aside to honor the women of the ceremonial ground. Four women are selected to lead this dance. The day starts with members taking medicine prepared by the medicine man. In the evening, the Ribbon Dance begins. Four calls are made to tell the women to start getting ready. The women wear bright-colored dresses and ribbons in their hair and on their dresses.

The Ribbon Dance consists of four series of dances, concluding with the long dance. During these dances, the men sit in the arbors, and two of them sing while the women dance. The women are the only people dancing at this time. Supper is served when the dance is over. After supper, members and visitors dance until midnight.

The next day is the day of the big celebration—the Green Corn Ceremony. It begins when the medicine man prepares medicine for the women, who, after they take it, are released to start their meal preparation. The men, too, begin their day by taking medicine. Then they sit under the brush arbors until late in the afternoon. All those who have taken medicine will continue to fast until the medicine man releases them from fasting. Fasting is an important part of Mvskoke religion—before members begin any task on the days of the Arbor Dance, the Ribbon Dance, or the Green Corn Ceremony, they fast.

Late in the evening of the Green Corn Ceremony, members of some grounds perform a Buffalo Dance. Everyone wears colorful clothes. A singer leads the dancers from the dance circle out to the ball pole and back again. (The ball pole, a prominent feature at most grounds, is a target in a ball game played between men and women.) After this dance, all visitors are fed, and people have a chance to talk for some time.

Once supper is over, the stick men come around to the camps to let members know it is time to start getting ready for the dance that night. After the third call, all members of the ground should be at their places around the ground. When the fourth call is made, the dance begins. It goes on until dawn.

The purpose of the Green Corn Ceremony is to thank the Creator for all that he has given. Taking medicine during these dances cleans a person's body and rededicates him or her to the Creator. By sharing with other members and visitors, one shows his or her love. Mvskoke people are always told to have love in their hearts when at these dances. Each of the four ceremonies that are performed throughout the season, the most prominent of which is the Green Corn, is begun by fasting and taking medicine prepared by the medicine man.

If you are interested in hearing a Mvskoke speech in the style used at the ceremonial ground by the *oponayv*, listen to track 25 of CD B. A translation is provided in track 26. The song style performed at the grounds is provided on track 27 of CD B. This musical style is quite different from the music performed by Plains Indian tribes. We hope you enjoy listening to it.

Suggested Readings

The various forms of the h-grade and its usage in the languages of the Muskogean family have been discussed by a number of researchers. David Cline ("Oklahoma Seminole and the Muskogean H-Grade," 1987), Mary Haas ("Ablaut and Its Function in Muskogee," 1940), and Donald E. Hardy ("The Semantics of Creek Morphosyntax," 1988:145–49) each focus on the use of the h-grade in Mvskoke and/or Oklahoma Seminole. All three discuss the different forms of the infixes, when they are used, and their meaning. Haas's and Hardy's work covers the h-grade forms used in Mvskoke. Haas also covers other means used by Mvskoke speakers to change the verb stem to denote time of completion and aspectual information; these forms are introduced in later chapters in this book. Cline shows that the forms of the h-grade used in Oklahoma Seminole are a little different from the forms used in Mvskoke, but these differences will not pose problems for those using this book to learn how to converse with speakers of Oklahoma Seminole.

Readers interested in how this grade arose in the Muskogean languages and how it is represented in each are directed to Karen M. Booker's "Com-

Figure 8.2. One team starting the men's stickball game (Little Brother of War), Greenleaf Ceremonial Ground, September 1989. Other ceremonial grounds are invited to participate in the stickball game, which is played in the morning after the last dance of the year at the ceremonial ground. *Photograph courtesy of Bertha Tilkens and Linda Alexander.*

parative Muskogean" (1980). Those interested in comparing Mvskoke forms of the h-grade to its forms in some related languages might consult Michele Nathan's "Grammatical Description of the Florida Seminole Dialect of Creek" (1977:91–92), Pamela Munro's "Chickasaw Accent and Verb Grades" (1985), and Geoffrey Kimball's "A Descriptive Grammar of Koasati" (1985: 254ff.). Except for Oklahoma Seminole, each of these languages uses forms of the h-grade that are fairly divergent from the forms found in Mvskoke, and the rules governing the use of these forms also vary from the rules used in Mvskoke. Readers may be interested in the variation but should not seek to learn how to use the Mvskoke h-grade from these works.

Information about the stompdance tradition is available from several very good sources. Readers might wish to consult James H. Howard and Willie Lena's *Oklahoma Seminoles* (1984:104–209); John R. Swanton's "Religious Beliefs and Medical Practices of the Creek Indians" (1928b:521–614); Amelia R. Bell's "Creek Ritual: The Path to Peace" (1984); Pamela Innes's "From One to Many, from Many to One" (1997b); Jason Baird Jackson's

"Yuchi Ritual" (1998); and three works by Frank G. Speck: *The Creek Indians of Taskigi Town* (1907), *Ethnology of the Yuchi Indians* (1909), and *Ceremonial Songs of the Creek and Yuchi Indians* (1911). Howard and Lena investigate the Seminole stompdance tradition and its associated symbolism. Swanton, Bell, Innes, and Speck, in his 1907 book, each explore the Muskogee (Creek) stompdance tradition and symbolism. Speck's 1909 book and Jackson's article both describe the practices of the Yuchi, who are members of Muskogee (Creek) Nation but who speak a language unrelated to those in the Muskogean family. In his 1911 book, Speck presents some of the ceremonial and curing songs used by the Muskogee and Yuchi and discusses their use in the ceremonial context.

CHAPTER 9

Middle, Distant, and Remote Past Tenses

In chapter 8 you learned about the h-grade, which tells a listener that an action being discussed was completed in the very recent past. In Mvskoke, there are three other ways of showing that an action took place in the past, each involving the addition of a suffix to the verb stem. These three past tense markers, in order of remoteness, with their time-marking translations and their abbreviations, are as follows:

Remoteness from Present	Suffix	Translation	Abbreviation
Middle	-vnk-	From yesterday to one year ago	mp
Distant	-mvt-	From yesterday to a long time ago	dp
Remote	-vtē-	From yesterday to the mythic past	rp

As you can see, with the h-grade and these three past tense forms, Mvskoke speakers can make it relatively clear to a listener when an action happened in the past simply by modifying the verb.

This is not to imply that the addition of the past tense markers tells a listener exactly when the action took place. As you can see from the translations, each of the past tense markers introduced in this chapter refers to a relatively long span of time. While any of the past tenses may be used to denote actions performed yesterday, the middle past tense is most often used to refer to this time. Actions that occurred more than one year ago but in the memorable past are most often referred to in the distant past tense. The remote past, although it may refer to actions that happened fairly recently, is most often used to speak about actions that happened a very long time ago—generally, so long ago that no living person witnessed them.

The context in which a tense marker is used, as well as time-marking words that define how long ago something happened, often clarifies exactly when an action happened. Without such means of clarifying the time at which an action took place, it becomes difficult to determine whether something happened fairly recently or a very long time ago simply from the past tense marker. In general, use of the distant and remote markers shows that an action happened farther in the past than does use of the middle past tense marker.

The middle, distant, and remote past tense suffixes do not include information about whether or not the action has been completed (**aspect**). Aspectual information about the completive or incompletive nature of the activity is indicated by changing the verb stem. Verb stem changes that carry aspectual information will be discussed as each tense suffix is introduced. We begin with a discussion of how the past tense suffixes are added to type I verbs.

Middle Past *-vnk-*

As the preceding chart showed, the middle past tense is used when the action took place approximately one day to one year ago. When the middle past tense marker is used without a particular time being stated (that is, without saying something like *paksvnkē ohhonayiyvnks* 'I was reading yesterday'), it is considered to indicate that a short but indeterminate time has lapsed since the action occurred. When no time span is specified in the Mvskoke sentence and the context does not clarify the time span to which the marker is referring, the verb is the only item that shows the past tense in the English translation (*ohhonayiyvnks* 'I was reading'). Occasionally, people will use the middle past tense even when talking about things that happened more than one year ago when they know something occurred in the not-too-distant past but are uncertain exactly how long ago. When the context makes it clear that the action happened around a year ago, translate this marker as 'not too long ago'.

Middle Past and the Completive Aspect

When the action was completed during the times denoted by the middle past and distant past tenses, another verb grade is required to show the completive aspect: the falling tone grade (abbreviated as "ft_grd"). This grade causes two changes in the verb stem. First, the final vowel of the stem is lengthened, just as in the l-grade. Second, the tone of the vowel drops while the vowel is held. For most speakers, an example of falling tone occurs in English when we pronounce the exclamation "uh-oh." If you listen carefully, you should hear that the "uh" has a higher pitch than the "oh" of the exclamation. This is precisely what happens in the Mvskoke falling tone grade except that there is no break as the tone falls (in "uh-oh" we break between the two parts of the exclamation instead of making the sound continuous). In Mvskoke, the tone falls while the vowel sound is held, so there is a fairly distinct lowering of the pitch throughout the vowel. It is the use of the falling tone grade that indicates that the action is over (that is, it indicates the completive aspect); the past tense suffixes simply indicate how long ago the action was completed.

The falling tone grade causes the final vowel of the verb stem to become a key syllable vowel. This means that the high tone on this vowel acts as the highest tone in the entire word. All syllables following this vowel, including the 2S type I suffix, will have a lower tonal quality. Because the 2S type I suffix is another "always key" syllable, it will have a higher tone than the syllables following it, but it will not have as high a tone as the final vowel of the verb stem when the falling tone grade is operating on that vowel.

Once the stem vowel has been modified with the falling tone grade, the subject and object markers are added, then the past tense form, and finally the declarative marker. In examples 1 and 2, each portion of the verb is separated so that you can see how the pieces are put together:

1. pohetv 'to hear'
   Paksvnkē efv poheckvnks.
   Paksvnkē efv poh-eck-vnk-s
   yesterday dog-def_obj hear-ft_grd-2S-mp-dec
   'You heard the dog yesterday'.

2. mēkusvpetv 'to pray'
   Erkenvkv mēkusapvnks.
   Erkenvkv mēkusap-vnk-s

preacher-def_subj pray-ft_grd-3S-mp-dec
'The preacher prayed (not too long ago)'.

Notice that the length and tonal change in the /o/ of the verb stem in example 1 are not marked—there is no way of showing that an *o* is affected by the falling tone grade in the Mvskoke writing system. In example 2, however, the final vowel of the verb stem is visibly changed to show that it has lengthened (from *mēkusvp-* to *mēkusap-*), although there is nothing to mark the tonal change. These examples show that you will need to remember that when the middle and distant past tenses are used, the stem vowel in the verb stem is lengthened and its tone falls, even though these qualities may not be indicated in the written form of the verb.

In examples 3 and 4, the length of the last vowel in only one stem is marked. Even when vowel length is marked, falling tone is not indicated by any symbol in the Mvskoke alphabet:

3. vpeletv 'to smile, laugh'—vowel length is marked
Hvtēyvnke, coko vfastv vpēliyvnks.
Hvtēyvnke, coko vfastv vpēl-i-yvnk-s
little_while_ago, deacon-def_obj 3SD-smile-ft_grd-1S-mp-dec
'I smiled at the deacon a little while ago'.

4. yvhiketv 'to sing'—vowel length is not marked
Mvt yvhiketv escokv yvhikiyvnks.
Mvt yvhiketv escokv yvhik-i-yvnk-s
that hymn-def_obj sing-ft_grd-1S-mp-dec
'I sang that hymn (not too long ago)'.

In both examples 3 and 4, the form of the middle past suffix is changed from *-vnk-* to *-yvnk-*. This change occurs when the first person subject suffix is used on a type I verb. The *y* of the suffix acts as a glide between the vowel of the subject suffix *-i-* and the vowel *v* of the middle past suffix *-vnk-*. Whenever the middle past suffix is placed immediately after another suffix that ends in a vowel, the *-yvnk-* form is used. The differences in the steps taken to form verbs with a 1S subject versus those with a 2S or 3S subject are presented in table 9.1.

Middle Past and the Incompletive Aspect

It is possible in English to discuss actions that were not completed at the time they took place in the past. In the English sentence "John was reading," the

TABLE 9.1. Use of *-yvnk-* and *-vnk-* Forms of Middle Past Depending on Subject Suffix

Step	Verb and 1S Subject	Verb and 2S or 3S Subject
1. Find infinitive form 'to smile, laugh'	vpeletv	vpeletv
2. Derive verb stem	vpel-	vpel-
3. Make changes for ft-grade	vpēl- (length + falling tone)	vpēl- (length + falling tone)
4. Add subject suffix	vpēli-	vpēleck- (2S) vpēl- (3S)
5. Add middle past suffix form	vpēliyvnk- (-yvnk- form)	vpēleckvnk- (2S)
		vpēlvnk- (3S) (both take -vnk- form)
6. Add declarative suffix	vpēliyvnks 'I smiled'	vpēleckvnks 'you smiled' vpēlvnks 'he/she/it smiled'

action is still in the process of being performed, even though the sentence is obviously referring to a point in the past. Mvskoke speakers form sentences of this sort, combining the past tense and the incompletive aspect, by making changes to the verb stem associated with the l-grade and then adding the proper suffix. This has been done to create the verb form in example 5:

5. Hvtēyvnke, coko vfastv vpēliyvnks.
   Hvtēyvnke, coko vfastv vpēl-i-yvnk-s
   little_while_ago, deacon-def_obj 3SD-smile-1S-mp-dec
   'I was smiling at the deacon a little while ago'.

Notice that the form of the verb in example 5 is very close to the form of the verb in example 3. The only difference involves the lack of falling tone in example 5. The final vowel of the verb stem has been lengthened, but the tone does not descend as the vowel is pronounced. You will need to listen carefully for the tonal qualities of the final vowels in the verb stems when past tense suffixes are used. This is not something that English speakers generally need to attend to, and it may seem difficult for some time. When you translate the verbs in sentences utilizing the l-grade and a past tense suffix, use a past tense form of 'to be' (such as 'was' or 'were') and an English verb form ending in the suffix '-ing'.

The two forms of the middle past suffix, *-vnk-* and *-yvnk-*, are used on verbs in the incompletive aspect, depending upon the form of the subject suffix used to denote who was performing the action. When the subject suffix ends in a vowel, the y-glide form (*-yvnk-*) is used to denote the middle past. When the subject suffix ends in a consonant, the regular form of the middle past (*-vnk-*) is used. The steps taken to construct a verb in the middle past tense and the incompletive aspect are basically the same as those followed to construct a verb in the completive aspect, as shown in table 9.1. The only difference is that the verb stem undergoes only vowel lengthening, and a falling tone is not evident as the lengthened vowel is pronounced.

Distant Past *-mvt-*

The distant past marker, *-mvt-*, shows that the action happened sometime during the period from yesterday to a long time ago. The exact time in the past may be stated along with the use of this marker (for example, a speaker might say, "I did it three years ago"), but Mvskoke speakers commonly use the distant past marker without specifying the exact time at which the action happened. When this is the case, the marker should be translated only by indicating the past tense change on the English form of the verb. When the context of the utterance makes it clear that the action happened in the rather distant past, translate this marker as 'a long time ago'.

Distant Past and Completive Aspect

Just as in the case of the middle past tense, when the action associated with the distant past marker was completed in the past (completive aspect), the verb stem takes the falling tone grade. Thus, when the distant past is used in conjunction with the completive aspect, the final vowel of the verb stem is lengthened and the tone falls as it is pronounced. Subject and object prefixes and/or suffixes remain unchanged, as does the declarative suffix. The distant past marker, *-mvt-*, is used in example 6. In it and following examples, the verb is pulled apart in the second line so that you can see how each prefix and suffix is added:

6. Nokosen hēcimvts.
Nokosen hēc-i-mvt-s
bear-ind_obj see-ft_grd-1S-dp-dec
'I saw a bear'.

The distant past suffix is also used in examples 7–9. Notice, however, that in these examples the form of the suffix differs from the form seen in example 6. In examples 7–9, the distant past suffix is now *-emvt-* rather than *-mvt-*. This occurs because, in these examples, the distant past suffix (*-mvt-*) follows a consonant (in 7 and 9, this is the *k* of the 2S suffix; in 8, the past tense suffix follows the *c* of the verb stem because the 3S subject is not indicated by any sound). When the distant past suffix is added directly after a consonant, an *e* is added to create a glide between the two consonants. When the distant past suffix is added directly after a vowel, it remains *-mvt-*.

7. Cepvwv encokopericeckemvts.
Ce-pvwv en-cokoperic-eck-emvt-s
your_uncle-def_obj 3SD-visit-ft_grd-2S-dp-dec
'You visited your uncle'.

8. Hofonofen, mvt honvnwv holwvyēcemvts.
Hofonofen, mvt honvnwv holwvyēc-emvt-s
long_time_ago, that man-def_subj 3S-mean-ft_grd-dp-dec
'That man was mean a long time ago'.

9. Hvtēyvnke, cvnafkeckemvts.
Hvtēyvnke, cv-nafk-eck-emvt-s
little_while_ago, 1Sdo-hit-ft_grd-2S-dp-dec
'You hit me a little while ago'.

The steps followed to form a verb in the distant past tense and completive aspect are shown in table 9.2. The same verb is constructed with 1S and 3S subjects in order to show the features determining which form of the distant past suffix (*-mvt-* or *-emvt-*) is chosen. The forms of the distant past suffix shown in the table in conjunction with the completive aspect (the falling tone grade) are also used with verbs in the incompletive aspect. The form of the distant past suffix depends solely upon the construction of the subject suffix, not on the aspect of the verb.

Distant Past and Incompletive Aspect

The distant past suffix may also be added to verbs in the incompletive aspect. This combination relays information about when the action occurred and

TABLE 9.2. Use of *-mvt-* and *-emvt-* Forms of Distant Past Depending on Subject Suffix

Step	Verb and 1S subject	Verb and 2S or 3S Subject
1. Find infinitive form 'to see'	hecetv	hecetv
2. Derive verb stem	hec-	hec-
3. Make changes for ft-grade	hēc- (length + falling tone)	hēc- (length + falling tone)
4. Add subject suffix	hēci-	hēceck- (2S) hēc- (3S suffix is null)
5. Add distant past suffix form	hēcimvt-	hēceckemvt- (2S) hēcemvt- (3S)
6. Add declarative suffix	hēcimvts 'I saw'	hēceckemvts 'you (sg.) saw' hēcemvts 'he/she/it saw'

tells that the action was not finished at that time. As in the present and middle past tenses, the incompletive aspect in the distant past tense is indicated by the use of the l-grade. Thus, to say in Mvskoke, "A long time ago I was running (and hadn't yet stopped)," the final vowel of the verb stem is lengthened, retaining an even tone as it is pronounced, and then the appropriate suffixes are added. The resulting Mvskoke form is shown in example 10:

10. Hofonofen lētkimvts.
    Hofonofen lētk-i-mvt-s
    long_time_ago run-1S-dp-dec
    'I was running a long time ago'.

Because the falling tone grade is not employed (the tone of the *ē* in *lētkimvts* remains level), a Mvskoke speaker knows that the action was ongoing in the past. Because the tone of the vowel communicates such important information, it is necessary that you monitor the tone of the lengthened vowel as you pronounce verbs utilizing the completive and incompletive aspects and the distant past tense.

REMOTE PAST *-VTĒ-*

The remote past, indicated by the marker *-vtē-*, may be used to talk about actions that took place sometime between yesterday and the very distant past.

The context tends to indicate when this marker is referring to the mythic past, as when it is used in stories dealing with actions that took place before the speaker was born, and in myths. When the remote past tense is used in such contexts, it is an indication that the actions being discussed took place before the speaker was alive or, if the speaker is very old, during his or her childhood. You will hear this tense used if you listen to traditional stories or historical tales. The English translation for this sense of the remote past tense is 'a long, long time ago'.

The remote past also may indicate that the action occurred in the rather recent but indeterminate past. This meaning is construed when the marker *-vtē-* is used in a context other than the telling of a historic tale or a myth. When the context does not clearly indicate that the marker is referring to an action that took place in the very remote past, simply show the past tense on the English verb without any other modifications or additions to the sentence.

Remote Past and Incompletive Aspect

As in the cases of the middle and distant past tenses, the incompletive aspect is shown for the remote past by using the l-grade. Thus, when the action was still occurring at the time to which the remote past suffix refers, the final vowel in the verb stem is lengthened, but the tone of the vowel does not fall as it is pronounced. After the vowel is lengthened, subject and object prefixes and suffixes are added as normal, the remote past suffix *-vtē-* is added, and then the declarative suffix. This pattern appears in examples 11–13. In each case, the verb is separated in the second line of the example to show you the order of the prefixes and suffixes added to the verb:

11. Este vculat pokkēcvtēs.
    Este vculat pokkēc-vtē-s
    man old-def_subj play_ball-3S-rp-dec
    'The old man was playing ball'.

12. Hvtēyvnke, cvrke Cokvrakko ohhonayvtēs.
    Hvtēyvnke, cvrke Cokvrakko ohhonay-vtē-s
    little_while_ago, my_father-def_subj Bible-def_obj read-3S-rp-dec
    "A little while ago, my father was reading the Bible."

13. Locv Cufe etemarvtēs.
Locv Cufe etemar-vtē-s
Turtle-def_subj Rabbit-def_obj race-3S-rp-dec
'Turtle was racing Rabbit a long, long time ago'.
(As though part of a story)

When the remote past marker is added after the 1S suffix (*-i-*), the form of the remote past suffix is changed. The *v* of the remote past suffix is lengthened to *a* and the 1S suffix is dropped; in effect, the 1S suffix is absorbed by the first vowel of the remote past suffix. Examples 14 and 15 show how this is done:

14. Cvrvhv nafkatēs.
Cvrvhv nafk-atē-s
my_older_brother/sister-def_obj hit-1S-rp-dec
'I was hitting my older brother (male speaking)/older sister (female speaking)'.

15. Hvtēyvnke, mvt ohmēkusvpkv ohlikatēs.
Hvtēyvnke, mvt ohmēkusvpkv ohlik-atē-s
little_while_ago, that pew-def_obj sit_on-1S-rp-dec
'I was sitting on that pew a little while ago'.

The steps that are followed in order to form a verb in the incompletive aspect and remote past tense are shown in table 9.3. Note that the verb is being formed with 1S and 2S subjects, so that the features determining the use of the two forms of the remote past tense suffix (*-vtē-* and *-atē-*) are clearly marked.

Remote Past and Completive Aspect

When the action being referred to in the remote past tense was completed in the past, the verb stem is affected by the use of the falling tone grade. Thus, the combination of the completive aspect and remote past follows the pattern found in each of the other past tense forms: if the action was completed, then the final vowel of the verb stem is lengthened and its tone descends as it is pronounced. All other suffixes and prefixes retain the forms used with the incompletive aspect. Verbs using both the completive

TABLE 9.3. Use of *-vtē-* and *-atē-* Forms of Remote Past Depending on Subject Suffix

Step	Verb and 1S Subject	Verb and 2S Subject
1. Find infinitive form 'to play ball'	pokkecetv	pokkecetv
2. Derive verb stem	pokkec-	pokkec-
3. Make changes for l-grade	pokkēc-	pokkēc-
4. Add subject suffix	pokkēci-	pokkēceck-
5. Add remote past suffix form	pokkēcatē- (1S suffix absorbed)	pokkēceckvtē-
6. Add declarative suffix	pokkēcatēs 'I was playing ball'	pokkēceckvtēs 'you were playing ball'

aspect and the remote past tense are presented in examples 16–18. Note that the form of the remote past is affected by the use of the 1S subject in example 16.

16. Rakkon ohlikatēs.
horse-ind_obj ride-ft_grd-1S-rp-dec
'I rode a horse'.

17. Hvtēyvnke, mvt ohmēkusvpkv ohlikeckvtēs.
little_while_ago that pew-def_obj sit_on-ft_grd-2S-rp-dec
'You sat on that pew a little while ago'.

18. Locv Cufe etemarvtēs.
Turtle-def_subj Rabbit-def_obj race-ft_grd-3S-rp-dec
'Turtle raced Rabbit a long, long time ago'.
(As though part of a story)

Example 18 is very similar to example 13, presented earlier. The difference between the completive form (example 18) and the incompletive form (example 13) lies in the falling tone of the final vowel of the verb stem in example 18. It is this feature, and this feature alone, that tells a Mvskoke speaker whether the action is ongoing or has been completed. The importance of being aware of the tonal quality of the vowel cannot be overstressed, and you should take every opportunity to listen to the tonal qualities of your pronunciations.

Type II Verbs and the Past Tense Suffixes

Type II Verbs and Completive Aspect

Use of the falling tone grade in a type II verb depends on whether the verb is stative or active in nature. The changes associated with the completive aspect (the falling tone grade) are not often made to the stems of stative type II verbs (verbs that have to do with a state of being). Instead, when the state denoted by a stative type II verb stopped affecting the subject in the past, the falling tone grade and the past tense marker are most frequently placed on an auxiliary verb. This practice is discussed in the next section.

Some type II verbs are not stative in nature. Instead, they are active, meaning that they denote that some activity is taking place. Type II verbs that take objects ({II;D} verbs) and express actions or states over which the subject appears to have some control make up the class of active type II verbs. Active type II verbs undergo the same kinds of changes to the final vowel of their stems that were discussed for type I verbs. Thus, if an action was completed in the past, the falling tone grade is applied to the final vowel of the verb stem.

Example 19 makes use of the type {II;D} verb *ohsolotketv* 'to slide toward', which notes that an action ('sliding') is taking place and that this action is affecting someone or something besides the subject (the D object). The circumflex symbol (^) over the final vowel of the verb stem in the second line of the example denotes that the falling tone grade is operating on that vowel (it denotes the tonal contour as the vowel is pronounced). The lengthened character and the falling tone, however, are not indicated in the Mvskoke writing system.

19. Cvnecohsolotkvnks.
    Cvn-ec-ohsolôtk-vnk-s
    1SD-2S-slide_toward-ft_grd-mp-dec
    'You slid toward me'.

That this action was completed in the past is shown by the use of the falling tone grade.

The same changes are operating on the {II;D} verb in example 20. There, the verb *em merretv* 'to feel sorry for' appears to be stative in nature, because the subject is under the power of a feeling or state of being. This verb has the quality of other active type II verbs, however, perhaps because one has some control over whether or not one feels sorry for someone else. One may consciously choose not to feel sorry, whereas one cannot consciously choose not to be sleepy. Because of the verb's more active nature, the final vowel in the verb stem of *em merretv* takes on the vowel length and falling tone associated with the completive aspect grade. Thus, the middle past tense, completive aspect form of this verb is the form shown in example 20:

20. Paksvnkē encvmērrvnks.
Paksvnkē en-cv-mêrr-vnk-s
yesterday 3SD-1S-feel_sorry_for-ft_grd-mp-dec
'Yesterday I felt sorry for him'.

The circumflex symbol over the *e* of the verb stem denotes that the falling tone grade is operating on that vowel. There is no symbol in the Mvskoke writing system to show that this grade is being used, so this symbol appears in the second line only for clarity in the example.

Active Type II Verbs and Incompletive Aspect

Active type II verbs can be formed to show that an action either was ongoing at the time referred to by one of the past tense markers or is still ongoing, if no past tense marker is used. As with type I verbs, the lengthened grade is used to show that the verb is in the incompletive aspect—the action had not been completed at the time specified. The final vowel of the verb *es fekcvkhē* 'to be jealous of' undergoes lengthening but does not assume a falling tone in example 21, which tells a Mvskoke speaker that the act of being jealous was still going on at the time spoken of in the sentence.

21. Cvpvwv enecesfekcakhemvtos.
Cv-pvwv en-ec-esfekcakh-emvt-os
My_uncle-def_subj 3SD-2S-be_jealous_of-l_grd-dp-ss-aux_vb-dec
'You were jealous of my uncle'.

The lengthened quality of the vowel is represented by the *a* in the verb stem.

Stative Type II Verbs and Incompletive Aspect

When a past tense construction of a stative type II verb includes the incompletive aspect, the final vowel of the verb stem is not affected by either the falling tone grade or the lengthened grade. The only change that is made to a stative type II verb stem involves deleting the final ē before the appropriate past tense suffix is added. Thus, when a past tense marker is added to a stative type II verb in the incompletive aspect, it will lead to one of the following structures:

22. Paksvnkē pipuce cvyayvkvnks.
    Paksvnkē pipuce cvyayvk-vnk-s
    Yesterday baby-def_subj 3S-quiet-mp-dec
    'The baby was quiet yesterday'.

23. Hofonofen, hvcce tvphemvtos.
    Hofonofen, hvcce tvph-emvt-os
    Long_time_ago river-def_subj 3S-wide-dp-ss-aux_vb-dec
    'The river was wide a long time ago'.

24. Cufe holwvkvtēs.
    Cufe holwvk-vtē-s
    Rabbit-def_subj 3S-naughty-rp-dec
    'Rabbit was naughty a long, long time ago'.
    (As though part of a story)

In examples 22–24, the final vowel in the verb stem remains short (*v* in each of the examples), and the final ē of the stem has been deleted. The subject in examples 22–24 is 3S, which means that no prefix appears to be added to the verb stem. Examples 25–27 show that the past tense markers do not affect subject prefixes when these are apparent on stative type II verbs.

25. Cvnehvnks.
    Cv-neh-vnk-s
    1S-fat-mp-dec
    'I was fat'.

26. Hofonofen, celopicemvtos.
    Hofonofen, ce-lopic-emvt-os

Long_time_ago, 2S-nice-dp-ss-aux_vb
'You were nice a long time ago'.

27. Cvyekcvtēs.
Cv-yekc-vtē-s
1S-strong-rp-dec
'I was strong'.

Marking the Past Tense on the Auxiliary Verb

Notice that in each of the examples that utilized an auxiliary verb (examples 21, 23, and 26), the auxiliary verb suffix remained in the present tense form. When the past tense is indicated on the primary verb, the auxiliary verb does not need to incorporate the past tense marker. It is possible, however, to put the past tense marker after the auxiliary verb rather than placing it on the primary verb. The auxiliary verb suffix is frequently followed by the middle, distant, or remote past tense form and only rarely takes the h-grade form.

If the past tense suffix is placed after the auxiliary verb suffix, the primary verb still retains the subject and object markers, but its stem does not undergo the changes associated with the falling tone or lengthening grade. Instead, the vowel of the auxiliary verb suffix will be affected by the changes necessary for the use of either the completive or the incompletive aspect. If the action was completed in the time indicated by the past tense suffix, then the alterations associated with the falling tone grade will take place on the vowel of the auxiliary. If the incompletive aspect is used with the past tense marker, then the vowel of the auxiliary verb is lengthened and its tone remains level.

Other changes also occur to the auxiliary verb suffix when the past tense suffix is placed after it. Up to this point, all examples in this chapter using auxiliary verbs have shown the verb suffix to be *-os*. When the auxiliary verb suffix takes on a past tense suffix, however, the auxiliary verb suffix occurs as *-om-*, the uncontracted verb stem derived from the infinitive form *ometv* 'to be'. Thus, when a past tense suffix follows the auxiliary verb suffix, the past tense suffix is added to the stem *-om-*, not to **-os-*.

Examples 28 and 29 show how the past tense marker is added to the auxiliary verb suffix occurring with a type I verb. Example 28 is in the incompletive aspect and utilizes the lengthening grade alone. Example 29, on the other hand, is in the completive aspect, so the *o* of the auxiliary verb stem both is lengthened and undergoes the falling tone grade.

28. Rakko lvsten hecitomvnks.
horse black-ind_obj see-1S-ss-aux_vb-mp-dec
'I was seeing a black horse'.

29. Arakkicecketomvtēs.
worship-2S-ss-aux_vb-ft_grd-rp-dec
'You worshipped'.

The 1S and 2S subject suffixes are added directly to the primary verb in each sentence, as has been the pattern in past examples. The past tense suffix and the changes associated with the verb aspect have been applied to the auxiliary verb suffix. In both cases, the English translations of the sentences are the same as when the past tense marker and the verb aspect were added to the primary verb.

The aspectival changes may also be applied to the auxiliary verb suffix, and the past tense suffix may follow the auxiliary suffix, in sentences in which the primary verb is a type II verb. The subject and object markers remain on the type II primary verb. The final *e* of the primary verb is shortened, the same-subject suffix is added to the verb, and the past tense suffix is moved to a point following the auxiliary verb suffix. The vowel of the auxiliary suffix *-om-* is affected by the verbal aspect, so it undergoes either lengthening alone or lengthening and falling tone. Examples 30 and 31 show how these changes are accomplished:

30. Kafen cvyacetomvnks.
Kafen cv-yace-t-om-vnk-s
coffee-gen_obj 1S-want-ss-aux_vb-ft_grd-mp-dec
'I wanted some coffee'.

31. Otvwoskuce hiyetomvtēs.
Otvwoskuce hiye-t-om-vtē-s
September hot-ss-aux_vb-rp-dec
'It was hot last September'.

The distant past suffix is generally not used on the auxiliary verb *ometv*. Thus, you should concentrate on using the middle and remote past suffixes on auxiliary verbs.

Vocabulary

Church Objects and People

Mvskoke	English
mēkusvpkv-coko	church
Cokvrakko	Bible
Cēsvs	Jesus
erkenvkv	preacher
coko vfastv *or* tēkvnv	deacon
yvhiketv escokv	hymn
cokv esyvhiketv	hymnal
mēkusvpkv	prayer, service
ohmēkusvpkv	pew
(e)tohwelēpkv	cross
hoktvke semevpayv	women's leader
ponvkv hērv honayetv	sermon
hvlwe tvlofv	heaven
naorkv	sinner
Aksomkvlke *or* Ue Aksomkvlke	Baptists
Ohkalvlke *or* Uewv Ohkalvlke	Methodists
Ohfēskvlke *or* Uewv Ohfēskvlke	Presbyterians
(E)Tohwelēpvlke *or* Enhonnv lvstē	Catholics
Cosvlke	Jewish people

Verbs

Mvskoke	English
mēkusvpetv {I}	to pray
em mēkusvpetv {I;D}	to pray for
ohhonayetv {I}	to read
yvhiketv {I}	to sing
erkenvketv {I;D}	to preach
vnokecetv {I;II}	to love someone
mvto kicetv {I;II}	to give thanks, say thanks
vkerricetv {I;II}	to think about
enhonrē {II}	hopeful

kometv *or* kowetv {I;3}	to hope for
arakkicetv {I;II}	to worship
aksomketv {II}	to be baptized

Months of the Year

Mvskoke	English
Rvfo Cuse	January
Hotvlē Hvse	February
Tasahcuce	March
Tasahce Rakko	April
Kē Hvse	May
Kvco Hvse	June
Hvyuce	July
Hvyo Rakko	August
Otvwoskuce	September
Otvwoskv Rakko	October
Eholē	November
Rvfo Rakko	December

Time-Reference Words

Mvskoke	English
paksvnkē	yesterday
hvtēyvnke	a little while ago
hofonofen	long ago
fvccvlik hoyanen	afternoon
hofonē haken	after a long time
nerē-isē	last night

Conversational Sentences

Hoktē 1: Hensci. Mēkusvpkv-coko ayeckvnkv Tecakuce?	Woman 1: Hello. Did you go to church on Sunday?
Hoktē 2: Ehi, mēkusvpkv-coko ayiyvnks. Erkenvkv henrē	Woman 2: Yes, I went to church. The preacher preached a good

erkenakvnks. Mēkusvpkv-coko coko-rakko etem hvnkahanetos, makvnks. Estecatē emvliketv mvo oponicet.	sermon. He told us our church is related to a tribal town. He talked about the clans, too.
Hoktē 1: Cemvliketvtot cemetvlwv kērreckv?	Woman 1: Do you know your clan and tribal town?
Hoktē 2: Ehi, Tvlvhvsset vmetvlwvts. Wotkot vmvliketvts. Cemetvlwvtot cemvliketv kērreckv?	Woman 2: Yes, I am from Tallahassee. I am Raccoon Clan. Do you know your tribal town and clan?
Hoktē 1: Vmvliketv kērretowiyesen, vmetvlwv kerrvks. Foswvt vmvliketvts.	Woman 1: I know my clan, but I don't know my tribal town. I am Bird Clan.
Hoktē 2: Cemvculvkēn tamen cemetvlwvtat empohet kērreckv. Stowet hofone awvtē cemvculvket cekerricewitēs.	Woman 2: You should ask your elders about your tribal town. They will help you learn about your history.
Hoktē 1: Vkerrickv hēnrēs. Mon owat vmvculvkēn vmvnicerēn empoharēs. Mvto.	Woman 1: That's a good idea. I will ask my elders for help. Thank you.

Exercises

Exercise 1

Transform the following incompletive aspect, present tense sentences into incompletive aspect, past tense sentences. The past tense form to be used in the new sentence is indicated in parentheses. If the present tense sentence contains an auxiliary verb, you may choose to mark the past tense and aspect on the auxiliary. You also may add appropriate time-reference words to your new sentences. Translate your new sentences and be prepared to pronounce them in class.

1. Mēkusapis. (rp)
2. Cokvrakko ohhonayeckes. (mp)
3. Hoktvke semevpayv yvhiketos. (mp)
4. Cēsvs arakkicis. (dp)

Figure 9.1. Toney E. Hill, traditional ceremonial ground chief and elder, talking to members of Greenleaf Ceremonial Ground, August 1990. *Photograph courtesy of Bertha Tilkens and Linda Alexander.*

The ground chief and other elders at the grounds routinely talk to the younger members of the ground about correct conduct, traditional practices, and the importance of continuing Muskogee and Seminole traditions. This practice takes place at Muskogee and Seminole churches as well. In this way, younger members are informed about the past and about expectations for the future.

5. Naorkvn emmēkusapeckes. (rp)
6. Vcaksomketos. (dp)
7. Wotko tvskocēs. (rp)
8. Cepanē holwvkētos. (mp)
9. Cepoca tosēnv cekfen nēses. (dp)
10. Cvckuce cvtvhakvn norices. (mp)

Exercise 2

In this in-class exercise, your teacher will present you with a short present tense sentence. Your teacher will then ask you to modify it to reflect either middle, distant, or remote past tense. An example is provided:

Teacher:	Sokhvpeswvn hompis.
	Distant past.
Student:	Sokhvpeswvn hompimvts.
Teacher:	Remote past.
Student:	Sokhvpeswvn hompatēs. [And so forth]

Exercise 3

Write a short paragraph about some event or activity you remember from your childhood. If you need some vocabulary that has not been presented in the textbook, ask your teacher for help. Your paragraph must contain past tense sentences, sentences containing a 1S subject, and some object pronouns.

Present your paragraph in class if your teacher asks you to do so. You may find that your paragraph begins a conversation about traditional or innovative activities.

Exercise 4

Change each of the following incompletive aspect, present tense sentences into completive aspect, past tense sentences. The past tense form to be used in the new sentence is indicated in parentheses. If the present tense sentence contains an auxiliary verb, you may choose to mark the past tense and aspect on the auxiliary. You also may add appropriate time-reference words to your new sentences. When you have changed the sentence to mark the appropriate past tense and completive aspect, identify each of the meaningful units in a line underneath your sentence. Translate your new sentences and be prepared to pronounce them in class.

1. Vtotkis. (dp)
2. Ceposet nockelēs. (mp)
3. Mvt naorkvt ponvkv hērv honayetv vkerrices. (mp)
4. Erkenvkv yvhiken vmmēkusapes. (rp)
5. Nettvcako, yvhiketv escokvn yvhikecketos. (dp)
6. Honvnwv hotosēt elvwētos. (rp)
7. Hoktuce lowakat cvtakkes. (mp)
8. Cerket Cokvrakko cekfēn cvyayvken ohhonayetos. (dp)
9. Ēwvnwvt honvnwv afvckan vce tvklik kvmokse vsemetos. (rp)
10. Pipuce wakvpesēn awotsanes. (mp)

Exercise 5

Break each word in the following sentences into its meaningful parts, just as was done in the second and third lines of examples 1–4 in this chapter. Remember that nouns, adjectives, and adverbs, as well as verbs, may have multiple meaningful units. You may choose to break apart sentences utilizing the past tense markers as though they are formed with either the incompletive or the completive aspect.

1. Hofonofen, vcaksomkvnks.
2. Hoktvlē kocoknē lopicēt vklopetos.
3. Cufet Hvlpvtv holwvyēcēn vwenayvtēs.
4. Mvnte enhvyvtke efv oklanē pvfnat vmakkvnks.
5. Ceccuste tosēnvn laffvtēs.
6. Paksvnkē hoktvke semevpayv mēkusapvnks.
7. Coko vfastv mvto kices.
8. Pipuce feknokken selaksēhkes.
9. Ceckuce vcahvlatemvts.
10. Cencvmēriyes.

Exercise 6

Listen to tracks 28 and 30 on CD B. Identify words that you have learned in chapters 1–9. Write down the words that you recognize, in the order in which they occur in the songs. Then listen to the translations (tracks 29 and 31). If there were words you should have identified earlier, listen again to the tracks and try to find them. If you found most of the words you should have been able to recognize, congratulations!

Christianity in the Mvskoke Community

Christianity was introduced to the Mvskoke people after their removal to Indian Territory (Oklahoma). White people looked upon the Mvskoke as hostile and uncivilized. It was thought that they could be tamed and civilized through conversion to Christianity. Therefore, Christian religions were introduced to the Mvskoke by missionaries.

The predominant Christian denominations in the Mvskoke community are Baptist, Methodist, and Presbyterian. Despite being places for

Figure 9.2. Presbyterian church and schoolhouse. *Photograph courtesy of the Western History Collections, University of Oklahoma Libraries, Seminole Nation Museum Collection.*

Christian worship, most Mvskoke churches share some practices with the traditional ceremonial grounds. In churches the number four is noticeable; for example, the call to worship involves ringing the bell or blowing the cow horn four times. Also, as in traditional grounds, all things are done facing east, and almost all older churches face east. This is a traditional practice because the sun rises in the east, bringing in a new day, bright and clear.

The leaders in the churches hold responsibilities similar to those of personnel at the ceremonial grounds. The pastor or preacher of the church is equal in position to the *mekko,* or chief, of the ceremonial ground. The deacon has many of the same responsibilities and duties as the stick men at the ceremonial grounds. Women leaders are found in the churches just as they are at the grounds.

Church members and ceremonial ground members also have similar views about their worship. Members of both churches and grounds believe in one God or Creator. In both belief systems, it is this God or Creator that gives each of us the blessing of life. Without this God or Creator, there would be nothing.

Suggested Readings

Use of the different past tense markers and aspects in Mvskoke is discussed in Mary Haas's "Ablaut and Its Function in Muskogee" (1940) and in Donald E. Hardy's "The Semantics of Creek Morphosyntax" (1988:134–44). In both sources, the completive or incompletive content of the various verb grades is discussed in great detail. Haas offers a thorough discussion of the time depth represented by the different past tense markers.

Michele Nathan ("Grammatical Description of the Florida Seminole Dialect of Creek," 1977) treats the past tense markers separately from the aspectual (verb grade) changes. However, her analysis of the past tense markers (pp. 112–15) and aspects (pp. 107–9) leads to results similar to those presented in this work.

Those interested in learning more about Christian religious communities among the Muskogee and Seminole are encouraged to read Jack M. Schultz's *The Seminole Baptist Churches of Oklahoma* (1999) or R. M. Loughridge's "History of Mission Work among the Creek Indians from 1832 to 1888" (1888). Those especially interested in interaction between missionaries and Muskogees may wish to investigate the A. E. W. Robertson collection at the University of Tulsa. Mrs. Robertson was the daughter of a respected missionary among the Muskogee, and she married such a missionary herself. She was fluent in the language and appeared to have had the confidence of many Christian Muskogee people, as well as their political leaders.

CHAPTER 10

Negation

Negation, which indicates that an action is not occurring, is indicated on the verb in Mvskoke. Negating a verb is done by adding a suffix, *-eko-*, to the verb stem. The negative suffix is added before any past tense suffix. If there is no past tense suffix, then the negative suffix falls directly before the declarative suffix or same-subject suffix. Diagram 10.1 shows the order of the various prefixes and suffixes as they are added to type I verb stems. Diagram 10.2 shows the order of the prefixes and suffixes as they occur on type II verb stems. Notice that the negating suffix comes immediately after the subject marker on type I verbs and immediately after the verb stem on type II verbs.

The negating suffix, *-eko-*, may have different forms, depending upon the types of sounds surrounding it. The various forms of the negating suffix are presented in Table 10.1.

Type I verbs without an auxiliary verb:

(Type II Object)	(Type D Object)	Verb Stem	Type I Subject	(Neg. Suffix)	(Past Tense Suffix)	(Decl. Suffix)

Type I verbs with an auxiliary verb:

(Type II Object)	(Type D Object)	Verb Stem	Type I Subject	(Neg. Suffix)	(Past Suffix)	(S-S Suffix)	(Aux. Verb)	(Decl. Suffix)

Diagram 10.1. Affix Order in Type I Verbs

Type II verbs without an auxiliary verb:

Type II Subject	(Type D Object)	Verb Stem	(Negation Suffix)	(Past Tense Suffix)	(Declarative Suffix)

Type II verbs with an auxiliary verb:

Type II Subject	(Type D Object)	Verb Stem	(Negation Suffix)	(Past Tense Suffix)	(S-S Suffix)	(Aux. Verb)	(Declarative Suffix)

Diagram 10.2. Affix Order in Type II Verbs

TABLE 10.1. Negating Suffix Forms

Position of Negating Suffix	Suffix Form
Between two consonants, neither of which is the declarative suffix (-*s*)	-eko-
Between a vowel and a consonant other than the /s/ of the declarative suffix	-ko-
Between a consonant and a vowel or between a consonant and the declarative suffix (-*s*)	-ek-
Between vowels or between a vowel and the declarative suffix (-*s*)	-k-

As the table shows, when the negating suffix occurs after a vowel, the initial *e* of the suffix is dropped. When the negating suffix appears before the declarative suffix or before a vowel, the final *o* of the suffix is dropped. If the suffix is added between a vowel and the declarative suffix or between two vowels, both the initial *e* and the final *o* are dropped, which results in the form -*k*-.

The initial /e/ of the negating suffix takes the tonal stress associated with an "always key" syllable. If the form of the negating suffix added to a verb does not have an initial /e/ (that is, it is -*ko*- or -*k*-), then the suffix does not have high stress. When the negating suffix is added to a verb with the 2S type I suffix, then the tone of the initial /e/ is still raised, but it is lower than the tone of the preceding 2S type I suffix syllable. Thus, in examples 1 and 2 the tonal contours of the words, listed below the Mvskoke sentence, show that in the verb, the tone of the negating suffix is equal to or higher than the last syllable but does not reach the level of the 2S type I suffix.

1. Sasvkwv hvtkan hompeckekotos.
sâ·svk·wv hvt·kán hom·péc·ké·kot·os
24-3-d 3-3 i-2-3-3-d
'You didn't eat the white goose'.

2. Cvhececkekos.
cv·hec·éc·ké·kos
i·3·2·3·d
'You don't see me'.

Negation of Type I Verbs in the Incompletive Aspect

When a present tense type I verb in the incompletive aspect is negated, the final vowel in the verb stem is not lengthened. Thus, in the verbs presented in examples 3b and 3c, which are in the present tense and incompletive aspect, the *e* of the verb stem is not lengthened. Also, because the negative suffix is added after the 1S type I suffix, which is a vowel, the negative suffix has the forms *-k-* and *-ko-* in examples 3b and 3c, respectively. Finally, the 1S suffix changes its form to *-v-* when the negative suffix is added to the verb.

Example 3a is the positive form of the sentence, example 3b is the negative form without an auxiliary verb, and example 3c is the negative form with an auxiliary verb. Notice that the negating suffix is added to the primary verb, not the auxiliary verb, in example 3c.

3a. Wakvpesēn ēskis.
Wakvpesēn ēsk-i-s
milk-ind_obj drink-l_grd-1S-dec
'I am drinking some milk'.

3b. Wakvpesēn eskvks.
Wakvpesēn esk-v-k-s
milk-ind_obj drink-1S-neg-dec
'I am not drinking some milk'.

3c. Wakvpesēn eskvkotos.
Wakvpesēn esk-v-ko-t-os
milk-ind_obj drink-1S-neg-ss-aux_vb-dec
'I am not drinking some milk'.

Examples 4a–4c and 5a–5c show how the negative suffix appears when added to sentences containing type I verbs modified for 2S and 3S subjects. In examples 4b–4c and 5b–5c, the negative suffix has the form *-ek-* because it appears between a subject marker ending in a consonant and the declarative suffix *-s*. As in examples 3a–3c, the positive form of the sentence is provided in examples 4a and 5a so that you can see how the verb stem changes when the action is negated.

4a. Cokon hayeckes.
Cokon hay-eck-es
house-ind_obj build-l_grd-2S-dec
'You are building a house'.

4b. Cokon hvyeckeks.
Cokon hvy-eck-ek-s
house-ind_obj build-2S-neg-dec
'You are not building a house'.

4c. Cokon hvyeckekotos.
Cokon hvy-eck-eko-t-os
house-ind_obj build-2S-neg-ss-aux_vb-dec
'You are not building a house'.

In examples 5a–5c, the verb is formed for a 3S subject:

5a. Hoktē naken vpohes.
Hoktē naken vpoh-es
woman-def_subj something-ind_obj buy-l_grd-3S-dec
'The woman is buying something/shopping'.

5b. Hoktē naken vpoheks.
Hoktē naken vpoh-ek-s
woman-def_subj something-ind_obj buy-3S-neg-dec
'The woman is not buying something/shopping'.

5c. Hoktē naken vpohekotos.
Hoktē naken vpoh-eko-t-os
woman-def_subj something-ind_obj buy-3S-neg-ss-aux_vb-dec
'The woman is not buying something/shopping'.

The steps necessary to correctly form a negated type I verb in the present tense and incompletive aspect are shown in the following list. Note that when the 1S subject suffix is added to a verb, it has the form *-v-*. Also, remember that the form of the negating suffix will depend upon the sounds that surround it.

1. Obtain verb stem (without *-etv* suffix)
2. Add correct subject suffix
3. Add correct form of negating suffix
4. Add declarative suffix or same-subject suffix and auxiliary verb

The verb forms resulting from each of these steps as they are applied to *etohkvletv* 'to add', a type I verb modified for 1S, 2S, and 3S subjects, are presented in table 10.2, in which the steps correspond to those in the preceding list.

Negation of Type I Verbs in the Past Tense

Recent Past

Negation of type I verbs in each of the past tenses operates in a fashion similar to that used to negate verbs in the present tense and incompletive aspect. Examples 6a–6c present negation of a verb in the very recent past (the h-grade). First, the verb stem is modified to show the immediate past. Second, the proper subject and object suffixes and prefixes are added. Note that the

Table 10.2. Steps in the Negation of Type I Verbs in Present Tense and Incompletive Aspect for 1S, 2S, and 3S Subjects

Step	1S Subject	2S Subject	3S Subject
1	etohkvl-	etohkvl-	etohkvl-
2	etohkvlv-	etohkvleck-	etohkvl-
3	etohkvlvk- *or* etohkvlvko-	etohkvleckek- *or* etohkvleckeko-	etohkvlek- *or* etohkvleko-
4	etohkvlvks *or* etohkvlvkotos 'I am not adding'	etohkvleckeks *or* etohkvleckekotos 'you (sg.) are not adding'	etohkvleks *or* etohkvlekotos 'he/she/it is not adding'

form of the 1S subject suffix is again *-v-* before the negating suffix. Third, the negative suffix is placed after the subject suffix. The last step involves adding the declarative or same-subject suffix. Following is a convenient list of these steps:

1. Obtain verb stem (without *-etv* suffix)
2. Insert appropriate h-grade infix form
3. Add correct subject suffix and object prefixes
4. Add correct form of negating suffix
5. Add declarative suffix or same-subject suffix and auxiliary verb suffix

Table 10.3 illustrates each of these steps as they are applied to the verb *vketēcetv* 'to watch after'. In the table, this verb has been modified for each of the singular subjects. The 2S direct object prefix is used with the 1S and 3S subjects, the 1S direct object prefix with the 2S subject.

Examples 6a through 8c present sentences that result from the application of these steps to three more verbs in the h-grade. In each set of examples, the first sentence demonstrates the unnegated form, the second shows the negated form without an auxiliary verb, and the third shows the negated form with an auxiliary verb. Examples 6a–6c utilize the 1S subject suffix.

TABLE 10.3. Steps in the Negation of Type I Verbs in Recent Past Tense for 1S, 2S, and 3S Subjects

Step	1S Subject	2S Subject	3S Subject
1	vketēc-	vketēc-	vketēc-
2	vketēhc-	vketēhc-	vketēhc-
3	cemvketēhcv-	vmvketēhceck-	cemvketēhc-
4	cemvketēhcvk- *or* cemvketēhcvko-	vmvketēhceckek- *or* vmvketēhceckeko-	cemvketēhcek- *or* cemvketēhceko-
5	cemvketēhcvks *or* cemvketēhcvkotos 'I was not watching after you (just now)'	vmvketēhceckeks *or* vmvketēhceckekotos 'you (sg.) were not watching after me (just now)'	cemvketēhceks *or* cemvketēhcekotos 'he/she/it was not watching after you (just now)'

6a. Honvnwvn hehcis.
man-ind_obj see-h_grd-1S-dec
'I just saw him/a man'.

6b. Honvwvn hehcvks.
man-ind_obj see-h_grd-1S-neg-dec
'I didn't see him (just now)'.

6c. Honvnwvn hehcvkotos.
man-ind_obj see-h_grd-1S-neg-ss-aux_vb-dec
'I didn't see him (just now)'.

Examples 7a–7c present a verb with the 2S subject suffix.

7a. Hoktuce hotososen vketēhceckes.
girl thin-ind_obj 3Sdo-watch_after-h_grd-2S-dec
'You were watching after a thin girl (just now)'.

7b. Hoktuce hotososen vketēhceckeks.
girl thin-ind_obj 3Sdo-watch_after-h_grd-2S-neg-dec
'You were not watching after a thin girl (just now)'.

7c. Hoktuce hotososen vketēhceckekotos.
girl thin-ind_obj 3Sdo-watch_after-h_grd-2S-neg-ss-aux_vb-dec
'You were not watching after a thin girl (just now)'.

The sentences in examples 8a–8c show a verb formed with the 3S subject suffix.

8a. Cepanē vhvnkvhts.
boy-def_subj count-h_grd-3S-dec
'The boy was counting (just now)'.

8b. Cepanē vhvnkvhteks.
boy-def_subj count-h_grd-3S-neg-dec
'The boy was not counting (just now)'.

8c. Cepanē vhvnkvhtekotos.
boy-def_subj count-h_grd-3S-neg-ss-aux_vb-dec
'The boy was not counting (just now)'.

Negating Type I Verbs Using More Distant Past Tense Forms

If the past tense involves the addition of a suffix (that is, if you are referring to the middle, distant, or remote past), then the negating suffix is added immediately before the past tense suffix. If the past tense normally takes the falling tone grade, this is not used along with the negating suffix—the final vowel of the verb stem is not lengthened, nor does the tone drop as the vowel is pronounced. Examples 9a through 11b show how the negating suffix is added to verbs in the middle, distant, and remote pasts.

9a. Paksvnkē cepanet cvnvfkekvnks.
Paksvnkē cepanet cv-nvfk-ek-vnk-s
yesterday boy-ind_subj 1Sdo-hit-3S-neg-mp-dec
'A boy did not hit me yesterday'.

9b. Paksvnkē cepanet cvnvfkekvnketos.
Paksvnkē cepanet cv-nvfk-ek-vnk-et-os
boy-ind_subj 1Sdo-hit-3S-neg-mp-ss-aux_vb-dec
'A boy did not hit me yesterday'.

Notice that the forms of the verb in 9a and 9b are not **cvnafkekvnks* and **cvnafkekvnketos* (with long vowels in the verb stem). The last vowel in the verb stem is not lengthened, nor does it have a falling tone, due to the presence of the negating suffix.

Examples 10a and 10b show how the negating suffix is placed in a verb containing the distant past tense suffix, *-mvt-*.

10a. Hofonofen cvpoheckekomvts.
Hofonofen cv-poh-eck-eko-mvt-s
long_time_ago 1Sdo-hear-2S-neg-dp-dec
'You did not hear me a long time ago'.

10b. Hofonofen cvpoheckekomvtos.
Hofonofen cv-poh-eck-eko-mvt-os
long_time_ago 1Sdo-hear-2S-dp-neg-dp-ss-aux_vb-dec
'You did not hear me a long time ago'.

The falling tone grade is not operating on the verb in either example 10a or 10b because of the presence of the negating suffix. The verb form in 10b appears different from what one might expect, in that it does not have the form **cvpoheckekomvtetos*. It would appear that the same-subject suffix (*-t*) has not been added to the verb in example 10b. In this example, however, the final *t* of the past tense marker (*-mvt-*) acts as the same-subject suffix. Whenever the final suffix on the primary verb that precedes the auxiliary verb ends in *t*, that *t* takes on the role of the same-subject suffix.

Examples 11a and 11b show how the negating suffix is added to verbs formed with the remote past tense suffix.

11a. Cufe Nokose vwenayekvtēs.
Cufe Nokose vwenay-ek-vtē-s
Rabbit-def_subj Bear-def_obj smell-3S-neg-rp-dec
'Rabbit did not smell Bear a long, long time ago'.
(As though part of a story)

11b. Cufe Nokose vwenayekvtētos.
Cufe Nokose vwenay-ek-vtē-t-os
Rabbit-def_subj Bear-def_obj smell-3S-neg-rp-ss-aux_vb-dec
'Rabbit did not smell Bear a long, long time ago'.
(As though part of a story)

Although it is not immediately obvious in examples 11a and 11b, because the final vowel in the verb is already a long vowel (*a*), the l-grade is not operating on verbs having both the negating suffix and the remote past suffix. (Remember that the remote past, when added to a verb without the negating suffix, takes either the l-grade or the ft-grade.) In this, as in each of the preceding examples of past tense with negating suffix, the final vowel in the verb stem retains the length it has in the infinitive form. If the vowel is short in the infinitive form, it remains short when the verb is negated. If the vowel is long in the infinitive form, it remains long when the verb is negated.

Negation of Type II Verbs in the Present Tense

As shown in diagram 10.1, when type II verbs in the present tense are negated, the negating suffix is added between the verb stem and the declarative suffix or the same-subject suffix, depending on which is used. All subject and object prefixes are added as you have learned up to this point. What is not apparent in the diagram is that when the negating suffix is added, the *e* of the negating suffix replaces the final *ē* of the verb stem. Thus, when the negating suffix is added to a type II verb, the *e* between the verb stem and the negating suffix is short, not long.

Examples 12a–12c show how the negating suffix is added to a type II verb in the present tense. The first example, 12a, presents the sentence in a non-negative state—the verb is formed exactly as shown in chapter 6.

12a. Hvcce cahkētos.
Hvcce cahkē-t-os
river-def_subj 3S-shallow-ss-aux_vb-dec
'The river is shallow'.

Examples 12b and 12c give the negated form of the sentence presented in 12a, with 12c adding an auxiliary verb to the sentence.

12b. Hvcce cahkeks.
Hvcce cahk-ek-s
river-def_subj 3S-shallow-neg-dec
'The river is not shallow'.

12c. Hvcce cahkekotos.
Hvcce cahk-eko-t-os
river-def_subj 3S-shallow-neg-ss-aux_vb-dec
'The river is not shallow'.

Notice that in 12b and 12c, the long final ē on the verb stem has been dropped, and the short *e* of the negating suffix takes its place.

The same pattern is followed when the subject is indicated by a prefix on the verb stem. Examples 13a–13c show how this is accomplished.

13a. Cvwvnhkēs.
cv-wvnhkē-s
1S-thirsty-dec
'I am thirsty'.

13b. Cvwvnhkeks.
cv-wvnhk-ek-s
1S-thirsty-neg-dec
'I am not thirsty'.

13c. Cvwvnhkekotos.
cv-wvnhk-eko-t-os
1S-thirsty-neg-ss-aux_vb-dec
'I am not thirsty'.

Note that the subject prefix has the same form and position as you had been taught in chapter 6. Again, the *e* between the verb stem and the negating suffix is short, not the long form ē.

In examples 14a–14c, both subject and object prefixes have been added to the verb. In these examples, the subject and object prefix order is just as you have seen in previous examples; the only difference between the positive and negative form of the verb is that a short *e* comes between the verb stem and the negative suffix.

14a. Cencvpenkvlēs.
cen-cv-penkvlē-s
2SD-1S-afraid_of-dec
'I am afraid of you'.

14b. Cencvpenkvleks.
cen-cv-penkvl-ek-s
2SD-1S-afraid_of-neg-dec
'I am not afraid of you'.

14c. Cencvpenkvlekotos.
cen-cv-penkvl-eko-t-os
2SD-1S-afraid_of-neg-ss-aux_vb-dec
'I am not afraid of you'.

As you can see, neither the order nor the form of subject prefixes and object prefixes is affected by the addition of the negating suffix.

Negation of Type II Verbs in the Past Tense

When type II verbs are in the past tense, they add the negating suffix before the past tense marker, just as type I verbs do (see diagram 10.1). If a type II verb is affected by the h-grade, then the negating suffix is added to the verb stem after the h-grade infix has been added, as shown in examples 15a–15c and 16a–16c. The form of the h-grade infix is not affected by the addition of the negating suffix. As in the examples presented previously, sentences are first presented in a positive form (no negation has occurred), and then the negating suffix is added, first without and then with an auxiliary verb. Examples 15a–15c show the negating suffix added to a type II verb taking the *-h-* form of the h-grade infix.

15a. Cvlvhwēs.
cv-lvhwē-s
1S-hungry-h_grd-dec
'I was hungry (just now)'.

15b. Cvlvhweks.
cv-lvhw-ek-s
1S-hungry-h_grd-neg-dec
'I was not hungry (just now)'.

15c. Cvlvhwekotos.
cv-lvhw-eko-t-os
1S-hungry-h_grd-neg-ss-aux_vb-dec
'I was not hungry (just now)'.

Examples 16a–16c show the negating suffix added to a type II verb taking the *-i-* form of the h-grade infix. Notice that the verbs in examples 15 and 16 take two different forms of the h-grade infix because of the different structures of the verb stems.

16a. Cewvnikēs.
ce-wvnikē-s
2S-thirsty-h_grd-dec
'You were thirsty (just now)'.

16b. Cewvnikeks.
ce-wvnik-ek-s
2S-thirsty-h_grd-neg-dec
'You were not thirsty (just now)'.

16c. Cewvnikekotos.
ce-wvnik-eko-t-os
2S-thirsty-h_grd-neg-ss-aux_vb-dec
'You were not thirsty (just now)'.

When a type II verb takes a past tense suffix, as with the distant, middle, and remote pasts, the negating suffix is added between the verb stem and the past tense marker, just as in type I verbs. The subject and object prefixes retain their usual forms and positions on the verb. As mentioned in chapter 9, the final vowel in a type II verb stem is not lengthened or affected by falling tone grade when the middle, distant, or remote past tense suffix is added. The only change that occurs to type II verb stems that have undergone past tense addition involves the use of a short *e* between the verb stem and the negating suffix.

When the negating suffix is added to a type II verb modified with a past tense suffix, the verb stem is constructed just as if it were in a positive sentence. The negating suffix is then added to the verb stem, just before the past tense suffix. This process leads to forms like those found in examples 17a through 19c. Sentences 17a–17c provide examples of negation occurring with the middle past tense.

17a. Cenkērrepvnketos.
cen-kērrep-vnk-et-os
1S-understand-mp-ss-aux_vb-dec
'I understood (some time ago)'.

17b. Cenkērrepekvnketos.
cen-kērrep-ek-vnk-et-os
1S-understand-neg-mp-ss-aux_vb-dec
'I did not understand (some time ago)'.

17c. Cenkērrepekvnks.
cen-kērrep-ek-vnk-s
1S-understand-neg-mp-dec
'I did not understand (some time ago)'.

Examples 18a–18c show how the negating suffix is added to a type II verb with the distant past tense.

18a. Cecvpakkemvtos.
ce-cvpakk-emvt-os
2S-angry-ft_grd-dp-ss-aux_vb-dec
'You were angry a while ago'.

18b. Cecvpakkekomvtos.
ce-cvpakk-eko-mvt-os
2S-angry-neg-dp-ss-aux_vb-dec
'You were not angry a while ago'.

18c. Cecvpakkekomvts.
ce-cvpakk-eko-mvt-s
2S-angry-neg-dp-dec
'You were not angry a while ago'.

Finally, examples 19a–19c present the forms realized when the negating suffix is added to type II verbs utilizing the remote past tense. Each of these sentences is presented as though it is being said in the narration of a story.

19a. Hofonofen Nokose nockelvtēs.
hofonofen Nokose nockel-vtē-s
long_ago Bear-def_subj 3S-sleepy-rp-dec
'A long time ago, Bear was sleepy'.

19b. Hofonofen Nokose nockelekvtētos.
hofonofen Nokose nockel-ek-vtē-t-os
long_ago Bear-def_subj 3S-sleepy-neg-rp-ss-aux_vb-dec
'A long time ago, Bear was not sleepy'.

19c. Hofonofen Nokose nockelekvtēs.
hofonofen Nokose nockel-ek-vtē-s
long_ago Bear-def_subj 3S-sleepy-neg-rp-dec
'A long time ago, Bear was not sleepy'.

The long vowels found in the verbs in examples 17a–17c and 18a–18c are not the result of vowel lengthening. Instead, the infinitive form of the verb, in each case, contains a long vowel. The length of the final vowel in the verb stem is not affected by the addition of either the negating or the past tense suffix.

Vocabulary

School Objects and People

Mvskoke	English
cokv-heckv *or* mvhakv-cuko	school
ahkopvnkv-ēkvnv	playground
cukhofv *or* nvthofv	room in a building or house

cokv-heckv cukhofv	classroom
mvhayv	teacher
cokv-hēcv	student
vpohkv	question
eshoccickv	pencil
owvlvste eshoccickv	pen
cokv	book or paper
vhvnkvtkv *or* vhvmkvtkv	number
eshoccickv lvste	blackboard chalk
vhoccickv	blackboard
nak-eshoccicetv cokv	notebook

SCHOOL ACTIVITIES

Mvskoke	English
cvyayvkē {II}	to be quiet
spvlketv {I;3}	to spell a word
ohhonvyetv {I}	to read
vpohetv {I;D}	to ask someone
kerretv {I;II}	to know
mvhayetv {I;D}	to teach
kērrepetv {II}	to understand
vslēcetv {I}	to erase
vhvnkvtetv {I;II} *or* vhvmkvtetv {I;II}	to count
hoccicetv {I;3}	to write
etohkvletv {I}	to add
vketēcetv {I;II}	to watch after
em mapohicetv {I:D}	to listen to someone
lvpotēcetv {I;D}	to correct

Exercises

EXERCISE 1

Translate the following sentences from Mvskoke into English. When translating the sentences, show the meaningful units as is done in the second line of each example in the chapter. An example is provided for you.

Cokv-hēcvt vhvnkvtekomvtos.
student-ind_subj count-3S-neg-dp-ss-aux_vb-dec
'A student was not counting a while ago'.

1. Mvhayv vnohhonayeks.
2. Cerke cvyayvkekvnks.
3. Hoktuce mahat kerrvkotos.
4. Cepanē yekcet vhoccickvn pvfnēt vslēcvtētos.
5. Este vculet henehan emoponvhyekotos.
6. Wotko Foswv hvtkan hecekvtētos.
7. Mucv-nettv cvnockelekotos.
8. Hoktvke semevpayvn emmēkusvpeckvnks.
9. Heles hayv etokonhe hvlvlatkēt vhvmkvhtetos.
10. Cecke vce tvklik kvmoksen tvcekomvtos.

Exercise 2

Negate the following sentences, then translate your sentences into English. When translating the sentences, show the meaningful units as is done in the second line of each example in the chapter.

1. Pipuce feknokket selaksēkemvts.
2. Nettvcako ecuse etkolētomvnks.
3. Cvpocv locv honnan lopicēt atvkkēsetos.
4. Mekko emenhonriyvtēs.
5. Cokv-hēcvt cokv ohhonayetos.
6. Cvnahvmke owvlvste eshoccickv asvnwiyetos.
7. Mucv-nettv erkenvkv ponvkv hērv honayetv hoccicetos.
8. Ceckuce Nettv opvnkv opanemvts.
9. Cepanē 'cukhofv' spvliketos.
10. Totkv hayētos.

Exercise 3

Translate the following sentences from English into Mvskoke. Show the meaningful units within the words in your translation, as is done in the second line of each example in the chapter.

1. I am thinking about you.
2. You thought about your mother a short while ago.

3. The girl did not watch after her sister.
4. I did not cook the little white goose.
5. Your paternal aunt did not pass me the salt a long time ago.
6. I feel sorry for you.
7. The speaker made peace with the deacon a little while ago.
8. My grandfather is not drinking hot coffee.
9. The teacher shook hands with my maternal uncle yesterday.
10. His/her grandmother poured the milk a little while ago.

EXERCISE 4

Create ten sentences using verbs and nouns presented in chapters 1–10 and including negation. Pronounce your sentences to your partner. Your partner is to change the sentences into an unnegated form. Your partner should then translate your (negated) sentences. Record any sentences about which you and your partner disagree over the form of the sentence, the negated form of the verb, or the translation. Ask your instructor about these sentences in class.

EXERCISE 5

Each of the following sentences is in the negated form. Change each sentence so that it is no longer negated, then show the meaningful units within each word in your sentence.

1. Rakko sopakhvtkan cempenkvlekotos.
2. Coko vfastv yvhiketv escokv hvlvlatkēt yvhikekvnks.
3. Cvkērrepekomvtos.
4. Nerē-isē, hvlpvtvt tolose lanen hompekvnks.
5. Cvcke vpeswv lvfiyekotos.
6. Rakko yekcen eto honnē mahan ahvlatekvtēs.
7. Hvtēyvnke, celvwēcekvnks.
8. Hotvle Hvse, eccus honvnwvt encokopericekomvts.
9. Eholē, honvnwv nockelat opvnkv ekvnv vyekvnks.
10. Cokv-hēcv vhonehcekotos.

EXERCISE 6

Write a short story in Mvskoke containing at least twelve sentences. Use some past tense markers and negation in your story. Translate your story. Be prepared to tell your story in class.

Figure 10.1. Ribbon Dance at Greenleaf Ceremonial Ground, August 1988. The four dancers at the front of the line are, from left to right, Mary Cully, Bonnie Gibson, Anna Cooper, and Bertha Tilkens. *Photograph by Linda Alexander.*

The Ribbon Dance takes place during the day on the Friday of the Green Corn Ceremony. Women wear bright colors and many ribbons on their dresses during this dance. One man can be seen sitting in the arbor to the left of the women. The men encourage the women dancers from their places under the arbors.

The Impact of Education on the Mvskoke

When Europeans first began to colonize the Americas, including the original Mvskoke homeland, they knew they wanted the native people's land. From the very beginning, the Europeans knew the Mvskoke didn't understand them, and they didn't understand the Mvskoke. Europeans began trading by making signs to the friendly Mvskoke, and a means of communication was established.

Soon, Euro-Americans began teaching English to the Mvskoke. Eventually they introduced the Mvskoke to the Bible and began to translate it into Mvskoke. One reason they started this was so that the Mvskoke would forget their traditional ways, their culture, and their language. The Euro-Americans did not know that the Mvskoke would not forget their ways and language, nor would they forget what they had already learned about their environment.

For instance, the Mvskoke knew how to survive in many environments. Mvskoke people raised their own food, including vegetables such as corn and beans. They knew how to obtain enough meat to feed their families—rabbits, squirrels, buffalo, birds, and fish. They also knew how to pick berries and wild plants for fruit and vegetables. The Mvskoke used the bow and arrow to kill game, using medicine on the end when they needed to kill large animals.

The Mvskoke also knew about using herbs and the roots and leaves of wild plants to cure illnesses. They had songs for each individual medicine. They also had songs that helped them kill game or obtain plant foods.

At one point, Euro-Americans tried to starve the Mvskoke into submission. The Mvskoke had such varieties of foods to choose from, and knew how to obtain and store enough food, that the Euro-Americans were unsuccessful in breaking their will. Instead, Euro-Americans began to learn about the availability and uses of wild foods from the Mvskoke!

The Mvskoke also understood the importance of exercise. They walked, climbed, swam, and danced for their exercise.

Before the arrival of Europeans, the Mvskoke had developed a calendar system for keeping track of the months in a year. They used a large piece of tree bark with holes punched in it representing days. A stick was placed in each of the holes in turn, until the month was over. The Mvskoke had named each month according to its weather. This is the same calendar cycle that is used today:

January	Rufo Cuse	Winter's Little Brother
February	Hotvlē Hvse	Windy Month
March	Tasahcuce	Little Spring Month
April	Tasahce Rakko	Big Spring Month
May	Kē Hvse	Mulberry Month
June	Kvco Hvse	Blackberry Month
July	Hvyuce	Little Harvest or Little Summer
August	Hvyo Rakko	Big Harvest or Big Summer
September	Otvwoskuce	Little Chestnut Month
October	Otvwoskv Rakko	Big Chestnut Month
November	Eholē	Frost Month
December	Rvfo Rakko	Big Winter

Suggested Readings

Little work has been done on negation in Mvskoke. Donald E. Hardy ("The Semantics of Creek Morphosyntax," 1988) provides examples of sentences containing the negating suffix, but he does not explore its use or incorporation into the verb. Pamela Munro's discussion of the negating suffix in Chickasaw ("Auxiliaries and Auxiliarization in Western Muskogean," 1984: 338–42) is of interest because it suggests that the Mvskoke negating suffix may be derived from a combination of suffixes. The examples of negation provided in Munro's data, however, are taken from Chickasaw, and students may find the comparison difficult to follow.

Sources regarding the effects of Anglo-European schooling on the Muskogee and Seminole communities are also rather scarce. K. Tsianina Lomawaima's exploration of Indian students' experiences at the Chilocco boarding school (*They Called It Prairie Light*, 1994) provides one portrayal of the treatment to which many Indian children were subjected in the early and mid-1900s. Many of the student interviews Lomawaima presents are from members of the Muskogee and Seminole Nations. Information about the numbers of schools and their financial situations is available in the Creek Nation files at the Oklahoma Historical Society, Oklahoma City. Unfortunately, no analytical or descriptive works have been written about students' experiences at neighborhood schools or about the quality of the education offered at these schools.

CHAPTER 11

Interrogatives

Interrogatives are questions. As in many other facets of the language, Mvskoke signals that a question is being asked by modifying the verb. All of the examples presented in the chapters up to this point have been declarative sentences—sentences that make statements. In each case, the declarative form has been indicated by the *-(e)s* suffix located on the verb.

Generally, when a question is created in Mvskoke, an interrogative suffix, generally ending in a vowel, is placed on the end of the verb, as in examples 1–4. The interrogative suffix takes the position of the declarative suffix in verb forms, as shown in diagram 11.1.

INTERROGATIVE FORM WHEN LAST SUFFIX DOES NOT END IN *Ē* OR *T*

In examples 1–4, the interrogative suffix is *-v*, which is used when the preceding verbal element, including the negating suffix and the past tense suffixes,

Type I verbs:

(Type II Object Prefix)	Verb Stem	Type I Subject	(Negating Suffix)	(Tense Suffix)	(Interrogative Suffix)

Type II verbs:

(Type D Prefix)	Type II Prefix	Verb Stem	(Negating Suffix)	(Tense Suffix)	(Interrogative Suffix)

Diagram 11.1. Position of Interrogative Suffix on Verbs

does not end with a final long ē or the consonant *t*. A different suffix, presented later, is used to form questions with verbs that end in ē or *t* after all other suffixes have been added. The interrogative suffix is indicated by the abbreviation "int" in the second line of each example.

1. Pipuce hvlkv?
   baby-def_subj crawl-3S-int
   'Is the baby crawling?'

2. Hoktucet opanv?
   girl-ind_subj dance-l_grd-3S-int
   'Is a girl dancing?'

3. Hompeckv?
   eat-l_grd-2S-int
   'Are you eating?'

4. Mēkusvpkv-cukon ayeckv?
   church-ind_obj go-l_grd-2S-int
   'Are you going to church?'

When a question is formed with the verb in the incompletive aspect, the l-grade applies to the stem vowel of the verb stem. This means that the stem vowel of the verb stem is lengthened when the present tense sentence is interrogative, just as it is when the sentence is declarative. The verb in example 1 does not show vowel lengthening, because the syllable in which the vowel occurs ends in an /l/ (see chapter 3 for more detail).

As in the questions just presented, when a question is asked about something in the past tense or about something involving the use of the negating suffix, the interrogative marker is added at the end of the verb, following all other suffixes, as in example 5.

5. Wakvpesē esikeckv?
   milk-def_obj drink-h_grd-2S-int
   'Did you just drink the milk?'

In examples 6a and 6b, the interrogative suffix follows a number of other suffixes. In 6a, the interrogative suffix *-v* follows the 2S subject suffix and the middle past tense suffix.

6a. Tvcakuce Cokorakko ohhonayeckvnkv?
Sunday Bible-def_obj read-ft_grd-2S-mp-int
'Did you read the Bible on Sunday?'

In example 6b, the interrogative suffix *-v* follows the 2S subject suffix, the negating suffix, and the middle past suffix.

6b. Tvcakuce Cokorakko ohhonvyeckekvnkv?
Sunday Bible-def_obj read-ft_grd-2S-neg-mp-int
'Didn't you read the Bible on Sunday?'

Interrogative Form When Last Suffix Ends in *Ē* or *T*

In examples 7a–7b and 8a–8b, the form of the interrogative suffix differs from what you have seen to this point. The final forms of the verbs in examples 7a–7b and 8a–8b (*heleswv sēyocetv* 'to take Indian medicine' and *pokkeccetv* 'to play ball', respectively), end in *-t* and *-ē* prior to the addition of the interrogative suffix. When the interrogative suffix is to be added to verbs ending in these sounds, it takes the form *-(ē)te*. When the preceding suffix ends in *t*, as it does in examples 7a and 7b, the interrogative suffix has the form *-ēte*. You will see this form used with the distant past tense *-mvt-*, where the final consonant of the past tense suffix is *t*.

7a. Hvtēyvnke heleswvn sēyoceckemvtēte?
hvtēyvnke heleswvn sēyoc-eck-emvt-ēte
little_while_ago medicine-ind_obj take_medicine-l_grd-2S-dp-int
'Were you taking medicine a little while ago?'

7b. Hvtēyvnke heleswvn sēyoceckekomvtēte?
hvtēyvnke heleswvn sēyoc-eck-eko-mvt-ēte
little_while_ago medicine-ind_obj
take_medicine-2S-neg-dp-int
'Weren't you taking medicine a little while ago?'

In examples 8a and 8b, the interrogative suffix has the form *-te*. This form is added when the preceding suffix ends in ē, as the remote past tense suffix *-vtē-* does.

8a. Hofonofen este vculat pokkēccvtēte?
hofonofen este vculat pokkēcc-vtē-te
long_time_ago man old-def_subj play_ball-l_grd-3S-rp-int
'Did the old man play ball a long time ago?'

8b. Hofonofen este vculat pokkeccekvtēte?
hofonofen este vculat pokkecc-ek-vtē-te
long_time_ago man old-def_subj play_ball-3S-neg-rp-int
'Didn't the old man play ball a long time ago?'

The addition of the interrogative suffix did not change the use of the verb grade associated with the past tenses in sentences 7a and 8a, which had not been negated (that is, h-grade for immediate past, falling tone grade for middle and distant pasts, and lengthened grade for remote past). The verb grades generally associated with the past tense forms were not used in examples 7b and 8b because of the addition of the negating suffix, not because of the addition of the interrogative suffix.

Questions Formed with Auxiliary Verbs

The interrogative suffix may be placed on the auxiliary verb suffix rather than on the primary verb. The verb stem *om-* of the auxiliary verb *ometv* 'to be' is used as the base in such interrogative constructions. When the interrogative suffix follows the auxiliary verb suffix, the *o* of the auxiliary verb undergoes any necessary grade changes (vowel lengthening or falling tone), and if the sentence is in the past tense, the appropriate past tense suffix is added before the interrogative suffix. The primary verb retains the subject and object markers, and the negating suffix (if it is used) is placed between the primary verb and the same-subject suffix. In general, an auxiliary verb can be used in present, middle past, distant past, and remote past tense constructions. It is not often used in immediate past (h-grade) constructions. Samples of interrogative sentences utilizing auxiliary verbs are provided in examples 9–12.

9. Hoktuce hotososat hvkihketomv?
girl skinny-def_subj cry-3S-ss-aux_vb-l_grd-int
'Is the skinny girl crying?'

10. Ervhvn vhopvketomvnkv?
his_older_brother-ind_obj 3Sdo-push-3S-ss-aux_vb-ft_grd-mp-int
'Did he push his older brother?'

11. Hvtēynvke cvtvhakv hompecketomvtēte?
little_while_ago blue_bread-def_obj
eat-2S-ss-aux_vb-ft_grd-dp-int
'Did you eat blue bread a little while ago?'

12. Hofonofen Cufe Nokose envsemetomvtēte?
long_time_ago Rabbit-def_subj Bear-def_obj
3SD-serve-3S-ss-aux_vb-ft_grd-rp-int
'Did Rabbit serve Bear a long time ago?'

Although it is not obvious, because the Mvskoke alphabet does not distinguish between long and short /o/, the /o/s in the preceding auxiliary verb suffixes are all long. In examples 10 and 11, the /o/ of the auxiliary verb has a falling tone as well. The vowels in the primary verbs have not been affected by any grade changes—the grade affects the auxiliary verb in each case.

Questions Formed with Question Words

Questions may also include a question word at the beginning of the sentence: for example, *stimvt* 'who', *naken/estomē* 'what', *stomēcet* 'how', *nakstowen/stowen* 'why', *stofvn* 'when', and *stvmen* 'where'. Often, when question words are used in a sentence, the interrogative suffix is added after the auxiliary verb suffix. However, it is also possible to form sentences beginning with question words without using an auxiliary verb suffix. Examples 13–17 show how questions containing question words are formed; some of them contain auxiliary verb suffixes.

13a. Stimvt pasv?
who sweep-l_grd-3S-int
'Who is sweeping?'

13b. Stimvt pasetomv?
who sweep-l_grd-3S-ss-aux_vb-int
'Who is sweeping?'

14a. Naken efv hompvnkv?
what dog-def_subj eat-ft_grd-3S-mp-int
'What did the dog eat?'

14b. Naken efv hompetomvnkv?
what dog-def_subj eat-3S-ss-aux_vb-ft_grd-mp-int
'What did the dog eat?'

15. Stomēcet vpēttēn hayeckvnkv?
how arbor-ind_obj build-ft_grd-2S-mp-int
'How did you build the arbor?'

16. Stowen cepanē nvfikeckv?
why boy-def_obj 3Sdo-hit-h_grd-2S-int
'Why did you hit the boy (just now)?'

17. Stofvn cvpvwv cencokopericvnkv?
when my_uncle-def_subj 2SD-visit-ft_grd-3S-mp-int
'When did my uncle visit you?'

Questions about Location

Questions beginning with 'where' are slightly different, depending on the item about which you are asking. The verb you use to ask for the location of an object will vary depending upon the form of the object and how easily it may be moved, as shown in the following list:

Large, immovable or hard-to-move objects: *likv*
Flat, hard-to-move objects: *likēte*
Easily moved objects: *ocv*
Persons and animate beings: noun + *tv*

Questions about the location of large, immovable or hard-to-move objects use the verb *liketv* 'to sit, be located'. When the object in question is immovable, the question form of the verb uses the interrogative suffix *-v*. Examples 18–20 show the form of questions about objects that, in general, are immovable.

18. Stvmen cencokon likv?
where 2S-house-ind_obj be_located-3S-int
'Where is your house?'

19. Stvmen Tvllvhvsse likv?
where Tallahassee be_located-3S-int
'Where is Tallahassee?' (Tallahassee is a ceremonial ground.)

20. Stvmen mēkusvpkv-cuko likv?
where church-def_obj be_located-3S-int
'Where is the church?'

When the question is about something that is difficult but possible to move and is flat, *liketv* is still used. However, in these cases, the verb takes the interrogative suffix *-ēte* rather than *-v*. This leads to examples like 21 and 22.

21. Stvmen topv likēte?
where bed-def_obj be_located-3S-int
'Where is the bed?'

22. Stvmen ohhompetv likēte?
where table-def_obj be_located-3S-int
'Where is the table?'

Note that each of these items is longer and broader than it is tall. Each item is also difficult but not impossible to move.

Questions about the location of smaller, easily moved objects use the verb *ocetv* 'to have, be located'. When questions about small, easily moved items are formed, the verb takes the *-v* form of the interrogative suffix. This leads to forms like those found in examples 23–25.

23. Stvmen cvtvhakvn ocv?
where blue_bread-ind_obj be_located-l_grd-3S-int
'Where is the blue bread?'

24. Stvmen espaskv ocv?
where broom-def_obj be_located-l_grd-3S-int
'Where is a broom?'

25. Stvmen cenkapv ocv?
where 2S-coat-def_obj be_located-l_grd-3S-int
'Where is your coat?'

Finally, questions about the location of a person or animate being are formed by placing *-tv* at the end of the noun phrase—that is, the noun and its modifiers. Neither the question word *stvmen* nor a verb is necessary when asking for the location of a person or other animate being. When a question about an animate being's location is presented in written form, the *-tv* suffix is translated as a locational interrogative, abbreviated "loc_int." Examples 26–28 show all that is necessary for creation of these kinds of questions.

26. Cerketv?
2S-father-loc_int
'Where is your father?'

27. Wakvtv?
cow-loc_int
'Where is the cow?'

28. Estucetv?
baby-loc_int
'Where is the baby?'

Questions with Type II Verbs

Up to this point, all of the questions have been formed with type I verbs. It is also possible to ask questions using type II verbs—you have seen some questions of this sort in the short conversations in earlier chapters. Questions utilizing type II verbs may be about states of being or may ask about actions.

As with type I verbs, questions are signified by adding a suffix to the type II verb. In general, questions formed with type II verbs that describe states of being (stative verbs) and that are constructed for the positive (not negated) incompletive aspect, h-grade, or remote past tense are asked by adding *-te* as a suffix. This is the same form of the suffix used with type I verbs ending in ē. Examples 29–32 show the position and form of the interrogative suffix on type II verbs.

29. Celvwēte?
2S-hungry-int
'Are you hungry?'

30. Owv kvsvppēte?
water-def_subj 3S-cold-int
'Is the water cold?'

31. Cecke lopicēte?
your_mother-def_subj 3S-kind/nice-int
'Is your mother nice?'

32. Wotko nuckelvtēte?
Raccoon-def_subj 3S-sleepy-rp-int
'Was Raccoon sleepy?' (As though in a story)

Questions formed with type II verb forms that do not end in a long ē take the *-v* suffix introduced earlier in the section for interrogatives formed with type I verbs. This suffix (*-v*) is added after all others (that is, tense and negation) have been attached to the verb. This leads to constructions such as the following:

33. Kafen ceyvcekv?
Coffee-ind_obj 2S-want-neg-int
'Don't you want some coffee?'

34. Cencvmmērrv?
2SD-1S-feel_sorry_for-int
'Do I feel sorry for you?'

35. Kafen ceyacvnkv?
Coffee-ind_obj 2S-want-mp-int
'Did you want some coffee?'

When the type II verb ends in the distant past tense suffix (*-mvt-*), the form of the interrogative marker is *-ēte,* just as it was for type I verbs ending in this suffix. Note that the inclusion of the negating suffix does not change the form of the interrogative marker used when the distant past tense suffix is on the verb. Examples 36 and 37 show the form of the interrogative suffix and its position on verbs in the distant past tense.

Figure 11.1. Playing the men's stickball game, Greenleaf Ceremnial Ground, September 1989. *Photograph courtesy of Bertha Tilkens and Linda Alexander.*

The men are fighting to get the ball, which is somewhere in the midst of them. When a player gets the ball from the ground, he may either run with it toward his goal or pass it to another player. Because the men are allowed to catch and handle the ball only with their ball sticks, which have small pockets (see the stick in the hand of the player on the right), players often end up huddling like this as they try to grab the ball from the ground.

36. Cekv ennokkemvtēte?
 2S-head-def_subj 3S-hurt-dp-int
 'Was your head hurting?'

37. Cecke lopicvtēte?
 your_mother-def_subj 3S-kind/nice-dp-int
 'Was your mother nice a long time ago?'

Vocabulary

Body Parts

Mvskoke	English
ena {II}	body
era {II}	back (of the body)
hokpe {II}	chest
ekv {II}	head
ekv-esse {II}	hair
torofv {II} *or* tvrofv {II}	face
cokwv {II}	mouth
nute {II}	tooth
yopo {II}	nose
torwv {II}	eye/eyes
hvcko {II}	ear/ears
nokwv {II}	neck
folowv {II}	shoulder
svkpv {II}	arm
enke {II}	hand
enke-wesakv {II}	finger
hvfe {II} *or* sokso {II}	hip
hvfececkv {II} *or* hvfe {II}	thigh
elempakko {II} *or* elenpakko {II}	calf (of the leg)
torkowv {II}	knee
ele {II}	foot/feet or leg
ele-wesakv {II}	toe, but not the big toe
ele-ecke {II}	big toe

Verbs

Mvskoke	English
tasketv {I}	to jump
ētenetv {I}	to stretch, as when waking up
vmelletv {I;II}	to point at
ohyofecetv {I} *or* mesētticetv {I}	to wink or blink
hvktēsketv {II/I}	to sneeze

ohoketv {II/I}	to cough
enkvrahpoletv {D}	to burp
yvcaketv {I;3}	to chew
rvtvtakketv {I}	to snore
nokmeletv {I;3}	to swallow
lvpotēcetv {I}	to straighten
takpvtoketv {I;II}	to bend
comokletv {I;II}	to bend over, stoop
mahetv {II}	to grow (of a person or an animal)

Exercises

Exercise 1

Translate the following sentences into English. In your translations, show each meaningful unit within each Mvskoke word, as is done in the second line of the examples in the chapter.

1. Pipuce cetorwvn vmeliyv?
2. Cerke yekcēt rvtvtakketomvtēte?
3. Rakko lvstet torkowv lvpotēcekvnkv?
4. Cehvktēsikv?
5. Naken hvlpvtvt hompvtēte?
6. Nakstowen wakvpesē tvlokfe eskeckekv?
7. Ceppucetv?
8. Stvmen este vculat vhyv?
9. Stofvn sasvkwv tvmkvtēte?
10. Stimvt cokv-heckv cukhofv hvsvtēcvnkv?

Exercise 2

Translate the following sentences into Mvskoke. Beneath your Mvskoke sentences, show each meaningful unit within each word, as is done in the second line of the examples in the chapter.

1. Was the baby crying a while ago?
2. Did the skinny girl just swallow some milk?
3. Where is your paternal aunt?

4. When did your mother wink?
5. Is John afraid of you?
6. Why is the dog chewing the chalk?
7. Did you just bend over?
8. How is the boy singing?
9. Who jumped?
10. Does your tooth hurt?

Exercise 3

For each item listed below, provide the correct form of the verb you would use to ask about the location of the item. Then, explain why you chose that particular form of the verb. An example is provided for you:

house likv Because the object is immovable

1. goat
2. airplane
3. desk
4. married woman
5. stream
6. hill
7. big piece of plywood
8. refrigerator
9. mouse
10. chair

Exercise 4

For each of the sentences in the following list, create a question for which the sentence would be an appropriate answer. Do not be concerned that there is only one "correct" question; there may be multiple questions you could ask to receive some of the answers presented below. Simply come up with a question that would cause someone to answer with the sentence provided. An example follows:

> Answer: Paksvnkē, svtohkiyvnks. Question: Stofvn svtohkeckvnkv?
> Another possible question: Nake paksvnkē estomet cvnkv?

1. Mvnks, kafen cvyvceks.
2. Vpēttēt hvsaklatkv likes.
3. Nettvcako ecuse Joe hvpo hayemvts.
4. Nokose lvstat hēyvn hueretos.
5. Pipucet ohokētomvnks.
6. Ehi, cvtorkowv ennokkētos.
7. Mvnks, cepanē rakko hvtkan ohliketomvnks.
8. Cvpvwv nak-eshoccicetv cokvn oces.
9. Erkenvkvn vce tvklik-kvmoksē asemwiyiyvnks.
10. Hofonof Cufe ētenvtēs.

Exercise 5

Think of five questions you can ask other class members. In class, your teacher will ask you to ask another student one of your questions. The student you ask will have to answer your question. The student who has just answered your question will then turn to another student and ask him or her a question. The entire class should thus have to ask and answer at least one question. Here is an example of how this exercise will be performed in class:

Student 1: Mvhayvtv?
Student 2: Mvhayv mvhakv-cuko liketos.
Student 2: Stimvt cokv hoccicvnkv?
Student 3: Cokv hocciciyvnks. [And so forth]

Exercise 6

Create an answer for each of the following questions. Do not be concerned that there is only one "correct" answer; there may be multiple answers you could give to some of these questions. Simply come up with one answer that would be appropriate for each question. An example is provided for you:

Question: Stofvn cokv-hēcv ahkopvnkv-ēkvnv ayvnkv?
Answer: Cokv-hēcv ahkopvnkv-ēkvnv vhyes.
Another possible answer: Hofonof cokv-hēcv ahkopvnkv-ēkvnv ayemvts.

1. Stvmen sasvkwv tvmketomvnkv?
2. Nake efvt hompv?
3. Oewvn kvsvppēte?

4. Cerke rvtvtakikv?
5. Stomēcet pipucet hvlkv?
6. Nake cvckuce ascenwiyv?
7. Sokhvn ohlikeckvnkv?
8. Hoktuce eshoccickv lvsten atvkkēsvtēte?
9. Stimvt enkvrahpolvnkv?
10. Vcvmelleckv?

The Role of Elders in Mvskoke Life

As children, Mvskoke people are taught to respect their elders. The elders are to be respected because of the knowledge and wisdom they have gained through life experience.

Mvskoke elders usually like to tell stories that impress a picture in young people's minds and that carry morals. Elders give young people courage by offering them "food for thought" and letting them know about the old ways. Young people also learn by hearing what the elders have experienced in life—their lessons, their hardships, and their rewards. They give encouragement and insight into the surrounding world.

Mvskoke young people should ask their elders, "Why?" and then listen to them. They can give answers, though maybe not in a straightforward way. Instead, they may offer something to think about that will lead the younger person to search for the meaning. In their wisdom, elders know that one can learn from thinking through thoughts that are left with the hearer. From this, a young person can learn how to search for meaning in things he or she experiences or hears—and some of the things one hears from the elders may be stories about themselves or animals.

The stories Mvskoke elders tell about animals are usually about Rabbit, Fox, or Turtle. Rabbit is in many stories because of his crafty ways. Fox is very sly. Turtle is important because of his slow motion and his patience.

In today's society, elders are not always held in high esteem, as they should be. In the past, Mvskoke elders were highly respected in their community or ceremonial ground because of their knowledge and wisdom. They were often consulted for guidance.

Mvskoke children were taught never to call an elder by his or her given name. They were to call the elders grandma, grandpa, aunt, or uncle. This could be confusing, because children had both natural, paternal and maternal relatives and clan relatives. However, clan relatives were just as important as blood relatives. As children grew older, they began to understand the difference between the clan and blood relationships.

Whether you are Mvskoke or not, it is wise to look to and talk with elders for guidance in whatever you undertake in life. They have had experiences from which they have gained knowledge and wisdom, and you should try to learn from them. Mvskoke elders are willing to help young people to understand and grow strong in their beliefs so that Mvskoke culture and traditions will live on. After all, where would the Mvskoke people be today if it were not for the elders' wisdom and knowledge?

Suggested Readings

There are other ways of forming questions that we have not discussed in this chapter, primarily because linguists are still debating them. For information about these other forms, some of which are certainly used in the Mvskoke-speaking community, readers are directed to Karen M. Booker's "Nasalization and Question Formation in Creek" (1992) and Jack B. Martin's "Interrogation in Creek" (1988). In both sources, the term "nasalization" refers to an *n*-like quality added to a vowel sound. This quality is part of another verb grade, as well as of interrogatives, but it is best reserved for an advanced textbook.

Elders are extremely important in the Muskogee and Seminole communities. As stated in the essay, they are responsible for passing along traditional knowledge and lore to younger generations. Students can ascertain that elders have long been regarded as repositories of knowledge in these communities by paying attention to the kinds of consultants earlier anthropologists, such as John R. Swanton (see his works listed in the bibliography under the dates 1928a and 1928b), Alexander Spoehr (1942, 1947), and Frank G. Speck (1907, 1909, 1911), worked with to collect the information they published. Perhaps the best way of learning about the role of elders in current Muskogee and Seminole society is to attend some of the public celebrations held in eastern Oklahoma each year and talk with some of the people attending them. You will find that elders play a central role in the organization of these events, and if there are venues for teaching and learning, elders will be central figures at those sites. Listen to their words, treat them with respect, and behave as they suggest, and you will find yourself gaining knowledge that you may someday pass on to a younger generation.

Glossary

Mvskoke to English

The following glossary includes all the Mvskoke words used in this book. In addition to a pronunciation guide and an English translation for each entry, it provides information about whether and how a word is modified for usage in a Mvskoke sentence and a list of related forms for the same item or activity.

A typical noun entry contains the Mvskoke spelling of the word followed by the phonemic (linguistic) spelling in parentheses, the English translation, and any alternate forms of the same word. When applicable, the possessive prefix set used to indicate ownership or control over the noun is included in brackets following the phonemic spelling. Examples of two noun entries are the following:

ayo (á:·yo)	hawk
eccuste (ic·cós·ti) {II}	a man's daughter

The possessive prefix set used to mark the person to whom the daughter is related is shown in brackets after the phonemic spelling (in the example, the {II} following ic·cós·ti). Use of the possessive prefix sets is covered in chapter 6.

Verb entries follow the pattern of noun entries, but the symbols in brackets provide information about the prefix and suffix sets used to conjugate the verb. A representative type I verb entry is the following:

hecetv (hi·cí·ta) {I;II}	to see

A representative type II verb entry is the following:

cekfē (cík·fi:) {II} thick

The Mvskoke spelling of the verb is shown first, followed by the phonemic spelling in parentheses and then, in brackets, the prefix and suffix sets used in verb formation. Finally, the English translation is given, as well as any alternative or related forms of the verb. Many words equivalent to English adjectives will show that the type II prefix set is used, because these are actually stative verbs in Mvskoke. Many of the words may also be used as adjectives in noun phrases, however, and when this is the case they are treated as described in chapter 3. Chapters 5, 6, and 7 explain how the different forms of prefixes and suffixes are used to create verb forms appropriate for use in Mvskoke sentences.

In some of the verb translations, you will notice that "(of one)" appears after the English equivalent. This phrase indicates that the verb stem is changed significantly when plural subjects are performing the action, but you may use any of the singular subject markers with these verbs.

A

afvckē (a:·fác·ki:) {II}: happy
ahkopvnetv (ah·ko·pa·ni·tá) {I}: to play
ahkopvnkv-ēkvnv (a:h·ko·pan·ka·i:·ka·ná): playground
ahvlvtetv (a:·ha·la·ti·tá) {I;II}: to pull in the direction of the speaker
akketv (a:k·ki·tá) {I;II}: to bite
aksomketv (a:k·som·ki·tá) {II}: to be baptized
Aksomkvlke (a:k·som·kâl·ki): Baptists; *also* Ue Aksomkvlke
apvske (a:·pás·ki): a drink made of finely ground cornmeal from parched corn
arakkicetv (a:·ła:k·ke:·ci·tá) {I;II}: to worship
aswiyetv (a:s·we:·yi·tá) {I;3;D}: to pass (something) to someone
atvkkesetv (a:·tak·ki·sí·ta) {I;II}: to pick up
atvmo (a:·ta·mó): car
awotsvnetv (a:·wot·sa·ní·ta) {I;3}: to pour out a liquid
ayo (á:·yo): hawk

C

cahkē (cá:h·ki:) {II}: shallow (of water)
catē (cá:·ti:) {II}: red
catosē (ca:·to·sí:) {II}: pink
cekfē (cík·fi:) {II}: thick
cekhē (cík·hi:) {II;D}: piled up (for wood, rocks, trash, etc.)
celayetv (ci·la:·yi·tá) {I;II}: to touch, feel
cenvpaken (ci·na·pâ:·kin): eight
cepanē (ci·pá:·ni:): boy
cesse (cís·si): mouse
cetto (cít·to): snake
cetto mekko (cít·to mík·ko): rattlesnake
cēme (cí:·mi): you (one person); *also* cēmeu
cēmeu (cí:·mio): you (one person); *also* cēme
Cēsvs (cí:·sas): Jesus
cofe (co·fí): rabbit, Rabbit of legends; *also* cufe
coko (co·kó): house
coko vfastv (co·kó a·fá:s·ta): deacon; *also* tēkvnv
cokopericetv (co·ko·pi·łe:·ci·tá) {I;D}: to visit
cokv (co·ká): book or paper
cokv esyvhiketv (co·ká is·ya·he:·ki·tá): hymnal
cokv-heckv (co·ka·híc·ka): school; *also* mvhakv-cuko
cokv-heckv cukhofv (co·ka·híc·ka cok·ho·fá): classroom
cokv-hēcv (co·ka·hí:·ca): student
Cokvrakko (co·ka·łá:k·ko): Bible
cokwv (cók·wa) {II}: mouth
comokletv (co·mok·li·tá) {I;II}: to bend over, stoop
Cosvlke (co:·sâl·ki): Jewish people
cufe (co·fí): rabbit, Rabbit of legends; *also* cofe
cukhofv (cok·ho·fá): room in a building or house; *also* nvthofv
custake (cos·tá:·ki): egg
cutkosē (cot·ko·sí:) {II}: little
cvhkēpen (cah·kî:·pin): five
cvlvkloketv (ca·lak·lo:·ki·tá) {I}: to gobble (like a turkey)
cvmpē (cám·pi:) {II}: sweet
cvpakkē (ca·pá:k·ki:) {II}: angry
cvstvlē (cas·ta·lí:): watermelon

cvto (ca·tó): rock, stone
cvtvhakv (ca·ta·há:·ka): blue bread
cvyayvkē (ca·ya:·ya·kí:) {II}: quiet

E

eccus hoktē (ic·cós hók·ti:) {II}: a woman's daughter
eccus honvnwv (ic·cós ho·nán·wa) {II}: a woman's son
eccuste (ic·cós·ti) {II}: a man's daughter
ecerwv (i·cíł·wa) {II}: a woman's brother
ecerwv mvnetosat (i·cíł·wa ma·ni·to·sát) {II}: a man's younger brother
echaswv (ic·há:s·wa): beaver
Echaswvlke (ic·ha:s·wâl·ki): Beaver Clan
ecke (íc·ki) {II}: mother (of either a man or a woman)
eckuce (ic·ko·cí) {II}: maternal aunt (of either a man or a woman)
eco (i·có): deer
Ecovlke (i·co·âl·ki): Deer Clan
ecuse (i·có·si) {II}: a man's younger brother, a woman's younger sister
ecuse mvnetat (i·có·si ma·ni·tá:t) {II}: a woman's younger sister
efuce (i·fó·ci): puppy
  vmefuce (am·i·fo·cí): my puppy
efv (i·fá): dog
ehessē, hoktē (hók·ti: i·hís·si:): married woman
ehi (i·hé:): yes
ehicv, honvnwv (ho·nán·wa i·hé:·ca): married man
Eholē (i·ho·lí:): November ('Frost Month')
ekv (i·ká) {II}: head
ekv-esse (i·ka·is·sí) {II}: hair
ekvnhvlwuce (i·kan·hal·wo·cí): hill
ele (i·lí) {II}: foot, feet, or leg
ele-ecke (i·li·ic·kí) {II}: big toe
elempakko (i·lim·pá:k·ko) {II}: calf (of the leg); *also* elenpakko
elenpakko (i·lin·pá:k·ko) {II}: calf (of the leg); *also* elempakko
ele-ohsehoyetv (i·li·oh·si·ho·yí·ta): footstool
ele-wesakv (i·li·wi·sá:·ka) {II}: toe, but not the big toe
elvwē (i·láw·i:) {II}: hungry; *also* lvwē
em enhonretv (im in·hon·łi·tá) {I;D/II;D}: to believe in, trust, depend on (something or someone)
em enhotetv (im in·ho·tí·ta) {II;D}: to be uneasy about

em etetaketv (im i·ti·ta:·ki·tá) {I;D}: to be ready for something
em etetakuecetv (im i·ti·ta:·koy·ci·tá) {I;D}: to prepare something or someone
emetv (i·mí·ta) {I;3;D}: to give something to someone
em mapohicetv (im ma:·po·he:·ci·tá) {I;D}: to listen to; *also* mapohicetv
em merretv (im mił·łi·tá) {II;D}: to feel sorry for
em mēkusvpetv (im mi:·ko·sa·pi·tá) {I;D}: to pray for
em mvyattēcetv (im ma·ya:t·ti:·ci·tá) {I;D}: to wave at
em oponvyetv (im o·po·na·yí·ta) {I;D}: to talk to someone; *also* em ponvyetv
em penkvletv (im pin·ka·lí·ta) {II;D}: to be afraid of; *also* em penkvlē
em penkvlē (im pin·ka·lí:) {II;D}: to be afraid of; *also* em penkvletv
em ponvyetv (im po·na·yí·ta) {I;D}: to talk to someone; *also* em oponvyetv
em vcvnēyetv (ima·ca·ni:·yi·tá) {I;D}: to peek at; *also* mvcvnēyetv
em vkerretv (im a·kił·łi·tá) {I;D}: to fool, trick; *also* mvkerretv
em vnvtaksetv (im a·na·ta:k·si·tá) {I;D}: to look up at something or someone
em vsehetv (im a·si·hi·tá) {I;D}: to give a warning to
ena (i·ná:) {II}: body
enahvmke (i·na:·hám·ki) {II}: cousin (of a man or a woman); *also* enahvnke
enahvnke (i·na:·hán·ki) {II}: cousin (of a man or a woman); *also* enahvmke
encvpvkketv (in·ca·pak·ki·tá) {II;D}: to be mad at
enfotketv (in·fot·ki·tá) {I;D}: to whistle at
enheckv (in·híc·ka): color
enhomecetv (in·ho·mi·cí·ta) {II;D}: to be mad at, hate; *also* enhomecē; *also see* encvpvkketv
enhomecē (in·ho·mi·cí:) {II;D}: to be mad at, hate; *also* enhomecetv; *also see* encvpvkketv
Enhonnv lvstē (in·hón·na lás·ti:): Catholics; *also* Etohwelēpvlke and Tohwelēpvlke
enhonrē (in·hón·łi:) {II}: hopeful
enke (in·kí) {II}: hand
enke-wesakv (in·ki·wi·sá:·ka) {II}: finger
enkvpicetv (in·ka·pe:·ci·tá) {I;D}: to share with someone
enkvpvketv (in·ka·pa·kí·ta) {I;D}: to leave, go away from; *also* vyepetv
enkvrahpoletv (in·ka·ła:h·po·lí·ta) {D}: to burp
enletketv (in·lit·ki·tá) {I;D}: to run away from
enlvksetv (in·lak·si·tá) {I;D}: to lie to
ennokkē (in·nók·ki:) {D}: to hurt, be sore
Ennvrkvpv (in·nał·ka·pá): Wednesday
enokkē (i·nók·ki:) {II}: to be sick
epoca (i·po·cá:) {II}: grandfather (of either a man or a woman)

epose (i·pó·si) {II}: grandmother or paternal aunt (of either a man or a woman)
eppuce (ip·pó·ci) {II}: a man's son
epvwv (i·pá·wa) {II}: maternal uncle (of either a man or a woman); *also* pvwv
era (i·łá:) {II}: back (of the body)
erke (íł·ki) {II}: father (of either a man or a woman)
erkenvketv (ił·ki·na·kí·ta) {I;D}: to preach to
erkenvkv (ił·ki·na·ká): preacher
erkuce (ił·kó·ci) {II}: paternal uncle (of either a man or a woman)
ervhv (i·łá·ha) {II}: a man's older brother, a woman's older sister
ervhv hoktvlēcat (i·łá·ha hok·ta·lí:·ca:t) {II}: a woman's older sister
ervhv vculicat (i·łá·ha a·co·lé:·ca:t) {II}: a man's older brother
es enhomahtetv (is in·ho·ma:h·ti·tá) {I;D}: to lead a dance
es fekcvkhē (is fik·cák·hi:) {II;D}: to be jealous of
esetv (i·sí·ta) {I;II}: to take
eshoccickv (is·ho:c·cé:c·ka): pencil
eshoccickv lvste (is·ho:c·cé:c·ka lás·ti): blackboard chalk
eskerretv (is·kił·łi·tá) {I;II}: to remember
esketv (is·kí·ta) {I;3}: to drink
eslafkv (is·lá:f·ka): knife
espaskv (is·pá:s·ka): broom
este (ís·ti): person, man; *also* miste
este vcule (ís·ti a·có·li): old man
estenkehute (ist·in·ki·hó·ti): glove
estimvt (is·te:·mát): who; *also* stimvt
estomē (is·to·mí:): what; *also* naken
estomēcet (is·to·mí:·cit): how; *also* stomēcet
estuce (is·tó·ci): child
esyomen (is·yó:m·in): together with
etemvretv (i·ti·ma·łí·ta) {I;II}: to race (of two or more)
etenherketv (i·tin·hił·ki·tá) {I;II}: to make peace with each other
etepoyetv (i·ti·po·yí·ta) {I;II}: to fight
eteyametv (i·ti·ya:·mi·tá) {I;3}: to mix, stir
etkolē (it·ko·lí:) {II}: to feel cold (of an animate being)
eto (i·tó): tree, wood
etohkvletv (i·toh·ka·lí·ta) {I}: to add
etohwelēpkv (i·toh·wí·lí:p·ka): cross, crucifix; *also* tohwelēpkv
Etohwelēpvlke (i·toh·wí·li:p·âl·ki): Catholics; *also* Tohwelēpvlke and Enhonnv lvstē

etokonhe (i·to·kón·hi): ball stick; *also* tokonhe
ewvnhkē (i·wánh·ki:) {II}: thirsty; *also* wvnkē
eyvcetv (i·ya·ci·tá) {II;3}: to like, want, need

Ē

ēhotkē (i:·hót·ki:) {II}: to be dangerous
ēkvnv (i:·ka·ná): ground, earth, dirt
ēlvwēcetv (i:·la·wi:·ci·tá) {I}: to fast
ēpaken (i:·pâ:·kin): six
ētenetv (i:·ti·ní·ta) {I}: to stretch, as when waking up
ētvsē (i:·ta·sí:) {II}: to be a little different
ēwvnwv (i:·wán·wa) {II}: a man's sister
ēyvcayē (i:·ya·cá:·yi:) {II}: careful
ēyvcayēcetv (i:·ya·ca:·yi:·ci·tá) {I}: to be careful

F

fekcvkhē (fik·cák·hi:) {II}: to be jealous
fekhvmkē (fik·hám·ki:) {II}: to be brave
feknokkē (fik·nók·ki:) {II}: sad
Flati (flá:·te:): Friday
fo (fó:): bee
fo-encvmpē (fo:·in·cam·pí:): honey
folowv (fo·ló·wa) {II}: shoulder
foswv (fós·wa): bird; *also* fuswv
Foswvlke (fos·wâl·ki): Bird Clan
fuswv (fós·wa): bird; *also* foswv
fvccvlik hoyanen (fac·ca·lé:k ho·yâ:·nin): afternoon
fvmpē (fám·pi:) {II}: smelly or stinking

H

hayē (há:·yi:) {II}: hot; *also* hiyē
hecetv (hi·cí·ta) {I;II}: to see
heles hayv (hi·lís há:·ya): medicine man
heleswv (hi·lís·wa): medicine
heleswv sēyocetv (hi·lís·wa si:·yo·cí·ta) {I}: to take Indian medicine
heneha (hi·ni·há:): second chief

hensci (híns·ce:): hello
heromē (hi·łó·mi:) {**II**}: kind, generous
heromosē (hi·łô:·mo·si:) {**II;D**}: kind, generous to
Hesaketv Messē (hi·sa:·ki·tá mís·si:): 'Giver of Life/Breath,' Creator, God
hēnrē (hí:n·łi:) {**II**}: good
hēyvn (hí:·yan): here
hiyē (hé:·yi:) {**II**}: hot; *also* hayē
hoccicetv (hoc·ce:·ci·tá) {**I;3**}: to write
hocefketv (ho·cif·ki·tá) {**II**}: to be named
hockvte (hoc·ka·tí): flour
hofonē haken (ho·fó·ni: hâ:·kin): after a long time
hofonofen (ho·fô:·no·fin): a long time ago
hokkolen (hok·kô:·lin): two
hokpe (hók·pi) {**II**}: chest (of the body)
hoktē (hók·ti:): woman
hoktē ehessē (hók·ti: i·hís·si:): married woman
hoktuce (hok·to·cí): girl
hoktvke semevpayv (hok·ta·kí si·mi·a·pá:·ya): women's leader
hoktvlē (hok·ta·lí:): old woman
holattē (ho·lá:t·ti:) {**II**}: blue
holwvkē (hol·wa·kí:) {**II**}: naughty
holwvyēcē (hol·wa·yí:·ci:) {**II**}: mean, unkind
hompetv (hom·pi·tá): food
hompetv (hom·pi·tá) {**I;3**}: to eat, taste
hompetv hakv (hom·pi·tá há:·ka): meal
hompetv hayv (hom·pi·tá há:·ya): cook, chef
homuce (ho:·mo·cí): black pepper
honerv (ho·ní·ła): north; *also* kvsvppofv
honnē (hón·ni:) {**II**}: heavy
honvnwv (ho·nán·wa): man, male
honvnwv ehicv (ho·nán·wa i·hé:·ca): married man
hoporrenkv (ho·poł·łín·ka): penny
hopvketv (ho·pa·ki·tá) {**I;II**}: to push someone or something
hotosē (ho·tó·si:) {**II**}: tired
hotososē (ho·tô:·so·si:) {**II**}: skinny, thin (of an animate being)
hotvle (ho·tá·li): wind, breeze
Hotvlē Hvse (ho·tá·li: ha·sí): February ('Windy Month')
Hotvlkvlke (ho·tal·kâl·ki): Wind Clan
hoyv (hó:·ya): net

hueretv (hoy·łi·tá) {I}: to stand (of one)
hvcce (hác·ci): river
hvccuce (hac·co·cí): stream
hvcko (hác·ko) {II}: ear or ears
hvfe (ha·fí) {II}: hip; *also* sokso or thigh; *also* hvfececkv
hvfececkv (ha·fi·cíc·ka) {II}: thigh; *also* hvfe
hvkihketv (ha·ke:h·ki·tá) {I}: to cry (of one)
hvktēsketv (hak·ti:s·ki·tá) {II/I}: to sneeze
hvlketv (hal·ki·tá) {I}: to crawl (of one)
hvlpvtv (hal·pa·tá): alligator
Hvlpvtvlke (hal·pa·tâl·ki): Alligator Clan
hvlvlatkē (ha·la·lá:t·ki:) {II}: slow
hvlwe tvlofv (hál·wi ta·ló·fa): heaven
hvmken (hám·kin): one (numeral)
hvpo (ha·pó:) {II}: one's camp; *also* hvpohakv
hvpo hayetv (ha·pó: ha:·yi·tá) {I;3}: to make camp
hvpohakv (ha·po:·há:·ka) {II}: one's camp; *also* hvpo
hvsaklatkv (ha·sa:k·lá:t·ka): west
hvse (ha·sí): sun
hvsossv (ha·sós·sa): east
hvsvtecetv (ha·sa·ti·cí·ta) {I;3}: to clean (one thing)
hvte (ha·tí): now
hvtēyvnke (ha·ti:·yán·ki): a little while ago
hvtkē (hát·ki:) {II}: white
hvyetv (ha·yí·ta) {I;3}: to build or make
Hvyo Rakko (ha·yó ła:k·ko): August ('Big Harvest' or 'Big Summer')
Hvyuce (ha·yó·ci): July ('Little Harvest' or 'Little Summer')

I

imapohicetv (e:·ma:·po·he:·ci·tá) {I;D}: to eavesdrop on

K

kaccv (ká:c·ca): tiger
Kaccvlke (ka:c·câl·ki): Tiger Clan
kafe (ká:·fi): coffee
kapv (ká:·pa): coat
keco (ki·có): a mortar

kecvpe (ki·cá·pi): a pestle
kerretv (kił·łi·tá) {I;II}: to know (someone or something)
Kē Hvse (kí: ha·sí): May ('Mulberry Month')
kērrepetv (ki:ł·łi·pí·ta) {II}: to understand
kocoknē (ko·cók·ni:) {II}: short
kolēppa (ko·li:p·pá:): firefly
kolvpaken (ko·la·pâ:·kin): seven
kometv (ko·mí·ta) {I;3}: to hope for; *also* kowetv
kono (ko·nó): skunk
korretv (koł·łi·tá) {I;3}: to dig
kowetv (ko·wí·ta) {I;3}: to hope for; *also* kometv
Kvco Hvse (ka·có ha·sí): June ('Blackberry Month')
kvrpē (káł·pi:) {II}: dry
kvsvppē (ka·sáp·pi:) {II}: cold (of inanimate things)
kvsvppofv (ka·sap·pó:·fa): north; *also* honerv

L

lanē (lá:·ni:) {II}: green, yellow
lekothofv (li·kot·hó:·fa): south; *also* wvhvlv
letketv (lit·ki·tá) {I}: to run (of one)
liketv (le:·ki·tá) {I}: to sit (of one), to be located
locv (lo·cá): turtle, turtle shell, Turtle of stories
lopicetv (lo·pe:·ci·tá) {II;D}: to be nice to
lopicē (lo·pé:·ci:) {II}: nice, kind
lowakē (lo·wá:·ki:) {II}: weak
lvffetv (laf·fi·tá) {I;3}: to cut many times (as when making repeated slices)
lvpotēcetv (la·po·ti:·ci·tá) {I;D}: to correct or straighten
lvokē (láw·ki:) {II}: deep (of water)
lvstē (lás·ti:) {II}: black
lvtketv (lat·ki·tá) {II/I}: to fall
lvwē (la·wí:) {II}: hungry; *also* elvwē

M

mahetv (ma:·hi·tá) {II}: to grow (of a person or animal)
mahē (má:·hi:) {II}: tall
mahēcetv (ma:·hi:·ci·tá) {I;II}: to grow (of grain or plants)
maketv (ma:·ki·tá) {I;II}: to say, speak to someone

mapohicetv (ma:·po·he:·ci·tá) {**I;D**}: to listen to; *also* em mapohicetv
mecetv (mi·cí·ta) {**I;3**}: to try, attempt something
mehaketv ((i)m·i·ha:·ki·tá) {**I;D**}: to wait for (someone or something)
mekko (mík·ko): king, chief
melletv (mil·li·tá) {**I**}: to point
mesētticetv (mi·si:t·te:·ci·tá) {**I**}: to wink or blink; *also* ohyofecetv
mēkusvpetv (mi:·ko·sa·pi·tá) {**I**}: to pray
mēkusvpkv (mi:·ko·sáp·ka): prayer, service
mēkusvpkv-cuko (mi:·ko·sáp·ka có·ko): church
miste (mé:s·ti): man, person; *also* este
mucv-nettv (mo·ca·nít·ta): today
munkat (món·ka:t): or
mvcvnēyetv ((i)m·a·ca·ni:·yi·tá) {**I;D**}: to peek at; *also* em vcvnēyetv
mvhakv-cuko (ma·ha:·ka·có·ko): school; *also* cokv-heckv
mvhayetv (ma·ha:·yi·tá) {**I;D**}: to teach
mvhayv (ma·há:·ya): teacher
mvliketv (ma·le:·ki·tá): clan
mvnhēretv (man·hi:·łi·tá) {**II;D**}: to enjoy
mvkerretv ((i)m·a·kił·łi·tá) {**I;D**}: to fool, trick; *also* em vkerretv
mvnks (manks): no
Mvnte (mán·ti): Monday
Mvnte enhvyvtke (mán·ti in·ha·yát·ki): Tuesday
mvt (mat): that, that one
mvto (ma·tó): thank you
mvto kicetv (ma·tó ke:·ci·tá) {**I;II**}: to give thanks, say thanks (to someone)

N

nak-eshoccicetv cokv (na:k·is·ho:c·ce:·ci·tá co·ká): notebook
nake (ná:·ki): what
naken (ná:·kin): something, what; *also* estomē
nakstomen (na:k·sto:·mín): why; *also* nakstowen, stowen, and stomen
nakstowen (na:k·sto:·wín): why; *also* nakstomen, stowen, and stomen
naorkv (na:·ó:ł·ka): sinner
nehē (ni·hí:) {**II**}: to be fat
nerē-isē (ni·łí:·ê:·si:): last night
nesetv (ni·sí·ta) {**I;3**}: to buy
neskv-coko (nis·ka·có·ko): retail store, shop
Nettv opvnkv (nít·ta o·pán·ka): Ribbon Dance

Nettvcako (nit·ta·cá:·ko): Sunday; *also* Tvcakuce
Nettvcako ecuse (nit·ta·cá:·ko i·có·si): Saturday
nēha (ní:·ha:): oil, cooking fat
nocetv (no·cí·ta) {I/II}: to sleep (of one)
nockelē (noc·ki·lí:) {II}: to be sleepy; *also* nuckelē
nokmeletv (nok·mi·lí·ta) {I;3}: to swallow
nokose (no·kó·si): bear
Nokosvlke (no·ko·sâl·ki): Bear Clan
nokricetv (nok·łe:·ci·tá) {I;3}: to burn
nokwv (nók·wa) {II}: neck
noricetv (no·łe:·ci·tá) {I;3}: to cook
nuckelē (noc·ki·lí:) {II}: to be sleepy, *also* nockelē
nute (no·tí) {II}: tooth
nvfketv (naf·ki·tá) {I;II}: to hit
Nvrkvpv enhvyvtke (nał·ka·pá in·ha·yát·ki): Thursday
nvthofv (nat·ho·fá): room in a building or house; *also* cukhofv

O

ocetv (o:·ci·tá) {I;3}: to have, to be located
oewv (óy·wa): water; *also* owv and uewv
Ohfēskvlke (oh·fi:s·kâl·ki): Presbyterians; *also* Uewv Ohfēskvlke
ohhompetv (oh·hom·pi·tá): table
ohhonvyetv (oh·ho·na·yí·ta) {I}: to read
Ohkalvlke (oh·ka:·lâl·ki): Methodists; *also* Uewv Ohkalvlke
ohliketv (oh·le:·ki·tá) {I;3}: to ride (of one), to sit on
ohmēkusvpkv (oh·mi:·ko·sáp·ka): pew
ohoketv (o·ho:·ki·tá) {II/I}: to cough
ohrolopē (oh·ło·lo·pí:): year
ohrolopēyvnke (oh·ło·lo·pi:·yán·ki): last year
ohsolotketv (oh·so·lo:t·ki·tá) {II;D}: to slide toward
ohyofecetv (oh·yo·fi·cí·ta) {I}: to wink or blink; *also* mesētticetv
okcatē (ok·cá:·ti:) {II}: purple; *also* pvrkomv
okcvnwv (ok·cán·wa): salt
okhacē (ok·há:·ci:) {II}: amusing, funny
okhacē (ok·há:·ci:) {II;D}: to be amusing to
oklanē (ok·lá:·ni:) {II}: brown
okofkē (o·kóf·ki:): muddy
okotafketv (ok·o·ta:f·ki·tá) {I}: to float (of one); *also* okvtafketv

okvtafketv (ok·a·ta:f·ki·tá) {I}: to float (of one); *also* okotafketv
ometv (o·mí·ta) {I}: to be; *also* owetv
omiyetv (o·me:·yi·tá) {I}: to swim; *also* vklopetv
opanv (o·pá:·na): dancer
oponayv (o·po·ná:·ya): speaker
oponvkv (o·po·na·ká): story
oponvkv hērv honayetv (o·po·na·ká hí:·ła ho·na:·yi·tá): sermon; *also* ponvkv hērv honayetv
oponvyetv (o·po·na·yí·ta) {I}: to talk
opvnetv (o·pa·ni·tá) {I}: to dance
opvnkv ēkvnv (o·pán·ka i:·ka·ná): ceremonial ground (stompground); *also* pvnkv ēkvnv
oskē (os·kí:): rain
osten (ô:s·tin): four
ostvpaken (os·ta·pâ:·kin): nine
Otvwoskuce (o·ta·wo:s·ko·cí): September ('Little Chestnut Month')
Otvwoskv Rakko (o·ta·wó:s·ka łá:k·ko): October ('Big Chestnut Month')
owetv (o·wí·ta) {I}: to be; *also* ometv
owv (ó:·wa): water; *also* oewv and uewv
owvlvste eshoccickv (o:·wa·lás·ti is·ho:c·cé:c·ka): pen

P

paksvnkē (pa:k·san·kí:): yesterday
pale-hokkolen (pá:·li hok·kô:·lin): twenty
palen (pá:·lin): ten
palen-cenvpohkaken (pá:·lin ci·na·poh·ká:·kin): eighteen
palen-cvhkēpohkaken (pá:·lin cah·kî:·poh·ka:·kin): fifteen
palen-ēpohkaken (pá:·lin i:·poh·ká:·kin): sixteen
palen-hokkolohkaken (pá:·lin hok·ko·loh·ká:·kin): twelve
palen-hvmkentvlaken (pá:·lin ham·kin·ta·lá:·kin): eleven
palen-kolvpohkaken (pá:·lin ko·la·poh·ká:·kin): seventeen
palen-ostohkaken (pá:·lin os·toh·ká:·kin): fourteen
palen-ostvpohkaken (pá:·lin os·ta·poh·ká:·kin): nineteen
palen-tutcenohkaken (pá:·lin tot·cin·oh·ká:·kin): thirteen
penkvlē (pin·ka·lí:) {II;D}: afraid, scared (of something)
perro (píł·ło): boat
pipuce (pe:·po·cí): baby
pohetv (po·hí·ta) {I;II}: to hear

pohkē (póh·ki:) {II}: loud
pokkeccetv (pok·kic·ci·tá) {I}: to play ball
poloksv (po·lók·sa): circle
ponvkv hērv honayetv (po·ná·ka hí:·ła ho·na:·yi·tá): sermon; *also* oponvkv hērv honayetv
pose (po·sí) {II}: grandmother or paternal aunt of either a man or woman; *also* eposi
pose (pó:·si): cat
posketv (pos·ki·tá) {I}: to fast for the Green Corn Ceremony
pvfnē (páf·ni:) {II}: fast, quick
pvhe (pa·hí): grass
pvkpvkoce (pak·pa·kó·ci): flower
pvksen (pák·sin): tomorrow
pvlecetv (pa·li·ci·tá) {I;D}: to return something borrowed
pvnkv ēkvnv (pán·ka i:·ka·ná): ceremonial ground (stompground); *also* opvnkv ēkvnv
pvpetv (pa·pí·ta) {I;3}: to taste
pvrko cencvtvhake (páł·ko cin·ca·ta·há:·ki): grape dumplings
pvrkoce (pał·ko·cí): wild grapes, 'possum grapes
pvrkomv (pał·ko·má) {II}: purple; *also* okcatē
pvsetv (pa·sí·ta) {I;3}: to sweep
pvwv (pa·wá) {II}: uncle (maternal) of either a man or a woman; *also* epvwv

R

rakkē (łá:k·ki:) {II}: big
rakko (łá:k·ko): horse
rē (łí:): arrow
rvfo (ła·fó): winter
Rvfo Cuse (ła·fó co·sí): January ('Winter's Little Brother')
Rvfo Rakko (ła·fó łá:k·ko): December ('Big Winter')
rvfoksē (ła·fók·si:) {II}: level, broad (as of a lake or piece of ground)
rvro (ła·łó): fish
rvtvtakketv (ła·ta·ta:k·ki·tá) {I}: to snore

S

sasvkwv (sâ:·sak·wa): goose

selaksēketv (si·la:k·si:·ki·tá) {I}: to scream or yell
sē emmvhayetv (si:·im·ma·ha:·yi·tá) {I}: to practice
sem vtehkv (sim a·tíh·ka): pie
sofke (sóf·ki): a drink made from corn and lye (ash drippings)
sokhv (sók·ha): pig
sokhvpeswv (sok·ha·pís·wa): pork
sokso (sók·so) {II}: hip; *also* hvfe
sopakhvtkē (so·pa:k·hát·ki:) {II}: gray
sote (só:·ti): baking soda
sotv (so·tá): sky
spvlketv (spal·ki·tá) {I;3}: to spell a word
stimvt (ste:·mát): who; *also* estimvt
stofvn (sto:·fán): when
stomen (sto:·mín): why; *also* nakstomen, nakstowen, and stowen
stomēcet (sto·mí:·cit): how; *also* estomēcet
stowen (sto:·wín): why; *also* nakstomen, nakstowen, and stomen
stvmen (sta·mín): where
stvpokhe ((i)s·ta·pók·hi): bush
svkmorecetv (sak·mo·łi·ci·tá) {I;3}: to fry
svkpv (sák·pa) {II}: arm
svtohketv (sa·toh·ki·tá) {I;3}: to drive a car
svtv (sa·tá): apple

T

tafvmpuce (ta:·fam·po·cí): wild onion
takketv (ta:k·ki·tá) {I;II}: to kick
takpvtoketv (ta:k·pa·to·ki·tá) {I;II}: to bend
Tasahcuce (ta:·sa:h·co·cí): March ('Little Spring Month')
Tasahce Rakko (ta:·sá:h·ci łá:k·ko): April ('Big Spring Month')
tasketv (ta:s·ki·tá) {I}: to jump
tēkvnv (ti:·ka·ná): deacon; *also* coko vfastv
tohoknē (to·hók·ni:) {II}: light (in weight); *also* tvhoknē
tohwelēpkv (toh·wi·lí:p·ka): cross, crucifix; *also* etohwelēpkv
Tohwelēpvlke (toh·wi·li:p·âl·ki): Catholics; *also* Etohwelēpvlke and Enhonnv lvstē
tokonhe (to·kón·hi): ball stick; *also* etokonhe
tolose (to·ló·si): chicken

topv (to·pá): bed
torkowv (to:ł·ko·wá) {II}: knee
torofv (to·łó:·fa) {II}: face; *also* tvrofv
torwv (tół·wa) {II}: eye or eyes
tosēnv (to·sí:·na): salt pork, salt meat
totkv (tót·ka): fire
tutcēnen (toc·cî:·nin): three
Tvcakuce (ta·ca:·ko·cí): Sunday; *also* Nettvcako
tvcetv (ta·cí·ta) {I;3}: to cut once
tvhoknē (ta·hók·ni:) {II}: light (in weight); *also* tohoknē
tvklik (tak·lé:k): bread; *also* tvklike
tvklik-espakkueckv (tak·lé:k is·pa:k·kóyc·ka): baking powder
tvklike (tak·lé:·ki): bread; *also* tvklik
tvklike svkmorkē (tak·lé:·ki sak·mó:ł·ki:): fried bread
Tvllvhvsse (tal·la·hás·si): name of one of the Mvskoke ceremonial grounds (Tallahassee)
tvlofv (ta·ló:·fa): town
tvlwv (tál·wa): tribal town, traditional settlement
tvmketv (tam·ki·tá) {I}: to fly (of one)
tvphē (táp·hi:) {II}: wide
tvrofv (ta·łó:·fa) {II}: face; *also* torofv
tvskocē (tas·ko·cí:) {II}: thin (not of a person)

U

Ue Aksomkvlke (oy a:k·som·kâl·ki): Baptists; *also* Aksomkvlke
uewv (óy·wa): water; *also* owv and oewv
Uewv Ohfēskvlke (óy·wa oh·fi:s·kâl·ki): Presbyterians; *also* Ohfēskvlke
Uewv Ohkalvlke (óy·wa oh·ka:·lâl·ki): Methodists; *also* Ohkalvlke

V

vce (a·cí): corn
Vce lanē posketv (a·cí la:·ní: pos·ki·tá): Green Corn Ceremony
vce tvklike kvmoksē (a·cí tak·lé:·ki ka·mók·si:): sour cornbread
vcelaketv (a·ci·la:·ki·tá) {I;II}: to touch, brush up against, tag; *also* vcvlaketv
vculē (a·co·lí:) {II}: old
vcvkē (a·ca·kí:) {II}: short, stunted, dwarfish
vcvlaketv (a·ca·la:·ki·tá) {I;II}: to touch, brush up against, tag; *also* vcelaketv

vhēhketv (a·hi:h·ki·tá) {I;D}: to growl at
vhepvketv (a·hi·pa·kí·ta) {I;II}: to push, shove; *also* vhopvketv
vhoccickv (a·ho:c·cé:c·ka): blackboard
vholocē (a·ho·lo·cí:): cloud
vhonecetv (a·ho·ni·cí·ta) {II}: to stay awake
vhonecē (a·ho·ni·cí:) {II}: to be awake
vhopvketv (a·ho·pa·kí·ta) {I;II}: to push, shove; *also* vhepvketv
Vhvlvkvlke (a·ha·la·kâl·ki): Sweet Potato Clan
vhvmkvtetv (a·ham·ka·tí·ta) {I;II}: to count; *also* vhvnkvtetv
vhvmkvtkv (a·ham·kát·ka): number; *also* vhvnkvtkv
vhvnkvtetv (a·han·ka·tí·ta) {I;II}: to count; *also* vhvmkvtetv
vhvnkvtkv (a·han·kát·ka): number; *also* vhvmkvtkv
vhvoke (a·háw·ki): door
vkerricetv (a·kił·łe:·ci·tá) {I;II}: to think about
vketēcetv (a·ki·ti:·ci·tá) {I;II}: to watch after
vklopetv (ak·lo·pi·tá) {I}: to swim; *also* omiyetv
vkvsvmetv (a·ka·sa·mí·ta) {I;II}: to believe
vlke (al·kí): about, almost
vmelletv (a·mil·li·tá) {I;II}: to point at
vnahetv (a·na:·hi·tá) {II;3}: to run out of something (such as supplies or food)
vne (a·ní): I, me
vnokecetv (a·no·ki·cí·ta) {I;II}: to love someone
vnvttetv (a·nat·ti·tá) {II}: to get wounded
vpeletv (a·pi·li·tá) {I}: to laugh, smile
vpeswv (a·pís·wa): meat
vpēttē (a·pi:t·tí:): arbor
vpohetv (a·po·hi·tá) {I;D}: to ask someone
vpohetv (a·po·hi·tá) {I;3}: to buy, shop for something
vpohkv (a·póh·ka): question
vpvllakv (a·pal·lá:·ka): spool
vsemetv (a·si·mi·tá) {I;3;D}: to serve (something) to someone
vsēketv (a·si:·ki·tá) {I;II}: to shake hands with, greet
vslēcetv (as·li:·ci·tá) {I}: to erase
vsokolv (a·so:·ko·lá): sugar
vsse (ás·si): tea
vtotketv (a·tot·ki·tá) {I}: to work (as at a job)
vwenayetv (a·wi·na:·yi·tá) {I;II}: to smell, sniff, or sense
vwiketv (a·we:·ki·tá) {I;II}: to drop

vyepetv (a·yi·pi·tá) {I;II}: to leave, go away from; *also* enkvpvketv
vyetv (a·yí·ta) {I}: to go (of one)

W

wakv (wá:·ka): cow
wakvpesē (wa:·ka·pi·sí:): milk
wakvpesē neha (wa:·ka·pi·sí: ni·há:): butter
wakvpesē tvlokfe (wa:·ka·pi·sí: ta·lók·fi): buttermilk
wakvpeswv (wa:·ka·pís·wa): beef
wiyetv (we:·yi·tá) {I;3}: to sell
wotko (wó:t·ko): raccoon
Wotkvlke (wo:t·kâl·ki): Raccoon Clan
wvhvlv (wa·há·la): south; *also* lekothofv
wvkketv (wak·ki·tá) {I}: to lie down (of one)
wvnkē (wán·ki:) {II}: to be thirsty; *also* ewvnkē

Y

yekcē (yík·ci:) {II}: strong, loud
yopo (yo·pó) {II}: nose
yvcaketv (ya·ca:·ki·tá) {I;3}: to chew
yvhiketv (ya·he:·ki·tá) {I}: to sing
yvhiketv escokv (ya·he:·ki·tá is·có·ka): hymn
yvhikv (ya·hé:·ka): singer
yvkvpetv (ya·ka·pi·tá) {I}: to walk (of one)
yvlahomv (ya·la:·ho·má) {II}: orange (in color)
Yvnvsv opvnkv (ya·ná·sa o·pán·ka): Buffalo Dance

Glossary
English to Mvskoke

A

about, almost: vlke (al·kí)
to add: etohkvletv (i·toh·ka·lí·ta) {I}
afraid, scared: penkvlē (pin·ka·lí:) {II;D}
to be afraid of: em penkvletv (im pin·ka·lí·ta) {II;D}; *also* em penkvlē (im pin·ka·lí:) {II;D}
after a long time: hofonē haken (ho·fó·ni: hâ:·kin)
afternoon: fvccvlik hoyanen (fac·ca·lé:k ho·yâ:·nin)
alligator: hvlpvtv (hal·pa·tá)
Alligator Clan: Hvlpvtvlke (hal·pa·tâl·ki)
almost, about: vlke (al·kí)
amusing, funny: okhacē (ok·há:·ci:) {II}
to be amusing to: okhacē (ok·há:·ci:) {II;D}
angry: cvpakkē (ca·pá:k·ki:) {II}
apple: svtv (sa·tá)
April ('Big Spring Month'): Tasahce Rakko (ta:·sá:h·ci łá:k·ko)
apvske (a drink made of finely ground corn meal from parched corn): apvske (a:·pás·ki)
arbor: vpēttē (a·pi:t·tí:)
arm: svkpv (sák·pa) {II}
arrow: rē (łí:)
to ask someone: vpohetv (a·po·hi·tá) {I;D}

to attempt, try something: mecetv (mi·cí·ta) {I; 3}
August ('Big Harvest' or 'Big Summer'): Hvyo Rakko (ha·yó łá:k·ko)
aunt (maternal) of either a man or a woman: eckuce (ic·kó·ci) {II}
aunt (paternal) or grandmother of either a man or a woman: epose (i·pó·si) {II}; *also* pose (po·sí) {II}
awake: vhonecē (a·ho·ni·cí:) {II}
to stay awake: vhonecetv (a·ho·ni·cí·ta) {II}

B

baby: pipuce (pe:·po·cí)
back (of the body): era (i·łá:) {II}
baking powder: tvklik-espakkueckv (tak·lé:k is·pa:k·kóyc·ka)
baking soda: sote (só:·ti)
ball stick: tokonhe (to·kón·hi); *also* etokonhe (i·to·kón·hi)
Baptists: Aksomkvlke (a:k·som·kâl·ki); *also* Ue Aksomkvlke (oy a:k·som·kâl·ki)
to be baptized: aksomketv (a:k·som·ki·tá) {II}
to be, exist: owetv (o·wí·ta) {I}; *also* ometv (o·mí·ta) {I}
bear: nokose (no·kó·si)
Bear Clan: Nokosvlke (no·ko·sâl·ki)
beaver: echaswv (ic·há:s·wa)
Beaver Clan: Echaswvlke (ic·ha:s·wâl·ki)
bed: topv (to·pá)
bee: fo (fó:)
beef: wakvpeswv (wa:·ka·pís·wa)
to believe: vkvsvmetv (a·ka·sa·mí·ta) {I;II}
to believe in, trust, depend on (something or someone): em enhonretv (im in·hon·łi·tá) {I;D/II;D}
to bend: takpvtoketv (ta:k·pa·to·ki·tá) {I;II}
to bend over, stoop: comokletv (co·mok·li·tá) {I;II}
Bible: Cokvrakko (co·ka·łá:k·ko)
big: rakkē (łá:k·ki:) {II}
big toe: ele-ecke (i·li·ic·kí) {II}
bird: foswv (fós·wa); *also* fuswv (fós·wa)
Bird Clan: Foswvlke (fos·wâl·ki)
to bite: akketv (a:k·ki·tá) {I;II}
black: lvstē (lás·ti:) {II}
black pepper: homuce (ho:·mo·cí)

blackboard: vhoccickv (a·ho:c·cé:c·ka)
blackboard chalk: eshoccickv lvste (is·ho:c·cé:c·ka lás·ti)
to blink or wink: ohyofecetv (oh·yo·fi·cí·ta) {I}; *also* mesēٹticetv (mi·si:t·te:·ci·tá) {I}
blue: holattē (ho·lá:t·ti:) {II}
blue bread: cvtvhakv (ca·ta·há:·ka)
boat: perro (píł·ło)
body: ena (i·ná:) {II}
book, paper: cokv (co·ká)
boy: cepanē (ci·pá:·ni:)
to be brave: fekhvmkē (fik·hám·ki:) {II}
bread: tvklike (tak·lé:·ki); *also* tvklik (tak·lé:k)
  blue bread: cvtvhakv (ca·ta·há:·ka)
  fried bread: tvklike svkmorkē (tak·lé:·ki sak·mó:ł·ki:)
breeze, wind: hotvle (ho·tá·li)
broad, level (as of a lake or piece of ground): rvfoksē (ła·fók·si:) {II}
broom: espaskv (is·pá:s·ka)
brother (a man's older): ervhv vculicat (i·łá·ha a·co·lé:·ca:t) {II}
brother (a man's older) or a woman's older sister: ervhv (i·łá·ha) {II}
brother (a man's younger): ecerwv mvnetosat (i·cíł·wa ma·ni·to·sá:t) {II}
brother (a man's younger) or a woman's younger sister: ecuse (i·có·si) {II}
brother (a woman's): ecerwv (i·cíł·wa) {II}
brown: oklanē (ok·lá:·ni:) {II}
to brush up against, tag, touch: vcvlaketv (a·ca·la:·ki·tá) {I;II}; *also* vcelaketv (a·ci·la:·ki·tá) {I;II}
Buffalo Dance: Yvnvsv opvnkv (ya·ná·sa o·pán·ka)
to build or make: hvyetv (ha·yí·ta) {I;3}
to burn: nokricetv (nok·łe:·ci·tá) {I;3}
to burp: enkvrahpoletv (in·ka·ła:h·po·lí·ta) {D}
bush: stvpokhe ((i)s·ta·pók·hi)
butter: wakvpesē neha (wa:·ka·pi·sí: ni·há:)
buttermilk: wakvpesē tvlokfe (wa:·ka·pi·sí: ta·lók·fi)
to buy: nesetv (ni·sí·ta) {I;3}
to buy, shop for something: vpohetv (a·po·hi·tá) {I;3}

C

calf (of the leg): elempakko (i·lim·pá:k·ko) {II}; *also* elenpakko (i·lin·pá:k·ko) {II}

camp (someone's): hvpo (ha·pó:) {II}; *also* hvpohakv (ha·po:·há:·ka) {II}
to make camp: hvpo hayetv (ha·pó: ha:·yi·tá) {I;3}
car, automobile: atvmo (a:·ta·mó)
careful: ēyvcayē (i:·ya·cá:·yi:) {II}
to be careful: ēyvcayēcetv (i:·ya·ca:·yi:·ci·tá) {I}
cat: pose (pó:·si)
Catholics: Tohwelēpvlke (toh·wi·li:p·âl·ki); *also* Etohwelēpvlke (i·toh·wi·li:p·âl·ki) and Enhonnv lvstē (in·hón·na lás·ti:)
ceremonial ground (stompground): opvnkv ēkvnv (o·pán·ka i:·ka·ná); *also* pvnkv ēkvnv (pán·ka i:·ka·ná)
chef, cook: hompetv hayv (hom·pi·tá há:·ya)
chest (of the body): hokpe (hók·pi) {II}
to chew: yvcaketv (ya·ca:·ki·tá) {I;3}
chicken: tolose (to·ló·si)
chief, king: mekko (mík·ko)
  second chief: heneha (hi·ni·há:)
child: estuce (is·tó·ci)
church: mēkusvpkv-cuko (mi:·ko·sáp·ka có·ko)
circle: poloksv (po·lók·sa)
clan: mvliketv (ma·le:·ki·tá)
classroom: cokv-heckv cukhofv (co·ka·híc·ka cok·ho·fá)
to clean (one thing): hvsvtecetv (ha·sa·ti·cí·ta) {I;3}
cloud: vholocē (a·ho·lo·cí:)
coat: kapv (ká:·pa)
coffee: kafe (ká:·fi)
cold (of inanimate things): kvsvppē (ka·sáp·pi:) {II}
to feel cold (of an animate being): etkolē (it·ko·lí:) {II}
color: enheckv (in·híc·ka)
cook, chef: hompetv hayv (hom·pi·tá há:·ya)
to cook: noricetv (no·łe:·ci·tá) {I;3}
cooking fat, oil: nēha (ní:·ha:)
corn: vce (a·cí)
to correct or straighten: lvpotēcetv (la·po·ti:·ci·tá) {I;D}
to cough: ohoketv (o·ho:·ki·tá) {II/I}
to count: vhvmkvtetv (a·ham·ka·tí·ta) {I;II}; *also* vhvnkvtetv (a·han·ka·tí·ta) {I;II}
cousin (of a man or a woman): enahvmke (i·na:·hám·ki) {II}; *also* enahvnke (i·na:·hán·ki) {II}
cow: wakv (wá:·ka)

to crawl (of one): hvlketv (hal·ki·tá) {I}
Creator, God, 'Giver of Life/Breath': Hesaketv Messē (hi·sa:·ki·tá mís·si:)
cross, crucifix: tohwelēpkv (toh·wi·lí:p·ka); *also* etohwelēpkv (i·toh·wi·lí:p·ka)
crucifix, cross: tohwelēpkv (toh·wi·lí:p·ka); *also* etohwelēpkv (i·toh·wi·lí:p·ka)
to cry (of one): hvkihketv (ha·ke:h·ki·tá) {I}
to cut many times (as when making repeated slices): lvffetv (laf·fi·tá) {I;3}
to cut once: tvcetv (ta·cí·ta) {I;3}

D

to dance: opvnetv (o·pa·ni·tá) {I}
dancer: opanv (o·pá:·na)
to be dangerous: ēhotkē (i:·hót·ki:) {II}
daughter (a man's): eccuste (ic·cós·ti) {II}
daughter (a woman's): eccus hoktē (ic·cós hók·ti:) {II}
deacon: coko vfastv (co·kó a·fás·ta); *also* tēkvnv (ti:·ka·ná)
December ('Big Winter'): Rvfo Rakko (ła·fó łá:k·ko)
deep (of water): lvokē (láw·ki:) {II}
deer: eco (i·có)
Deer Clan: Ecovlke (i·co·âl·ki)
to depend on, believe in, trust (something or someone): em enhonretv (im in·hon·łi·tá) {I;D/II;D}
different, to be a little different: ētvsē (i:·ta·sí:) {II}
to dig: korretv (koł·łi·tá) {I;3}
dirt, ground, earth: ēkvnv (i:·ka·ná)
dog: efv (e·fá)
door: vhvoke (a·háw·ki)
to drink: esketv (is·kí·ta) {I;3}
drinks made of corn: apvske (a:·pás·ki) and sofke (sóf·ki)
to drive a car: svtohketv (sa·toh·ki·tá) {I;3}
to drop: vwiketv (a·we:·ki·tá) {I;II}
dry: kvrpē (káł·pi:) {II}
dwarfish, short, stunted: vcvkē (a·ca·kí:) {II}

E

ear, ears: hvcko (hác·ko) {II}
earth, dirt, ground: ēkvnv (i:·ka·ná)
east: hvsossv (ha·sós·sa)

to eat, taste: hompetv (hom·pi·tá) {I;3}
to eavesdrop on: imapohicetv (e:·ma:·po·he:·ci·tá) {I;D}
egg: custake (cos·tá:·ki)
eight: cenvpaken (ci·na·pâ:·kin)
eighteen: palen-cenvpohkaken (pá:·lin ci·na·poh·ká:·kin)
eleven: palen-hvmkentvlaken (pá:·lin ham·kin·ta·lá:·kin)
to enjoy: mvnhēretv (man·hi:·łi·tá) {II;D}
to erase: vslēcetv (as·li:·ci·tá) {I}
eye, eyes: torwv (tół·wa) {II}

F

face: torofv (to·łó:·fa) {II}; *also* tvrofv (ta·łó:·fa) {II}
to fall: lvtketv (lat·ki·tá) {II/I}
to fast: ēlvwēcetv (i:·la·wi:·ci·tá) {I}
to fast for the Green Corn Ceremony: posketv (pos·ki·tá) {I}
fast, quick: pvfnē (páf·ni:) {II}
to be fat: nehē (ni·hí:) {II}
father (of either a man or woman): erke (íł·ki) {II}
February ('Windy Month'): Hotvlē Hvse (ho·tá·li: ha·sí)
to feel, touch: celayetv (ci·la:·yi·tá) {I;II}
to feel sorry for: em merretv (im mił·łi·tá) {II;D}
feet, foot, or leg: ele (i·lí) {II}
fifteen: palen-cvhkēpohkaken (pá:·lin cah·kî:·poh·ka:·kin)
to fight: etepoyetv (i·ti·po·yí·ta) {I;II}
finger: enke-wesakv (in·ki·wi·sá:·ka) {II}
fire: totkv (tót·ka)
firefly: kolēppa (ko·li:p·pá:)
fish: rvro (ła·łó)
five: cvhkēpen (cah·kî:·pin)
to float (of one): okotafketv (ok·o·ta:f·ki·tá) {I}; *also* okvtafketv (ok·a·ta:f·ki·tá) {I}
flour: hockvte (hoc·ka·tí)
flower: pvkpvkoce (pak·pa·kó·ci)
to fly (of one): tvmketv (tam·ki·tá) {I}
food: hompetv (hom·pi·tá)
to fool or trick: em vkerretv (im a·kił·łi·tá) {I;D}; *also* mvkerretv ((i)m·a·kił·łi·tá) {I;D}
foot, leg, or feet: ele (i·lí) {II}
footstool: ele-ohsehoyetv (i·li·oh·si·ho·yí·ta)

four: osten (ô:s·tin)
fourteen: palen-ostohkaken (pá:·lin os·toh·ká:·kin)
Friday: Flati (flá:·te:)
fried bread: tvklike svkmorkē (tak·lé:·ki sak·mó:ł·ki:)
to fry: svkmorecetv (sak·mo·łi·ci·tá) {I;3}
funny, amusing: okhacē (ok·há:·ci:) {II}

G

generous, kind: heromē (hi·łó·mi:) {II}
to be generous to, kind to: heromosē (hi·łô:·mo·si:) {II;D}
girl: hoktuce (hok·to·cí)
to give a warning to: em vsehetv (im a·si·hi·tá) {I;D}
to give something to someone: emetv (i·mí·ta) {I;3;D}
to give thanks, say thanks (to someone): mvto kicetv (ma·tó ke:·ci·tá) {I;II}
'Giver of Life/Breath,' Creator, God: Hesaketv Messē (hi·sa:·ki·tá mís·si:)
glove: estenkehute (ist·in·ki·hó·ti)
to go (of one): vyetv (a·yí·ta) {I}
to go away from, leave: enkvpvketv (in·ka·pa·kí·ta) {I;D}; *also* vyepetv (a·yi·pi·tá) {I;II}
to gobble (like a turkey): cvlvkloketv (ca·lak·lo:·ki·tá) {I}
God, 'Giver of Life/Breath,' Creator: Hesaketv Messē (hi·sa:·ki·tá mís·si:)
good: hēnrē (hí:n·łi:) {II}
goose: sasvkwv (sâ:·sak·wa)
grandfather (of either a man or a woman): epoca (i·po·cá:) {II}
grandmother or paternal aunt (of either a man or a woman): epose (i·pó·si) {II}; *also* pose (po·sí) {II}
grape dumplings: pvrko cencvtvhake (páł·ko cin·ca·ta·há:·ki)
grapes (wild), 'possum grapes: pvrkoce (pał·ko·cí)
grass: pvhe (pa·hí)
gray: sopakhvtkē (so·pa:k·hát·ki:) {II}
green, yellow: lanē (lá:·ni:) {II}
Green Corn Ceremony: Vce lanē posketv (a·cí la:·ní: pos·ki·tá)
to greet, shake hands with: vsēketv (a·si:·ki·tá) {I;II}
ground, earth, dirt: ēkvnv (i:·ka·ná)
to grow (of a person or animal): mahetv (ma:·hi·tá) {II}
to grow (of grain or plants): mahēcetv (ma:·hi:·ci·tá) {I;II}
to growl at: vhēhketv (a·hi:h·ki·tá) {I;D}

H

hair: ekv-esse (i·ka·is·sí) {II}
hand: enke (in·kí) {II}
happy: afvckē (a:·fác·ki:) {II}
to hate, be mad at: enhomecetv (in·ho·mi·cí·ta) {II;D}; *also* enhomecē (in·ho·mi·cí:) {II;D}; *also see* encvpvkketv (in·ca·pak·ki·tá) {II; D}
to have, to be located: ocetv (o:·ci·tá) {I;3}
hawk: ayo (á:·yo)
head: ekv (i·ká) {II}
to hear: pohetv (po·hí·ta) {I;II}
heaven: hvlwe tvlofv (hál·wi ta·ló·fa)
heavy: honnē (hón·ni:) {II}
hello: hensci (híns·ce:)
here: hēyvn (hí:·yan)
hill: ekvnhvlwuce (i·kan·hal·wo·cí)
hip: hvfe (ha·fí) {II}; *also* sokso (sók·so) {II}
to hit: nvfketv (naf·ki·tá) {I;II}
honey: fo-encvmpē (fo:·in·cam·pí:)
to hope for: kometv (ko·mí·ta) {I;3}; *also* kowetv (ko·wí·ta) {I;3}
hopeful: enhonrē (in·hón·łi:) {II}
horse: rakko (łák·ko)
hot: hayē (há:·yi:) {II}; *also* hiyē (hé:·yi:) {II}
house: coko (co·kó)
how: estomēcet (is·to·mí:·cit); *also* stomēcet (sto·mí:·cit)
hungry: elvwē (i·lá·wi:) {II}; also lvwē (la·wí:) {II}
to hurt, be sore: ennokkē (in·nók·ki:) {D}
hymn: yvhiketv escokv (ya·he:·ki·tá is·có·ka)
hymnal: cokv esyvhiketv (co·ká is·ya·he:·ki·tá)

I

I, me: vne (a·ní)

J

January ('Winter's Little Brother'): Rvfo Cuse (ła·fó co·sí)
to be jealous: fekcvkhē (fik·cák·hi:) {II}
to be jealous of: es fekcvkhē (is fik·cák·hi:) {II;D}

Jesus: Cēsvs (cí:·sas)
Jewish people: Cosvlke (co:·sâl·ki)
July ('Little Harvest' or 'Little Summer'): Hvyuce (ha·yó·ci)
to jump: tasketv (ta:s·ki·tá) {I}
June ('Blackberry Month'): Kvco Hvse (ka·có ha·sí)

K

to kick: takketv (ta:k·ki·tá) {I;II}
kind, nice: lopicē (lo·pé:·ci:) {II}
kind, generous: heromē (hi·łó·mi:) {II}
to be kind to, generous to: heromosē (hi·łô:·mo·si:) {II;D}
king, chief: mekko (mík·ko)
knee: torkowv (to:ł·ko·wá) {II}
knife: eslafkv (is·lá:f·ka)
to know (someone or something): kerretv (kił·łi·tá) {I;II}

L

last night: nerē-isē (ni·łí:·ê:·si:)
last year: ohrolopēyvnke (oh·ło·lo·pi:·yán·ki)
to laugh, smile: vpeletv (a·pi·li·tá) {I}
to lead a dance: es enhomahtetv (is in·ho·ma:h·ti·tá) {I;D}
to leave, go away from: enkvpvketv (in·ka·pa·kí·ta) {I;D}; *also* vyepetv (a·yi·pi·tá) {I;II}
leg, foot, or feet: ele (i·lí) {II}
level, broad (as of a lake or piece of ground): rvfoksē (ła·fók·si:) {II}
to lie down (of one): wvkketv (wak·ki·tá) {I}
to lie to: enlvksetv (in·lak·si·tá) {I;D}
light (in weight): tohoknē (to·hók·ni:) {II}; *also* tvhoknē (ta·hók·ni:) {II}
to like, want, need: eyvcetv (i·ya·ci·tá) {II;3}
to listen to: em mapohicetv (im ma:·po·he:·ci·tá) {I;D}; *also* mapohicetv (ma:·po·he:·ci·tá) {I;D}
little: cutkosē (cot·ko·sí:) {II}
to be a little different: ētvsē (i:·ta·sí:) {II}
a little while ago: hvtēyvnke (ha·ti:·yán·ki)
to be located, to have: ocetv (o:·ci·tá) {I;3}
to be located, to sit (of one): liketv (le:·ki·tá) {I}
a long time ago: hofonofen (ho·fô:·no·fin)

to look up at something or someone: em vnvtaksetv (im a·na·ta:k·si·tá) {I;D}
loud: pohkē (póh·ki:) {II}
loud, strong: yekcē (yík·ci:) {II}
to love someone: vnokecetv (a·no·ki·cí·ta) {I;II}

M

to be mad at: encvpvkketv (in·ca·pak·ki·tá) {II;D}; *also see* enhomecetv (in·ho·mi·cí·ta) {II;D}; *also see* enhomecē (in·ho·mi·cí:) {II;D}
to be mad at, hate: enhomecetv (in·ho·mi·cí·ta) {II;D}; *also* enhomecē (in·ho·mi·cí:) {II;D}; *also see* encvpvkketv (in·ca·pak·ki·tá) {II;D}
to make or build: hvyetv (ha·yí·ta) {I;3}
to make peace with each other: etenherketv (i·tin·hił·ki·tá) {I;II}
male, man: honvnwv (ho·nán·wa)
man, person: este (ís·ti); *also* miste (mé:s·ti)
man, male: honvnwv (ho·nán·wa)
man, married: honvnwv ehicv (ho·nán·wa i·hé:·ca)
man, old: este vcule (ís·ti a·có·li)
March ('Little Spring Month'): Tasahcuce (ta:·sa:h·co·cí)
married man: honvnwv ehicv (ho·nán·wa i·hé:·ca)
married woman: hoktē ehessē (hók·ti: i·hís·si:)
maternal aunt (of either a man or a woman): eckuce (ic·kó·ci) {II}
maternal uncle (of either a man or a woman): epvwv (i·pá·wa) {II;1}; *also* pvwv (pá·wa) {II}
May ('Mulberry Month'): Kē Hvse (kí: ha·sí)
me, I: vne (a·ní)
meal: hompetv hakv (hom·pi·tá há:·ka)
mean, unkind: holwvyēcē (hol·wa·yí:·ci:) {II}
meat: vpeswv (a·pís·wa)
medicine: heleswv (hi·lís·wa)
to take Indian medicine: heleswv sēyocetv (hi·lís·wa si:·yo·cí·ta) {I}
medicine man: heles hayv (hi·lís há:·ya)
Methodists: Ohkalvlke (oh·ka:·lâl·ki); *also* Uewv Ohkalvlke (wí:·wa oh·ka:·lâl·ki)
milk: wakvpesē (wa:·ka·pi·sí:)
to mix, stir: eteyametv (i·ti·ya:·mi·tá) {I;3}
Monday: Mvnte (mán·ti)
mortar: keco (ki·có)
mother (of either a man or a woman): ecke (íc·ki) {II}
mouse: cesse (cís·si)

mouth: cokwv (cók·wa) {II}
muddy: okofkē (o·kóf·ki:)

N

to be named: hocefketv (ho·cif·ki·tá) {II}
naughty: holwvkē (hol·wa·kí:) {II}
neck: nokwv (nók·wa) {II}
to need, like, want: eyvcetv (i·ya·ci·tá) {II;3}
net: hoyv (hó:·ya)
nice, kind: lopicē (lo·pé:·ci:) {II}
to be nice to: lopicetv (lo·pe:·ci·tá) {II;D}
nine: ostvpaken (os·ta·pâ:·kin)
nineteen: palen-ostvpohkaken (pá:·lin os·ta·poh·ká:·kin)
no: mvnks (manks)
north: honerv (ho·ní·ła); *also* kvsvppofv (ka·sap·pó:·fa)
nose: yopo (yo·pó) {II}
notebook: nak-eshoccicetv cokv (na:k·is·ho:c·ce:·ci·tá co·ká)
November ('Frost Month'): Eholē (i·ho·lí:)
now: hvte (ha·tí)
number: vhvmkvtkv (a·ham·kát·ka); *also* vhvnkvtkv (a·han·kát·ka)

O

October ('Big Chestnut Month'): Otvwoskv Rakko (o·ta·wó:s·ka łá:k·ko)
oil, cooking fat: nēha (ní:·ha:)
old: vculē (a·co·lí:) {II}
old man: este vcule (ís·ti a·có·li)
old woman: hoktvlē (hok·ta·lí:)
older brother (a man's): ervhv vculicat (i·łá·ha a·co·lé:·ca:t) {II}
older brother (a man's) or older sister (a woman's): ervhv (i·łá·ha) {II}
older sister (a woman's): ervhv hoktvlēcat (i·łá·ha hok·ta·lí:·ca:t) {II}
one (numeral): hvmken (hám·kin)
or: munkat (món·ka:t)
orange (in color): yvlahomv (ya·la:·ho·má) {II}

P

paper, book: cokv (co·ká)
to pass (something) to someone: aswiyetv (a:s·we:·yi·tá) {I;3;D}

paternal aunt (of either a man or a woman) or grandmother: epose (i·pó·si) {II}; *also* pose (po·sí) {II}
paternal uncle (of either a man or a woman): erkuce (ił·kó·ci) {II}
to peek at: em vcvnēyetv (ima·ca·ni:·yi·tá) {I;D}; *also* mvcvnēyetv ((i)ma·ca·ni:·yi·tá) {I;D}
pen: owvlvste eshoccickv (o:·wa·lás·ti is·ho:c·cé:c·ka)
pencil: eshoccickv (is·ho:c·cé:c·ka)
penny: hoporrenkv (ho·poł·łín·ka)
pepper (black): homuce (ho:·mo·cí)
person, man: este (ís·ti); *also* miste (mé:s·ti)
pestle: kecvpe (ki·cá·pi)
pew: ohmēkusvpkv (oh·mi:·ko·sáp·ka)
to pick up: atvkkesetv (a:·tak·ki·sí·ta) {I;II}
pie: sem vtehkv (sim a·tíh·ka)
pig: sokhv (sók·ha)
piled up (for wood, rocks, trash, etc.): cekhē (cík·hi:) {II;D}
pink: catosē (ca:·to·sí:) {II}
to play: ahkopvnetv (a:h·ko·pa·ni·tá) {I}
to play ball: pokkeccetv (pok·kic·ci·tá) {I}
playground: ahkopvnkv-ēkvnv (a:h·ko·pan·ka·i:·ka·ná)
to point: melletv (mil·li·tá) {I}
to point at: vmelletv (a·mil·li·tá) {I;II}
pork: sokhvpeswv (sok·ha·pís·wa)
'possum grapes, wild grapes: pvrkoce (pał·ko·cí)
to pour out a liquid: awotsvnetv (a:·wot·sa·ní·ta) {I;3}
to practice: sē emmvhayetv (si: im·ma·ha:·yi·tá) {I}
to pray: mēkusvpetv (mi:·ko·sa·pi·tá) {I}
to pray for: em mēkusvpetv (im mi:·ko·sa·pi·tá) {I;D}
prayer, service: mēkusvpkv (mi:·ko·sáp·ka)
to preach to: erkenvketv (ił·ki·na·kí·ta) {I;D}
preacher: erkenvkv (ił·ki·na·ká)
to prepare something or someone: em etetakuecetv (im i·ti·ta:·koy·ci·tá) {I; D}
Presbyterians: Ohfēskvlke (oh·fi:s·kâl·ki); *also* Uewv Ohfēskvlke (óy·wa oh·fi:s·kâl·ki)
to pull in the direction of the speaker: ahvlvtetv (a:·ha·la·ti·tá) {I;II}
puppy: efuce (i·fó·ci)
  my puppy: vmefuce (am·i·fo·cí)
purple: okcatē (ok·cá:·ti:) {II}; *also* pvrkomv (pał·ko·má) {II}

to push, shove: vhepvketv (a·hi·pa·kí·ta) {I;II}; *also* vhopvketv (a·ho·pa·kí·ta) {I;II}
to push someone or something: hopvketv (ho·pa·ki·tá) {I;II}

Q

question: vpohkv (a·póh·ka)
quick, fast: pvfnē (páf·ni:) {II}
quiet: cvyayvkē (ca·ya:·ya·kí:) {II}

R

rabbit, Rabbit of legends: cofe (co·fí); *also* cufe (co·fí)
raccoon: wotko (wó:t·ko)
Raccoon Clan: Wotkvlke (wo:t·kâl·ki)
to race (of two or more): etemvretv (i·ti·ma·łí·ta) {I;II}
rain: oskē (os·kí:)
rattlesnake: cetto mekko (cít·to mík·ko)
to read: ohhonvyetv (oh·ho·na·yí·ta) {I}
to be ready for something: em etetaketv (im i·ti·ta:·ki·tá) {I;D}
red: catē (cá:·ti:) {II}
retail store, shop: neskv-coko (nis·ka·có·ko)
to return something borrowed: pvlecetv (pa·li·ci·tá) {I;D}
Ribbon Dance: Nettv opvnkv (nít·ta o·pán·ka)
to ride (of one), to sit on: ohliketv (oh·le:·ki·tá) {I;3}
river: hvcce (hác·ci)
rock, stone: cvto (ca·tó)
room in a building or house: cukhofv (cok·ho·fá); *also* nvthofv (nat·ho·fá)
to run (of one): letketv (lit·ki·tá) {I}
to run away from: enletketv (in·lit·ki·tá) {I;D}
to run out of something (such as supplies or food): vnahetv (a·na:·hi·tá) {II;3}

S

sad: feknokkē (fik·nók·ki:) {II}
salt: okcvnwv (ok·cán·wa)
salt meat, salt pork: tosēnv (to·sí:·na)
Saturday: Nettvcako ecuse (nit·ta·cá:·ko i·có·si)

to say, speak to someone: maketv (ma:·ki·tá) {I; II}
to say thanks, give thanks (to someone): mvto kicetv (ma·tó ke:·ci·tá) {I;II}
scared, afraid: penkvlē (pin·ka·lí:) {II;D}
school: cokv-heckv (co·ka·híc·ka); *also* mvhakv-cuko (ma·ha:·ka·có·ko)
to scream, yell: selaksēketv (si·la:k·si:·ki·tá) {I}
second chief: heneha (hi·ni·há:)
to see: hecetv (hi·cí·ta) {I;II}
to sell: wiyetv (we:·yi·tá) {I;3}
to sense, smell, sniff: vwenayetv (a·wi·na:·yi·tá) {I;II}
September ('Little Chestnut Month'): Otvwoskuce (o·ta·wo:s·ko·cí)
sermon: oponvkv hērv honayetv (o·po·na·ká hí:·ła ho·na:·yi·tá); *also* ponvkv hērv honayetv (po·ná·ka hí:·ła ho·na:·yi·tá)
to serve (something) to someone: vsemetv (a·si·mi·tá) {I;3;D}
service, prayer: mēkusvpkv (mi:·ko·sáp·ka)
seven: kolvpaken (ko·la·pâ:·kin)
seventeen: palen-kolvpohkaken (pá:·lin ko·la·poh·ká:·kin)
to shake hands with, greet: vsēketv (a·si:·ki·tá) {I;II}
shallow (of water): cahkē (cá:h·ki:) {II}
to share with someone: enkvpicetv (in·ka·pe:·ci·tá) {I;D}
shop, retail store: neskv-coko (nis·ka·có·ko)
to shop for something, buy: vpohetv (a·po·hi·tá) {I;3}
short: kocoknē (ko·cók·ni:) {II}
short, stunted, dwarfish: vcvkē (a·ca·kí:) {II}
shoulder: folowv (fo·ló·wa) {II}
to shove, push: vhepvketv (a·hi·pa·kí·ta) {I;II}; *also* vhopvketv (a·ho·pa·kí·ta) {I;II}
to be sick: enokkē (i·nók·ki:) {II}
to sing: yvhiketv (ya·he:·ki·tá) {I}
singer: yvhikv (ya·hé:·ka)
sinner: naorkv (na:·ó:ł·ka)
sister (a man's): ēwvnwv (i:·wán·wa) {II}
sister (a woman's older): ervhv hoktvlēcat (i·łá·ha hok·ta·lí:·ca:t) {II}
sister (a woman's older) or a man's older brother: ervhv (i·łá·ha) {II}
sister (a woman's younger): ecuse mvnetat (i·có·si ma·ni·tá:t) {II}
sister (a woman's younger) or a man's younger brother: ecuse (i·có·si) {II}
to sit (of one), to be located: liketv (le:·ki·tá) {I}
to sit on (of one), to ride: ohliketv (oh·le:·ki·tá) {I;3}
six: ēpaken (i:·pâ:·kin)
sixteen: palen-ēpohkaken (pá:·lin i:·poh·ká:·kin)

skinny, thin (of an animate being): hotososē (ho·tô:·so·si:) {II}
skunk: kono (ko·nó)
sky: sotv (so·tá)
to sleep (of one): nocetv (no·cí·ta) {I/II}
to be sleepy: nockelē (noc·ki·lí:) {II}; also nuckelē (noc·ki·lí:) {II}
to slide toward: ohsolotketv (oh·so·lo:t·ki·tá) {II;D}
slow: hvlvlatkē (ha·la·lá:t·ki:) {II}
to smell, sniff, sense: vwenayetv (a·wi·na:·yi·tá) {I;II}
smelly, stinking: fvmpē (fám·pi:) {II}
to smile, laugh: vpeletv (a·pi·li·tá) {I}
snake: cetto (cít·to)
to sneeze: hvktēsketv (hak·ti:s·ki·tá) {II/I}
to sniff, sense, smell: vwenayetv (a·wi·na:·yi·tá) {I;II}
to snore: rvtvtakketv (ła·ta·ta:k·ki·tá) {I}
sofke (a drink made from corn and lye [ash drippings]): sofke (sóf·ki)
something, what: naken (ná:·kin)
son (a man's): eppuce (ip·pó·ci) {II}
son (a woman's): eccus honvnwv (ic·cós ho·nán·wa) {II}
to be sore, hurt: ennokkē (in·nók·ki:) {D}
to feel sorry for: em merretv (im mił·łi·tá) {II;D}
sour cornbread: vce tvklike kvmoksē (a·cí tak·lé:·ki ka·mók·si:)
south: lekothofv (li·kot·hó:·fa); *also* wvhvlv (wa·há·la)
to speak, say to someone: maketv (ma:·ki·tá) {I; II}
speaker: oponayv (o·po·ná:·ya)
to spell a word: spvlketv (spal·ki·tá) {I;3}
spool: vpvllakv (a·pal·lá:·ka)
to stand (of one): hueretv (hoy·łi·tá) {I}
to stay awake: vhonecetv (a·ho·ni·cí·ta) {II}
stinking, smelly: fvmpē (fám·pi:) {II}
to stir, mix: eteyametv (i·ti·ya:·mi·tá) {I;3}
stompground (ceremonial ground): opvnkv ēkvnv (o·pán·ka i:·ka·ná); *also* pvnkv ēkvnv (pán·ka i:·ka·ná)
stone, rock: cvto (ca·tó)
to stoop, bend over: comokletv (co·mok·li·tá) {I;II}
story: oponvkv (o·po·na·ká)
to straighten or correct: lvpotēcetv (la·po·ti:·ci·tá) {I;D}
stream: hvccuce (hac·co·cí)
to stretch, as when waking up: ētenetv (i:·ti·ní·ta) {I}

strong, loud: yekcē (yík·ci:) {II}
student: cokv-hēcv (co·ka·hí:·ca)
stunted, dwarfish, short: vcvkē (a·ca·kí:) {II}
sugar: vsokolv (a·so:·ko·lá)
sun: hvse (ha·sí)
Sunday: Nettvcako (nit·ta·cá:·ko); also Tvcakuce (ta·ca:·ko·cí)
to swallow: nokmeletv (nok·mi·lí·ta) {I;3}
to sweep: pvsetv (pa·sí·ta) {I;3}
sweet: cvmpē (cám·pi:) {II}
Sweet Potato Clan: Vhvlvkvlke (a·ha·la·kâl·ki)
to swim: omiyetv (o·me:·yi·tá) {I}; *also* vklopetv (ak·lo·pi·tá) {I}

T

table: ohhompetv (oh·hom·pi·tá)
to tag, touch, brush up against: vcvlaketv (a·ca·la:·ki·tá) {I;II}; *also* vcelaketv (a·ci·la:·ki·tá) {I;II}
to take: esetv (i·sí·ta) {I;II}
to take Indian medicine: heleswv sēyocetv (hi·lís·wa si:·yo·cí·ta) {I}
to talk: oponvyetv (o·po·na·yí·ta) {I}
to talk to someone: em oponvyetv (im o·po·na·yí·ta) {I;D}; *also* em ponvyetv (im po·na·yí·ta) {I;D}
tall: mahē (má:·hi:) {II}
Tallahassee (name of one of the Mvskoke ceremonial grounds): Tvllvhvsse (tal·la·hás·si)
to taste: pvpetv (pa·pí·ta) {I;3}
to taste, eat: hompetv (hom·pi·tá) {I;3}
tea: vsse (ás·si)
to teach: mvhayetv (ma·ha:·yi·tá) {I;D}
teacher: mvhayv (ma·há:·ya)
ten: palen (pá:·lin)
thank you: mvto (ma·tó)
that, that one: mvt (mat)
thick: cekfē (cík·fi:) {II}
thigh: hvfe (ha·fí) {II}; *also* hvfececkv (ha·fi·cíc·ka) {II}
thin (not of a person): tvskocē (tas·ko·cí:) {II}
thin, skinny (of an animate being): hotososē (ho·tô:·so·si:) {II}
to think about: vkerricetv (a·kił·łe:·ci·tá) {I;II}

to be thirsty: ewvnhkē (i·wánh·ki:) {II}; *also* wvnkē (wán·ki:) {II}
thirteen: palen-tutcenohkaken (pá:·lin tot·cin·oh·ká:·kin)
three: tutcēnen (toc·cî:·nin)
Thursday: Nvrkvpv enhvyvtke (nał·ka·pá in·ha·yát·ki)
tiger: kaccv (ká:c·ca)
Tiger Clan: Kaccvlke (ka:c·câl·ki)
tired: hotosē (ho·tó·si:) {II}
today: mucv-nettv (mo·ca·nít·ta)
toe, big: ele-ecke (i·li·ic·kí) {II}
toe, but not the big toe: ele-wesakv (i·li·wi·sá:·ka) {II}
together with: esyomen (is·yó:m·in)
tomorrow: pvksen (pák·sin)
tooth: nute (no·tí) {II}
to touch, brush up against, tag: vcvlaketv (a·ca·la:·ki·tá) {I;II}; *also* vcelaketv (a·ci·la:·ki·tá) {I;II}
to touch, feel: celayetv (ci·la:·yi·tá) {I;II}
town: tvlofv (ta·ló:·fa)
traditional settlement, tribal town: tvlwv (tál·wa)
tree, wood: eto (i·tó)
tribal town, traditional settlement: tvlwv (tál·wa)
to trick or fool: em vkerretv (im a·kił·łi·tá) {I;D}; *also* mvkerretv ((i)m·a·kił·łi·tá) {I;D}
to trust, depend on, believe in (something or someone): em enhonretv (im in·hon·łi·tá) {I;D/II;D}
to try, attempt something: mecetv (mi·cí·ta) {I;3}
Tuesday: Mvnte enhvyvtke (mán·ti in·ha·yát·ki)
turtle, turtle shell, Turtle of stories: locv (lo·cá)
Tvllvhvsse (name of one of the Mvskoke ceremonial grounds): Tvllvhvsse (tal·la·hás·si)
twelve: palen-hokkolohkaken (pá:·lin hok·ko·loh·ká:·kin)
twenty: pale-hokkolen (pá:·li hok·kô:·lin)
two: hokkolen (hok·kô:·lin)

U

uncle (maternal) of either a man or a woman: epvwv (i·pá·wa) {II}; *also* pvwv (pá·wa) {II}
uncle (paternal) of either a man or a woman: erkuce (ił·kó·ci) {II}
to understand: kērrepetv (ki:ł·łi·pí·ta) {II}

to be uneasy about: em enhotetv (im in·ho·tí·ta) {II;D}
unkind, mean: holwvyēcē (hol·wa·yí:·ci:) {II}

V

to visit: cokopericetv (co·ko·pi·łe:·ci·tá) {I;D}

W

to wait for (someone or something): mehaketv ((i)m·i·ha:·ki·tá) {I;D}
to walk (of one): yvkvpetv (ya·ka·pi·tá) {I}
to want, need, like: eyvcetv (i·ya·ci·tá) {II;3}
to warn, give a warning to: em vsehetv (im a·si·hi·tá) {I;D}
to watch after: vketēcetv (a·ki·ti:·ci·tá) {I;II}
water: oewv (óy·wa); *also* owv (ó:·wa) and uewv (óy·wa)
watermelon: cvstvlē (cas·ta·lí:)
to wave at: em mvyattēcetv (im ma·ya:t·ti:·ci·tá) {I;D}
weak: lowakē (lo·wá:·ki:) {II}
Wednesday: Ennvrkvpv (in·nał·ka·pá)
west: hvsaklatkv (ha·sa:k·lá:t·ka)
what: estomē (is·to·mí:); *also* naken (ná:·kin) and nake (ná:·ki)
what, something: naken (ná:·kin); *also* estomē (is·tó·mi:)
when: stofvn (sto:·fán)
where: stvmen (sta·mín)
to whistle at: enfotketv (in·fot·ki·tá) {I;D}
white: hvtkē (hát·ki:) {II}
who: estimvt (is·te:·mát); *also* stimvt (ste:·mát)
why: nakstomen (na:k·sto:·mín); *also* nakstowen (na:k·sto:·wín), stomen (sto:·mín), and stowen (sto:·wín)
wide: tvphē (táp·hi:) {II}
wild grapes, 'possum grapes: pvrkoce (pał·ko·cí)
wild onion: tafvmpuce (ta:·fam·po·cí)
wind, breeze: hotvle (ho·tá·li)
Wind Clan: Hotvlkvlke (ho·tal·kâl·ki)
to wink or blink: ohyofecetv (oh·yo·fi·cí·ta) {I}; *also* mesētticetv (mi·si:t·te:·ci·tá) {I}
winter: rvfo (ła·fó)
woman: hoktē (hók·ti:)
woman, married: hoktē ehessē (hók·ti: i·hís·si:)

woman, old: hoktvlē (hok·ta·lí:)
woman's leader: hoktvke semevpayv (hok·ta·kí si·mi·a·pá:·ya)
wood, tree: eto (i·tó)
to work: vtotketv (a·tot·ki·tá) {I}
to worship: arakkicetv (a:·ła:k·ke:·ci·tá) {I;II}
to get wounded: vnvttetv (a·nat·ti·tá) {II}
to write: hoccicetv (hoc·ce:·ci·tá) {I;3}

Y

year: ohrolopē (oh·ło·lo·pí:)
last year: ohrolopēyvnke (oh·ło·lo·pi:·yán·ki)
to yell, scream: selaksēketv (si·la:k·si:·ki·tá) {I}
yellow, green: lanē (lá:·ni:) {II}
yes: ehi (i·hé:)
yesterday: paksvnkē (pa:k·san·kí:)
you (one person): cēme (cí:·mi); *also* cēmeu (cí:·mio)
younger brother (a man's): ecerwv mvnetosat (i·cíł·wa ma·ni·to·sát) {II}
younger brother (a man's) or younger sister (a woman's): ecuse (i·có·si) {II}
younger sister (a woman's): ecuse mvnetat (i·có·si ma·ni·tá:t) {II}

Glossary

Linguistic Terms

A

Adjective (adj). A word that describes a noun.

Adverb (adv). A word describing how an action is being performed.

Adverbial suffix. A suffix attached to modifiers describing how an action is being performed. The adverbial suffix in Mvskoke is *-ēn*.

Affix. A unit added at the beginning, middle, or end of another word that modifies the meaning of the word to which it has been added.

Always key syllable. A syllable in a Mvskoke word that always affects the tonal pattern of the syllables surrounding it. If more than one "always key" syllable occurs in a word, the first of these will have the highest tone.

Aspect. Information about the performance of an activity in relation to time. Mvskoke has incompletive, completive, and stative aspects.

Aspirated consonant. A sound produced with a discernable puff of air following the release of the consonant.

Auxiliary verb (aux_vb). A verb used in conjunction with another verb. The primary verb generally refers to the central action of the sentence, while the auxiliary verb, often called a helping verb or modal verb, refers to a secondary feature of the action.

D

Dative (D). A noun case showing that the noun is either an indirect or a direct object of a verb.

Declarative suffix (dec). A means of designating that the sentence is making a statement.

Definite noun. A noun whose referent is specific. In English, definite nouns often are preceded by "the," as opposed to "a" or "an."

Definite object marker (def_obj). A suffix attached to noun modifiers referring to definite object nouns. The definite object marker suffix in Mvskoke is *-an*.

Definite subject marker (def_subj). A suffix attached to noun modifiers referring to definite subject nouns. The definite subject marker suffix in Mvskoke is *-at*.

Definite suffix. A suffix attached directly to the noun that denotes that the noun is definite. The definite suffixes are null suffixes for both subjects and objects in Mvskoke.

Diminutive. A noun that has been modified to show smallness or littleness.

Diminutive suffix (dim). A suffix attached either directly to a noun or to the last adjective modifying the noun that shows that the noun is small or little.

Diphthong. A vowel sound produced with movement of the jaw, tongue, and/or lips during the production of the sound.

Direct object (do). An object directly affected by the action.

F

First person singular (1S). Linguistic term used to refer to subjects or objects designated by the English pronouns "I" or "me."

Ft-grade (falling tone grade) (ft_grd). A verb grade designating that the action described by the verb was completed in the middle, distant, or remote past. In Mvskoke, the ft-grade is indicated by lengthening the final vowel and then pronouncing the vowel with a descending tone.

G

Geminate consonants. Pairs of the same consonants, such as the two [k]s in the Mvskoke word *wakketv*.

H

H-grade (h_grd). A verb grade designating that the action described by the verb was completed in the very recent past. The h-grade infixes in Mvskoke are *-h-*, *-i-*, and *-iy-*.

Heavy syllable. A syllable composed of a long vowel alone, a consonant followed by a long vowel, or a vowel (either long or short) between two consonants.

I

Inalienable nouns. Nouns for which possession marking is mandatory.

Incompletive aspect. A verbal form showing that the action has not been completed at the time referred to in the sentence. In Mvskoke, incompletive aspect is indicated by lengthening the final vowel in the verb stem.

Indefinite noun. A noun whose referent is not specific. In English, indefinite nouns often are preceded by "a" or "an," as opposed to "the."

Indefinite object marker (ind_obj). A suffix attached to noun modifiers referring to indefinite object nouns. The indefinite object marker in Mvskoke is *-en*.

Indefinite subject marker (ind_subj). A suffix attached to noun modifiers referring to indefinite subject nouns. The indefinite subject marker in Mvskoke is *-et*.

Indefinite suffix. A suffix attached directly to the noun that denotes that the noun is indefinite. These suffixes are *-t* for subjects and *-n* for objects in Mvskoke.

Indirect object. An object not directly affected by the action.

Infinitive form. A form of the verb that has not been modified to show that any subject is performing the action.

Infix. An affix added to the middle of a word.

Initial syllable. The first syllable in a word.

Interrogative suffix (int). A suffix added to a verb to show that a question is being asked. The Mvskoke interrogative suffixes are *-v* and *-(ē)te*.

K

Key syllable. A syllable affecting the tonal contours of the syllables surrounding it.

L

L-grade (lengthened grade) (l_grd). A verb grade designating that the action described by the verb is incomplete at the time referred to in the sentence. The l-grade in Mvskoke is indicated by lengthening the final vowel of the verb stem.

Light syllable. A syllable in a Mvskoke word that is composed of a short vowel alone, a consonant followed by a short vowel, or a short vowel followed by a consonant.

Locational interrogative (loc_int). A question asking about the location of a being or object. In Mvskoke, locational interrogatives are formed by adding the suffix *-tv* to the noun.

Long vowel. A vowel sound held for a longer time than a short vowel sound. Long and short vowel distinctions vary somewhat from speaker to speaker, but all speakers hold long vowels for a longer time than they hold short vowels.

M

Mass noun. A noun made up of items that generally are not counted separately. Examples of English mass nouns are "oatmeal" and "sand."

N

Negating suffix (neg). A suffix added to the verb that indicates that the action is not occurring or was not performed. The Mvskoke negating suffix is *-(e)k(o)-*.

Noun phrase. A grammatical construction composed of a noun and its modifiers.

Null prefix. A prefix that does not have a pronounced form. In Mvskoke, the third person singular (3S) prefixes are null prefixes.

Null suffix. A suffix that does not have a pronounced form. In Mvskoke, the third person singular (3S) suffix is a null suffix.

O

Object. A grammatical role. The object of a sentence is the person or item affected by the action designated by the verb.

Orthography. A writing system.

P

Past tense marker. An affix added to the verb that shows that the action took place in the past. Past tense in Mvskoke is marked by the use of the h-grade infixes or by the suffixes *-vnk/-yvnk*, *-mvt/-emvt*, and *-vtē*.

Penultimate syllable. The next-to-last syllable in a word.

Phoneme. A sound recognized by speakers of a language as distinct from other sounds. Changes in phonemes will cause changes in meaning, as in the English words *pat* and *bat*, which differ only because of the change from /p/ to /b/.

Phonemic symbol. A means of representing a sound in a notation widely used by linguists.

Prefix. An affix added to the beginning of a word.

Pure vowel. A vowel produced with little or no movement of the mouth during the production of the vowel sound.

S

Same-subject suffix (ss). A suffix added to the primary verb in a construction including more than one verb. This marker, in Mvskoke the suffix *-t*, shows that the same subject is performing both actions.

Second person singular (2S). Linguistic term used to refer to single subjects or objects designated by the English pronoun "you."

Short vowel. A vowel sound held for a shorter time than a long vowel sound. Long and short vowel distinctions vary somewhat from speaker to speaker, but all speakers hold long vowels for a longer time than they hold short vowels.

Stative aspect. An aspect denoting that the action described is an ongoing state of being. In Mvskoke, the stative aspect is designated by a lack of lengthening of the final vowel of the verb stem.

Stative verb. A verb that denotes a state of being. These verbs may often be used as adjectives and always appear in the stative aspect.

Subject (S). A grammatical role. The subject of a sentence is the person or thing responsible for performing the activity designated by the verb.

Subject suffix. A suffix added after a verb stem to designate who or what is performing the action described by the verb.

Suffix. An affix added to the end of a word.

T

Third person singular (3S). Linguistic term used to refer to subjects or objects designated by the English pronouns "he," "she," and "it."

Tonal accent. The pattern of pitches assigned to syllables in a Mvskoke word.

Tone. The pitch of a syllable. In this book, tonal quality is denoted by numbers, with higher tones represented by lower numbers.
Type I verb. One of a class of Mvskoke verbs taking suffixes to denote the subject performing the action.
Type II verb. One of a class of Mvskoke verbs taking prefixes to denote the subject performing the action.
Type I/II or II/I verb. One of a class of Mvskoke verbs that may take either a suffix or a prefix to denote the subject performing the action. The preferred way of showing the subject is indicated by the first roman numeral indicated in the pair (I/II or II/I) contained in the glossary entry for the verb.

U

Unaspirated consonant. A sound produced with little or no puff of air following the release of the consonant.

V

Verb. A word designating an action or state of being.
Verb grade. An alteration of the verb stem that indicates aspect or tense.
Verb stem. That portion of the verb that causes the listener and speaker to know what action is being discussed.
Voiced sounds. Sounds produced while the vocal cords are vibrating.
Voiceless sounds. Sounds produced without vocal cord vibration.
Vowel length. A measure of the duration of a vowel sound. In Mvskoke, the amount of time one holds a vowel sound is heard as a phonemic distinction.

Bibliography

Bartram, William R.

1791 *Travels through North and South Carolina, Georgia, East and West Florida, the Cherokee Country, the Extensive Territories of the Muscogulges or Creek Confederacy, and the Country of the Choctaws.* Philadelphia: James and Johnson.

Bell, Amelia R.

1984 Creek Ritual: The Path to Peace. Ph.D. dissertation, University of Chicago.

Booker, Karen M.

1980 Comparative Muskogean: Aspects of Proto-Muskogean Verb Morphology. Ph.D. dissertation, University of Kansas.

1988 The Loss of Preconsonantal *k in Creek/Seminole. *International Journal of American Linguistics* 54:371–86.

1992 Nasalization and Question Formation in Creek. In *Proceedings of the 1992 Mid-America Linguistics Conference and Conference on Siouan-Caddoan Languages*, edited by Evan Smith and Flore Zephir, pp. 373–88.

1993 More on the Development of Proto-Muskogean $*k^w$. *International Journal of American Linguistics* 59:405–15.

Braund, Kathryn E. H.

1993 *Deerskins and Duffels: Creek Indian Trade with Anglo-America, 1685–1815.* Lincoln: University of Nebraska Press.

Campbell, Lyle

1997 *American Indian Languages: The Historical Linguistics of Native America*. Oxford: Oxford University Press.

Campbell, Lyle, and Marianne Mithun, eds.

1979 *The Languages of Native America: Historical and Comparative Assessment.* Austin: University of Texas Press.

Cline, David

1987 Oklahoma Seminole and the Muskogean H–Grade. In *Muskogean Linguistics: A Volume of Papers Begun at UCLA on Comparative, Historical, and Synchronic Muskogean Topics,* edited by Pamela Munro, pp. 36–50. Occasional Papers in Linguistics no. 6. Los Angeles: Department of Linguistics, University of California.

Cohn, Abigail

1987 Causative Formation in the Oklahoma Seminole Dialect of Creek. In *Muskogean Linguistics: A Volume of Papers Begun at UCLA on Comparative, Historical, and Synchronic Muskogean Topics,* edited by Pamela Munro, pp. 51–65. Occasional Papers in Linguistics no. 6. Los Angeles: Department of Linguistics, University of California.

Corkran, David

1967 *The Creek Frontier, 1540–1783*. Norman: University of Oklahoma Press.

Debo, Angie

1940 *And Still the Waters Run: The Betrayal of the Five Civilized Tribes.* Princeton, N.J.: Princeton University Press.

1941 *The Road to Disappearance: A History of the Creek Indians.* Norman: University of Oklahoma Press.

Foreman, Grant

1932 *Indian Removal: The Emigration of the Five Civilized Tribes of Indians.* Norman: University of Oklahoma Press.

Foster, Michael K.

1996 Language and the Culture History of North America. In *Handbook of North American Indians,* vol. 17, *Languages,* edited by Ives Goddard, pp. 64–110. Washington, D.C.: Smithsonian Institution Press.

Fromkin, Victoria, and Robert Rodman

1998 *An Introduction to Language.* Sixth edition. Fort Worth, Tex.: Harcourt Brace College Publishers.

Green, Michael D.

1982 *The Politics of Indian Removal: Creek Government and Society in Crisis.* Lincoln: University of Nebraska Press.

Haas, Mary
1940 Ablaut and Its Function in Muskogee. *Language* 16:141–50.
1941 The Classification of the Muskogean Languages. In *Language, Culture, and Personality: Essays in Memory of Edward Sapir,* edited by L. Spier, A. I. Hallowell, and S. S. Newman, pp. 41–56. Menasha, Wis.: Sapir Memorial Publication Fund.
1949 The Position of Apalachee in the Muskogean Family. *International Journal of American Linguistics* 15:121–27.
1977a Nasals and Nasalization in Creek. In *Proceedings of the Third Annual Meeting of the Berkeley Linguistics Society,* edited by Kenneth Whistler et al., pp. 194–203. Berkeley, Calif.: Berkeley Linguistics Society.
1977b Tonal Accent in Creek. In *Studies in Stress and Accent,* edited by Larry M. Hyman, pp. 195–208. Southern California Occasional Papers in Linguistics 4. Los Angeles: University of Southern California.
1977c From Auxiliary Verb Phrase to Inflectional Suffix. In *Mechanisms of Syntactic Change,* edited by Charles N. Li, pp. 525–37. Austin: University of Texas Press.
1979 Southeastern Languages. In *The Languages of Native America: Historical and Comparative Assessment,* edited by Lyle Campbell and Marianne Mithun, pp. 299–326. Austin: University of Texas Press.

Hardy, Donald E.
1988 The Semantics of Creek Morphosyntax. Ph.D. dissertation, Rice University.
1992 Figure and Ground in the Creek Auxiliary *oom. Word* 43(2):217–31.

Hassig, Ross
1974 Internal Conflict in the Creek War of 1813–1814. *Ethnohistory* 21(3): 251–71.

Hawkins, Benjamin
1848 A *Sketch of the Creek Country, in 1798 and* '99. Georgia Historical Society Collections, vol. 3. Savannah: Georgia Historical Society.

Howard, James H.
1968 *The Southeastern Ceremonial Complex and Its Interpretation.* Memoir of the Missouri Archaeological Society 6. Columbia: Missouri Archaeological Society.

Howard, James H., and Willie Lena
1984 *Oklahoma Seminoles: Medicines, Magic, and Religion.* Norman: University of Oklahoma Press.

Hudson, Charles
1976 *The Southeastern Indians.* Knoxville: University of Tennessee Press.

Innes, Pamela
1997a Demonstrating that One Can Work within Two Communities: Codeswitching in Muskogee (Creek) Political Discourse. *Florida Anthropologist* 50(4):201–8.
1997b From One to Many, from Many to One: Speech Communities among the Mvskoke Stompdance Population. Ph.D. dissertation, University of Oklahoma.

Jackson, Jason Baird
1996 "Everybody Has a Part, Even the Little Bitty Ones": Notes on the Social Organization of Yuchi Ceremonialism. *Florida Anthropologist* 49(3):121–30.
1998 Yuchi Ritual: Meaning and Tradition in Contemporary Ceremonial Ground Life. Ph.D. dissertation, Indiana University.

Kimball, Geoffrey
1985 A Descriptive Grammar of Koasati. Ph.D. dissertation, Tulane University.

Ladefoged, Peter
2000a *A Course in Phonetics*. Fourth edition. Fort Worth, Tex.: Harcourt Brace Jovanovich.
2000b *Vowels and Consonants: An Introduction to the Sounds of Languages.* Oxford: Blackwell Publishers.

Lomawaima, K. Tsianina
1994 *They Called It Prairie Light: The Story of Chilocco Indian School.* Lincoln: University of Nebraska Press.

Loughridge, R. M.
1888 History of Mission Work among the Creek Indians from 1832 to 1888. Special Collections, University of Tulsa.

Loughridge, R. M., and David M. Hodge
1890 [1964] *Dictionary Muskokee and English.* Okmulgee, Okla.: Baptist Home Mission Board.

Martin, Jack B.
1988 Interrogation in Creek. In *In Honor of Mary Haas: From the Haas Festival Conference on Native American Linguistics,* edited by W. Shipley and M. R. Haas. Berlin: Mouton de Gruyter.

Martin, Jack B., and Keith Johnson
2002 An Acoustic Study of "Tonal Accent" in Creek. *International Journal of American Linguistics* 68(1):28–50.

Martin, Jack B., and Margaret McKane Mauldin
2000 *A Dictionary of Creek/Muskogee.* Lincoln: University of Nebraska Press.

Moore, John H.
1988 The Mvskoke National Question in Oklahoma. *Science and Society* 52(2):163–90.

Munro, Pamela
1984 Auxiliaries and Auxiliarization in Western Muskogean. In *Historical Syntax*, edited by Jacek Fisiak, pp. 333–62. Trends in Linguistics: Studies and Monographs 23. Berlin: Mouton de Gruyter.
1985 Chickasaw Accent and Verb Grades. In *Studia Linguistica Diachronic et Synchronica*, edited by U. Pieper and G. Stickel, pp. 581–91. Berlin: Mouton de Gruyter.
1987 Introduction: Muskogean Studies at UCLA. In *Muskogean Linguistics: A Volume of Papers Begun at UCLA on Comparative, Historical, and Synchronic Muskogean Topics*, edited by Pamela Munro, pp. 1–6. Occasional Papers in Linguistics no. 6. Los Angeles: Department of Linguistics, University of California.
1993 The Muskogean II Prefixes and Their Significance for Classification. *International Journal of American Linguistics* 59:374–404.

Munro, Pamela, and Lynn Gordon
1982 Syntactic Relations in Western Muskogean: A Typological Perspective. *Language* 58:81–115.

Nathan, Michele
1977 Grammatical Description of the Florida Seminole Dialect of Creek. Ph.D. dissertation, Tulane University.

Pauketat, Timothy R., and Thomas E. Emerson
1991 The Ideology of Authority and the Power of the Pot. *American Anthropologist* 93(4):919–41.

Schuetze-Coburn, Stephan
1987 Exceptional *–t/–n* Marking in Oklahoma Seminole Creek. In *Muskogean Linguistics: A Volume of Papers Begun at UCLA on Comparative, Historical, and Synchronic Muskogean Topics*, edited by Pamela Munro, pp. 156–59. Occasional Papers in Linguistics no. 6. Los Angeles: Department of Linguistics, University of California.

Schultz, Jack M.
1999 *The Seminole Baptist Churches of Oklahoma: Maintaining a Traditional Community.* Norman: University of Oklahoma Press.

Speck, Frank G.
1907 *The Creek Indians of Taskigi Town.* Memoirs of the American Anthropological Association vol. 2, no. 2. Washington, D.C.: American Anthropological Association.

1909 *Ethnology of the Yuchi Indians.* Anthropological Publications of the University Museum, University of Pennsylvania, vol. 1, no. 1. Philadelphia: University Museum.

1911 *Ceremonial Songs of the Creek and Yuchi Indians.* Anthropological Publications of the University Museum, University of Pennsylvania, vol. 1, no. 2. Phildelphia: University Museum.

Spoehr, Alexander

1942 *Kinship System of the Seminole.* Anthropological Series, Field Museum of Natural History, vol. 33, no. 2. Chicago: Field Museum of Natural History.

1947 *Changing Kinship Systems: A Study in the Acculturation of the Creeks, Cherokee, and Choctaw.* Anthropological Series, Field Museum of Natural History, vol. 33, no. 4. Chicago: Field Museum of Natural History.

Stiggins, George

1989 *Creek Indian History: A Historical Narrative of the Genealogy, Traditions, and Downfall of the Ispocoga or Creek Indian Tribe of Indians.* Edited by Virginia Pounds Brown. Birmingham, Ala.: Birmingham Public Library Press.

Sturtevant, William C.

1971 Creek into Seminole. In *North American Indians in Historical Perspective,* edited by E. B. Leacock and N. O. Lurie, pp. 92–128. New York: Random House.

Swanton, John R.

1922 *Early History of the Creek Indians and Their Neighbors.* Bureau of American Ethnology Bulletin 73. Washington, D.C.: Smithsonian Institution.

1928a Social Organization and Social Usages of the Indians of the Creek Confederacy. In *Forty-Second Annual Report of the Bureau of American Ethnology,* pp. 174–242. Washington, D.C.: United States Government Printing Office.

1928b Religious Beliefs and Medical Practices of the Creek Indians. In *Forty-Second Annual Report of the Bureau of American Ethnology,* pp. 473–672. Washington, D.C.: United States Government Printing Office.

Usner, Daniel H., Jr.

1992 *Indians, Settlers, and Slaves in a Frontier Exchange Economy: The Lower Mississippi Valley before 1783.* Chapel Hill: University of North Carolina Press.

Waring, Antonio J.
1968 The Southern Cult and Muskhogean Ceremonial. In *The Waring Papers*, edited by Stephen Williams, pp. 30–69. Papers of the Peabody Museum of Archaeology and Ethnology, vol. 58. Cambridge, Mass.: Harvard University.

Wright, J. Leitch, Jr.
1986 *Creeks and Seminoles: The Destruction and Regeneration of the Muscogulge People*. Lincoln: University of Nebraska Press.

Index

Contents of Accompanying Audio CDs

Disc A

1. Introduction: Linda Alexander
2. Importance of knowing the Mvskoke alphabet

3-22. Sounds of the Mvskoke alphabet
23. Introduction to Mvskoke words
24-32. Exercise 1-4
33-38. Exercise 2-5
39. Introduction to Mvskoke nouns
40-50. Nouns from chapter 1
51. Introduction to verbs of motion
52-62. Verbs from chapter 1

Disc B

1. Introduction to simple Mvskoke sentences
2. Sentences combining “man” and verbs of motion from chapter 1
3. Sentences combining “woman” and verbs of motion from chapter 1
4. Sentences combining “boy” and verbs of motion from chapter 1
5. Sentences combining “girl” and verbs of motion from chapter 1
6. Sentences combining “child” and verbs of motion from chapter 1
7. Sentences combining “baby” and verbs of motion from chapter 1
8. Introduction to conversational sentences

9-23. Conversational sentences
24. Explanation of clans
25. "Thank you for coming" speech, representative of the kind of speech given at a stompground—Andrew Alexander, speaker, October 24, 2002
26. Interpretation of "Thank you for coming" speech—Andrew Alexander, speaker
27. Stomp Dance, led by Jimmy Roy Gibson, Okmulgee, Oklahoma, July 18, 1999
28. Church Song 1—Linda Alexander, singer
29. Interpretation of Church Song 1
30. Church Song 2—Linda Alexander, singer
31. Interpretation of Church Song 2
32. Turtle Story—Linda Alexander, speaker
33. Interpretation of Turtle Story
34. Introduction to numbers 1-20
35-56. Numbers 1-20

CDs recorded and produced by Marvin Alexander.